DESTINATION MARKETING

for Convention and Visitor Bureaus

Richard B. Gartrell

Under the Auspices of the
International Association of
Convention & Visitor Bureaus
P.O. Box 758
Champaign, Illinois 61820

KENDALL/HUNT PUBLISHING COMPANY
2460 Kerper Boulevard   P.O. Box 539   Dubuque, Iowa 52004-0539

CREDITS

Figure 4.1 The Dallas/Ft. Worth Area Tourism Council, The Ann Arbor, Greater Omaha, Lincoln, Wichita, and Tampa/Hillsborough Convention and Visitors Bureaus; Figure 4.2 The Greater Fort Lauderdale Convention and Visitors Bureau; Figure 4.3 The Greater Houston Convention and Visitors Bureau; Figure 4.4 The Wichita Convention and Visitors Bureau; Figure 4.5 The National Tour Association; Figure 4.6 The Denver Convention and Visitors Bureau; Figure 4.7 The Long Beach Area Convention and Visitors Council, Inc.; Figure 4.8 The San Diego Convention and Visitors Bureau; Figure 5.3 The Greater Lexington Convention and Visitors Bureau; Figure 5.4 The San Francisco and San Diego Convention and Visitors Bureaus; Figure 5.5 The San Diego (CA) Convention Center; Figure 5.6 The Anaheim Convention and Visitors Bureau; Figure 5.7 The Cincinnati Convention and Visitors Bureau; Figure 5.8 The Greater Lexington Convention and Visitors Bureau; Figure 5.9 The New York Convention and Visitors Bureau; Figure 5.10 The Nice Convention Bureau; Figure 6.3 The Ann Arbor Convention and Visitors Bureau; Figure 7.1 The Phoenix and Valley of the Sun Convention and Visitors Bureau, and the San Jose Convention and Visitors Bureau; Figure 7.2 The Boston Convention and Visitors Bureau; Figure 7.3 The San Francisco Convention and Visitors Bureau; Figure 7.4 The Boston Convention and Visitors Bureau; Figure 7.5 The Boston Convention and Visitors Bureau; Figure 7.6 The Greater Milwaukee Convention and Visitors Bureau; Figure 7.7 The San Francisco Convention and Visitors Bureau; Figure 8.2 The Sydney Convention and Visitors Bureau (Australia).

Printed in the United States of America
10 9 8 7 6 5 4 3 2

Dedication

This book is dedicated to past, present and future members of the International Association of Convention & Visitor Bureaus and to dedicated bureau professionals everywhere for their enthusiastic support, leadership and contributions to the growth and recognition of the industry.

Editorial Staff

Marie Earley, President, Champaign Urbana Convention and Visitors Bureau (Illinois).

Katherine Jones, Vice President-Sales, Ann Arbor Convention and Visitors Bureau (Michigan).

Shirley Miller, International Association of Convention & Visitor Bureaus, Champaign (Illinois).

William Snyder, President, Anaheim Area Convention and Visitors Bureau (California).

Kathryn Usitalo, Vice President of Communications, Metropolitan Detroit Convention and Visitors Bureau (Michigan).

Contributors

Keith Arnold, Executive Director/CEO, Metropolitan Richmond Convention and Visitors Bureau (Virginia).

Jeanne Baer, Corporate Training, Information, CENTEL, Inc, Lincoln (Nebraska).

Collin D. Barnes, Executive Director, Sydney Convention and Visitors Bureau, Ltd. (Australia).

Richard C. Bogren, Communication Department, International Association of Convention & Visitor Bureaus, Champaign, Illinois

Joe E. Boyd, President, Wichita Convention and Visitors Bureau (Kansas).

Carol Burgess, Director of Marketing, Reno-Sparks Convention and Visitors Authority (Nevada).

John Burt, Head of Convention Bureau, London Visitor and Convention Bureau (England).

Wayne C. Chappell, Executive Director, Baltimore Convention Bureau, Inc. (Maryland).

Ellyn Clifton, Vice President/Convention Sales, Phoenix and Valley of the Sun Convention and Visitors Bureau (Arizona).

Shirley Condiff, Director of Tourism, Wichita Convention and Visitors Bureau (Kansas).

Robert E. Cumings, President, Greater Boston Convention and Visitors Bureau, Inc. (Massachusetts).

Patricia R. Davidson, Director of Tourism, Long Beach Convention and Visitors Council (California).

Thomas Doering, Ph.D., Deputy Director, Division of Research, Department of Economic Development (Nebraska).

Deane C. Drury, Executive Director, Fort Collins Convention and Visitors Bureau (Colorado).

Julian R. Dugas, Director of Sales, Oakland Convention and Visitors Bureau (California).

William M. Duron, President, Metropolitan Toronto Convention and Visitors Association (Canada).

Marie Earley, President/CEO, Champaign Urbana Convention and Visitors Bureau (Illinois).

Roy B. Evans, Jr., Executive Vice President, Professional Convention Management Association, Birmingham (Alabama).

Susan Fielder, Information Specialist, Ann Arbor Convention and Visitors Bureau (Michigan).

Jane Foley, Director of Sales, Greater Lexington Convention and Visitors Bureau (Kentucky).

Charles Gillett, President, New York Convention and Visitors Bureau, Inc. (New York).

Ed Hall, Executive Director, Greater Birmingham Convention and Visitors Bureau (Alabama).

Thomas D. Hanlon, Executive Director, Fort Worth Convention and Visitors Bureau (Texas).

Marlyce Heidt, Executive Director, Cedar Rapids Area Convention and Visitors Bureau (Iowa).

Dean Henricksen, Executive Director, National Tour Association, Lexington (Kentucky).

Elizabeth Vann Howell, Director of Membership, Metropolitan Tucson Convention and Visitors Bureau (Arizona).

Richard Howell, Ph.D., Director, Recreation, Travel and Tourism Institute, Clemson University (South Carolina).

Richard M. Kinney, Vice President, Convention and Visitors Division, Nashville Area Chamber of Commerce (Tennessee).

George D. Kirkland, CAE, President, Greater Miami Convention and Visitors Bureau (Florida).

K. Carl Little, Executive Director, Chattanooga Area Convention and Visitors Bureau (Tennessee).

Charles "Sonny" Mares, Director, Jacksonville Convention and Visitors Bureau (Florida).

John A. Marks, Executive Director, San Francisco Convention and Visitors Bureau (California).

Ellen E. McCleskey, Publications Manager, Greater Los Angeles Visitors and Convention Bureau (California).

Dennis P. Miriani, Executive Vice President, Metropolitan Detroit Convention and Visitors Bureau (Michigan).

Steve Morris, Vice President-Marketing, Greater Houston Convention and Visitors Bureau (Texas).

Richard J. Newman, Executive Director/CEO, International Association of Convention & Visitor Bureaus, Champaign (Illinois).

Woody Peek, Director of Tourism, Tampa/Hillsborough Convention and Visitors Association, Inc. (Florida).

Burke M. Pease, President, San Jose Convention and Visitors Bureau (California).

William C. Peeper, Executive Director, Orlando/Orange County Convention and Visitors Bureau (Florida).

Joseph R. Phillips, Director of Convention Marketing, The Westin Bonaventure Hotel, Los Angeles (California).

Jacqueline Pietri, Executive Manager, Nice Convention Bureau (France).

David S. Radcliffe, Executive Director, Phoenix and Valley of the Sun Convention and Visitors Bureau (Arizona).

Don Raulie, Executive Director, Tulsa Convention and Visitors Bureau (Okiahoma).

Charles E. Rixse, Executive Director, Myrtle Beach Area Convention Bureau (South Carolina).

Bette L. Sammons, Convention Services Manager, Atlanta Convention and Visitors Bureau, Inc. (Georgia).

Gerald G. Sanderson, Director of Sales, Chicago Convention and Visitors Bureau, Inc. (Illinois).

Barry Shemer, Vice President/Finance and Operations, Phoenix and Valley of the Sun Convention and Visitors Bureau (Arizona).

Roger A. Smith, President/CEO, Denver Metropolitan Convention and Visitors Bureau (Colorado).

James H. Smither, Executive Director, Greater Lexington Convention and Visitors Bureau (Kentucky).

Ted G. Sprague, President, Atlanta Convention and Visitors Bureau, Inc. (Georgia).

Christopher "Butch" Spyridon, Executive Director, Baton Rouge Area Convention and Visitors Bureau (Louisiana).

Doug Stafford, President/CEO, Charlotte Convention and Visitors Bureau, Inc. (North Carolina).

Suzann Stewart, Director of Visitor Development, Tulsa Convention and Visitors Bureau (Oklahoma).

Stephen R. Stickford, Director of Sales, Convention and Visitors Bureau of Greater Kansas City (Missouri).

Tyler M. Stroh, Vice President and General Manager, Greater Los Angeles Visitors and Convention Bureau (California).

Karie Stupek, Convention Services Manager, Greater Milwaukee Convention and Visitors Bureau, Inc. (Wisconsin).

June T. Switken, Director, Greater Fort Lauderdale Convention and Visitors Bureau (Florida).

Warren L. Trafton, CAE, President/CEO, Greater Hartford Convention and Visitors Bureau, Inc. (Connecticut).

Victoria Tribble, Vice President of Administration, San Diego Convention and Visitors Bureau (California).

George S. Toly, Vice President/Tourism, Phoenix and Valley of the Sun Convention and Visitors Bureau (Arizona).

Dal Watkins, President, San Diego Convention and Visitors Bureau (California).

Nancy Whittlesey, Director of Membership, San Francisco Convention and Visitors Bureau (California).

LaMar B. Williams, Director of Marketing, Tampa/Hillsborough Convention and Visitors Association, Inc. (Florida).

Michael J. Wilson, President, Greater Cincinnati Convention and Visitors Bureau (Ohio).

Michael J. Wright, Vice President of Administration, Metropolitan Detroit Convention and Visitors Bureau (Michigan).

John F. Yee, Director of Finance and Administration, San Francisco Convention and Visitors Bureau (California).

Contents

Preface

Over the past decades, the growth of the travel and tourism industry has enhanced an awareness of its economic significance to cities, states, provinces, regions and nations. Though many still consider tourism a pleasure activity and attribute to it an aura of romance and glamor, travel and tourism as a composite industry is annually a multimillion dollar enterprise that provides employment for millions, income to destinations, attractions, and thousands of service companies, tax revenues to public bodies, and satisfaction to millions of consumers.

Though Herman Kahn saw the travel industry becoming one of the largest industries in the world by the year 2000, there are others who feel that its growth already has surpassed any such projections and today it is a critically significant economic enterprise among world economies.

This industry called travel and tourism has a very complex structure, with 98% of its organizations classified as small businesses. Among its many constituent entities are marketing organizations (such as national, state, provincial, regional or urban organizations), suppliers (such as attractions, hotels and restaurants) and distributors (such as travel agents, tour operators and meeting planners). The enormity of this diverse industry confuses many; yet each entity maintains a critical interrelationship and interdependence with other entities in order to deliver the desired products and services.

Significant among these many organizations has been the specific growth of those with primary responsibilities for marketing of their defined geographic areas. Hundreds of convention and visitor bureaus compete for meetings, conventions, group tours and visitors worldwide. And yet the first convention bureau was founded only 91 years ago in Detroit, Michigan (USA).

There also has been an influx of academic programs to prepare students for careers in the travel and tourism industry. These programs include such diverse concentrations as hospitality management, meetings management, travel agency operations, tour planning, attraction operations, facility planning and tourism management. The growing number of students in these programs plus the proliferation of programs indicates the recognition being given this relatively young industry as a source for professional careers.

As a result of these trends, a need has developed for a better understanding of the *marketing* role of convention and visitor bureaus in the life of their urban settings. People travel in relationship to a destination; destinations therefore influence their direction of travel as well as those activities engaged in once they arrive. Whether it be for leisure travel or planning a meeting, the destination becomes the critical planning variable. Understanding therefore the important marketing role that bureaus play in formulating images and influencing travelers and planners is fundamental for the smooth and efficient performance of the travel and tourism industry.

This book presents materials that will help develop an understanding of the pivotal marketing role that bureaus occupy and will serve as:

- a resource for people entering the travel and tourism industry, to explain the critical mission of convention and visitor bureaus in marketing destinations;
- a resource for individuals specifically employed with a bureau, to assist them in understanding the diversity of interrelated bureau activities to solicit and service conventions and other group business;
- a resource for boards of directors, to orient them to the multiple roles and responsibilities of bureaus in light of their mission as destination marketers;
- a resource for students to study in understanding the significance of these marketing functions as they impact the economic fabric of destinations and provide a potential for career opportunities;
- and a resource that will become an industry standard, providing insights and understanding into the dynamic marketing activities of convention and visitor bureaus and their interdependence with other travel and tourism enterprises.

This book will explore the mission of convention and visitor bureaus, the economic benefits and significance of the meetings markets, and the diverse marketing activities undertaken by bureaus on behalf of their destinations with meeting planners, tour planners, leisure travelers, media representatives and other targeted markets. Further this book will explore the internal structure and operations of bureaus as they pertain to membership development, financial resources, boards of directors, bureau staffing, allied associations, travel businesses and political structures.

Today, we live in a global village; bureaus worldwide are in competition, yet they function in a very similar manner. This book will outline these basic governing principles of operation, structure and responsibility. The economic importance of this young industry requires a more serious understanding of its many facets; selling a product is only effective when the consumer's needs have been met. The travel and tourism industry can no longer be considered a frivolous activity but big business that responds to the many challenges confronted by any business, whether political, social or economic. Today's travel professionals must be skilled, knowledgeable and resourceful to meet the challenges of a fast growing industry. This book will therefore focus on one organization within this diverse industry, to provide insights and information needed to understand the mission of convention and visitor bureaus and their fundamental role as destination marketing organizations.

Acknowledgments

Undertaking the writing of this text, particularly since this is the first of its kind, has been a challenging task. But had it not been for the assistance of many, this text would not have been completed. This author wishes to acknowledge the support and encouragement provided during the development of these materials from the Board of Directors of the International Association of Convention & Visitor Bureaus; William Duron, President of the Metropolitan Toronto Convention and Visitors Association; Dan Walker, Vice President and General Manager of the Campus Inn, Ann Arbor, Michigan; Tillie Geiser, Office Manager and Administrative Assistant, Ann Arbor Convention and Visitors Bureau; Paul Jaronski, Photographer; and my associates with the Ann Arbor Convention and Visitors Bureau. Needless to say, there may be many others who have provided words of encouragement during the development of these materials whose names I may have forgotten or mistakenly omitted; my apologies are offered but with deep gratitude for their caring spirit. Though I leave the following to last, by no means is this the case; for while many hours of labor have been committed to writing and editing this publication, there has also been a sacrifice on the part of my family who had to do without my presence. For their patience and understanding, words cannot express what I feel in my heart for what they gave up over these past months but I love and thank them deeply for allowing me to complete this significant personal and professional accomplishment.

Richard B. Gartrell
1988

DESTINATION MARKETING

for Convention and Visitor Bureaus

CONVENTION AND VISITOR BUREAUS: AN OVERVIEW

1

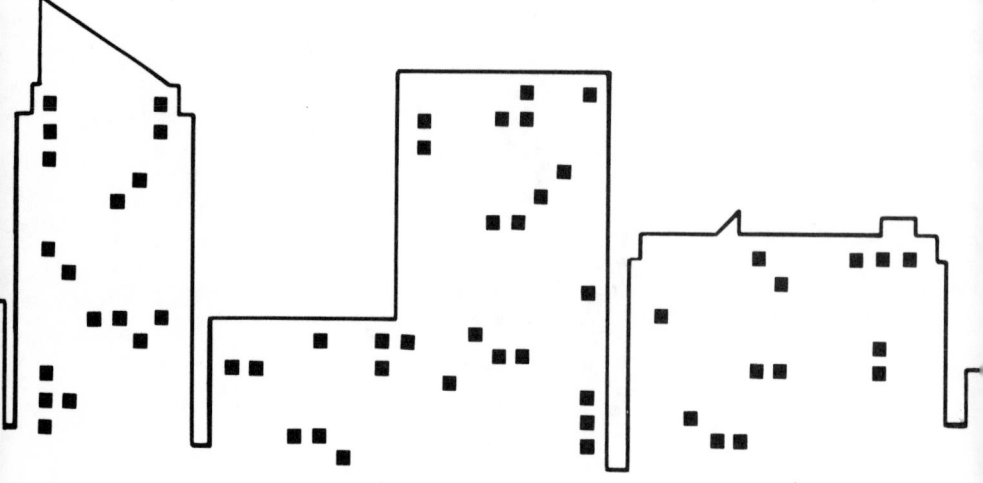

LEARNING OBJECTIVES

Upon reading this chapter, you will learn the
following:

- About the growth and evolution of the
  convention industry;

- About the formation of the first convention
  and visitor bureau;

- About what convention and visitor bureaus
  are, what they do, and how they are
  organized and funded;

- And about the International Association of
  Convention & Visitor Bureaus and its
  leadership role in the development of
  convention bureaus and the recognition of the
  convention and visitor industry.

Introduction

From the beginning of civilization, cities have been the focal point for people gathering, whether in the marketplace or the forums of public discourse. Cities have always had the dynamic financial, technical and intellectual resources that have made them a crucial factor in the history of mankind. As a result, cities continue to maintain a central focus in human behavior, not only as a gathering place for living but also as a gathering place for the sharing and exchange of information and ideas. This importance is no less significant today than it was in the days of the Greeks. People need to interact with one another, and gathering for a convention or trade show can serve as a catalyst for this dynamic interaction. Truly, cities are international gathering places where the mobility of transportation allows representatives from around the world to come together to exchange knowledge and technical expertise and to sell and acquire goods.[1]

Though there were many trade, professional, fraternal and religious associations with historical roots throughout Europe, it wasn't until the mid 1800's that such activity took place along the eastern seaboard of North America. These associations tended to be small and regional; but with the westward population movement across North America and the advent of convenient and fast transportation, many had the potential of becoming broader in scope. Cities grew up overnight and along with them, national trade and professional associations. As these trade and professional associations matured, a number of committees were formed to lure the growing convention business from these expanding and thriving associations.[2]

As more and more cities became aware of the value of convention business, it was inevitable that the solicitation of these conventions would be assigned to a full-time salesperson; and while this might have happened in any one of many major cities, history records that it first happened in Detroit, Michigan (USA) when a group of businessmen decided to place a full-time salesperson on the road to invite conventions to their city. Thus, in 1896, the first convention bureau was formed, and an industry emerged. Soon, other cities followed, forming their own convention bureaus: Cleveland (1904), Atlantic City (1908), Denver and St. Louis (1909), Louisville and Los Angeles (1910), Atlanta and Minneapolis (1913), Columbus and Omaha (1914) and Baltimore and Milwaukee (1915). Today, most major cities and many smaller or second-tier cities have formed bureaus. In fact, bureaus have become an essential part of a community's civic identity. These bureaus all have been established for the same reason, to more effectively make their cities dynamic meeting places by attracting conventions, trade shows and visitor business to their areas. The size and value of the convention and visitors markets has been increasing steadily over these past 90 years, and its significance can be seen in the economic revitalization of cities.

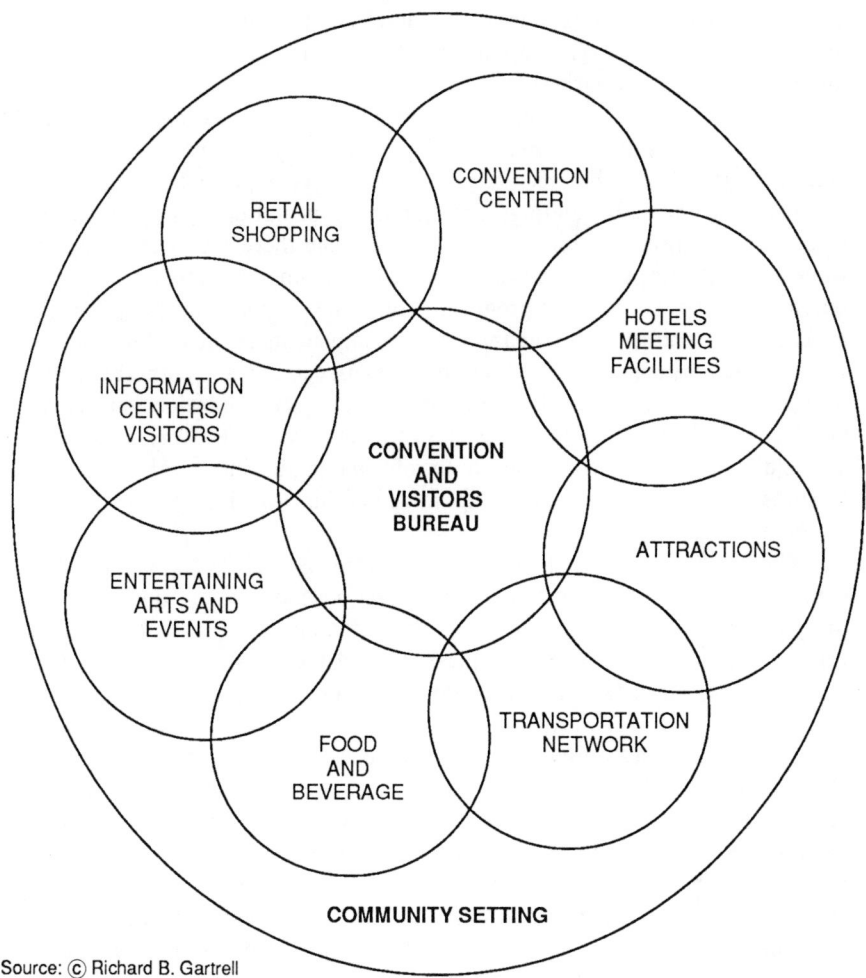

Source: © Richard B. Gartrell

Figure 1.1

Successful bureaus are formed around the same fundamental principle: convention and visitor business can be attracted to an area more effectively through coordinated group action than through independent individual actions. A bureau therefore serves like a cooperative, representing all components of the visitor industry including hotels, motels, restaurants, convention facilities, tour operators, attractions, transportation carriers as well as the retail and commercial resources that are important to visitors.[3] Each component of the visitor industry is extremely competitive; yet they share that competitive spirit with the bureau in order to make it an effective organization able to carry out a comprehensive, unified marketing program for their community.

The convention and visitor bureau is, therefore, a community's single most important marketing organization, projecting an image for that destination into various targeted markets.

Being a cohesive marketing entity for a city has its challenges. One immediate concern is an assessment and analysis of city resources. It is a basic fact of life that the ambitions a city may have for civic promotion are seldom supported by adequate funding; consequently, expectations generally exceed by a sizable margin the ability to deliver. A bureau therefore must determine ways in which it can get the best results from its financial investments. The bureau must have a focused program. And in developing that program, the bureau must carefully examine the various components of the visitor industry. For example, the convention segment includes association and corporate meetings of all descriptions, from small meetings of thirty to major conventions and trade shows that involve thousands of delegates. Most of these meetings are held by nonprofit associations; but profit-making businesses also hold conferences and these corporate meetings are emerging as an important economic segment of the industry.

The tourism segment of the industry is composed of several elements including the group tour market, which caters to senior citizens and other affinity groups who travel by motorcoach; the individual traveler, many of whom travel for business but others for pleasure; and the vacationing family, who may be visiting friends or relatives or simply enjoying a get-away weekend.

Selecting which of these lucrative markets to pursue is the responsibility of the convention and visitor bureau. Such decisions rely on many criteria including: Does the destination have the resources being sought by that market segment (e.g. convention facilities, hotel rooms, transportation access)? Can a decision-maker be identified with whom the bureau can work? Does the city have available dates? When is the next open date for the group's meeting? What criteria does the group have for making a decision? Historically, bureaus have focused their marketing endeavors exclusively on the convention and trade show markets. First, it has been an easily identifiable market within which to work; decision-makers, planners, rotation dates, convention requirements could be identified easily and placed into a tracking system for sales calls. Second, the larger conventions and trade shows usually exceeded the capacity of one hotel, requiring the coordinating expertise of the bureau for housing of convention delegates. And third, bureaus could more easily track these groups since they would generate overnight stays within the community. This also was important since overnight visitors tend to spend more money while in a community.

Though bureaus have focused on convention and trade show business, there has been an evolutionary process reflected, not only in their names which include the term "visitors", but also in their programming which now is broadened to include various tourism markets. Bureaus have found tourism markets difficult to work since the individual traveler is literally the decision-maker.

However, as programs have matured, bureaus have found certain aspects of that market to be beneficial, including the development of visitor information centers, visitor inquiry programs and the group tour market.

The convention and visitor bureaus of today are a far cry from the first small operation in Detroit. Bureau size differs from small cities like Wilmington, Delaware; Lincoln, Nebraska; or Ontario, California, to large cities such as New York, San Francisco, Toronto, Honolulu and Paris. They can employ as many as 300 specialists, as is the case in Hong Kong, all willing and able to offer professional attention and advice to meeting planners and city visitors. Bureaus are designed to pull together those resources that will make any visit to their city, whether for business or pleasure, a successful and memorable one.

Bureaus: What They Are

Convention and visitor bureaus are private, not-for-profit organizations. A majority of the bureaus are independent organizations, though some remain departments of governmental structures or divisions of chambers of commerce. With the growth and importance of bureaus in the development of a destination's image and in the coordination of diverse groups, bureaus have found that independence allows for greater market flexibility and strength in developing a viable destination image.

Typically, bureaus work with their area's larger hotels and convention hall facilities to solicit what is commonly termed "city-wide" conventions to their destination. These interdependent relationships require the astute impartiality of the bureau in making a competitive bid for targeted conventions and trade shows. Smaller cities may market in a similar manner, using the resources of multi-hotels in conjunction with a convention hall, city auditorium or university facilities to bid for a "city-wide" convention or trade show.

Though private, many bureaus receive funding through public sources, usually under mandated or enabling legislation or through a contractual arrangement with governing political entities. With the evolution of transient hotel room tax legislation, bureaus have benefited from the infusion of funds that have allowed them to be more aggressive in cultivating convention and tourism markets. But such public funds are usually coupled with other sources of revenue including memberships, grants, revenues from advertising and publication programs, and inkind gifts to the bureau, thereby providing a solid financial base for marketing activities. Funding for bureaus ranges anywhere from $100,000 to $16 million annually. Of course, bureaus in larger cities are usually the ones with the larger budgets.

Transient hotel room tax legislation has enabled bureaus to develop their resources and more effectively organize their services for meeting and group planners. Typically, this room tax is mandated by local governing bodies through legislation that stipulates its use for convention and visitor promotion.

Though imposed on transient hotel or motel guests, the local governing bodies have a fiduciary responsibility and must have a solid understanding as to the primary mission of a bureau. By attracting conventions, bureaus have traditionally been able to effectively track the room-nights and therefore the kinds of revenues that might be generated from those overnight stays. With the broader commitments to the tourism industry, bureaus have expanded their programs to target the pleasure traveler while recognizing the difficulty of identifying their economic impact on a community. This legislation also has brought about a new level of involvement from the lodging industry which has been important in developing a mutually beneficial interest and respect for bureau programming. Working within a competitive marketplace, bureaus are constantly challenged to stretch their organizational resources, both financial and personnel, to provide the maximum exposure of a destination and at the same time respond to the servicing needs of visitors. Bureau personnel are not magicians, but professionals who carefully and methodically develop their marketing programs, staff themselves with the best available professional talent, and work hard to satisfy the needs of many diverse constituents.

Bureaus: Their Purpose

It may be too simple to say that bureaus sell cities; but in reality, that is their primary mission. Bureaus are charged with the task of developing an image that will position their cities in the marketplace as a viable destination for meetings and visitors. They further must coordinate those constituent elements, which are quite independently diverse yet need to be homogenized, in order to attain that desired single image. Bringing together local political, civic, business and visitor industry representatives requires skilled and sophisticated leadership. Those bureaus which have been most consistently successful in their marketing endeavors have been those which have sought and obtained that kind of quality personnel.

Bureau professionals work within political climates. It is important that the bureau develop a leadership role within the community in order to be effective in the coordination and execution of its programs. Bureaus should be visible entities within a city, drawing attention to what they are doing so that the community understands the significance of the visitor industry.

Bureaus have another important role as well: that of working with meeting and group planners. It is an important role as the bureau serves as the key resource for planners who need assistance in a number of areas. The bureau can provide vital contact names and local information, locate necessary facilities, and act as a convention management consultant to the planner who, like bureau personnel, is a demanding professional requiring the best for the association, corporation or group. The bureau recommends reliable sources for services and supplies information on facilities and prices. The bureau will

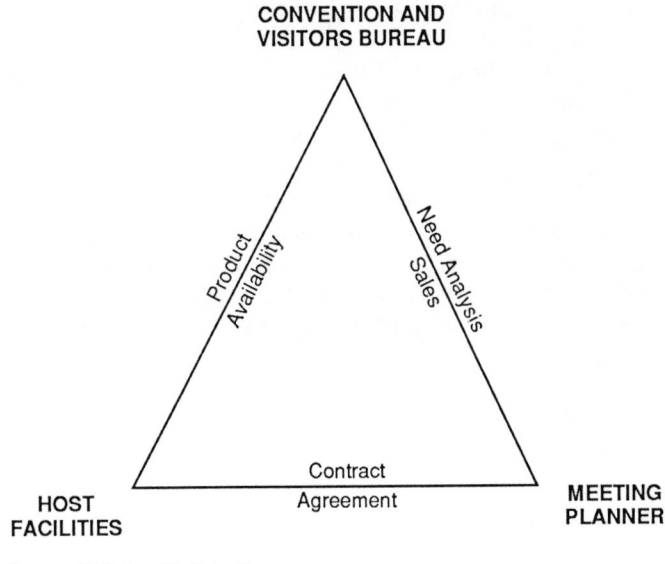

**CONVENTION AND
VISITORS BUREAU**

Product Availability

Need Analysis
Sales

Contract
Agreement

**HOST
FACILITIES**

**MEETING
PLANNER**

Source: © Richard B. Gartrell

Figure 1.2

present to a planner on behalf of the community a bid for his/her convention or group, assisting with the securing of meeting room and hotel room commitments. The bureau can suggest tour itineraries or other tour planning assistance. The bureau wants to make the meeting or tour planner's job easier; thus, the bureau serves as the broker or liaison between the planner and the host destination and its resources. From pre-convention planning through post-convention activities, bureaus are, for meeting and tour planners, the most efficient source for comprehensive city information and assistance.

This liaison role is difficult but essential. Cities have a reputation which is important. The bureau, through its stable presence, protects the components of its product from the unreasonable demands of its customers, the planners, while at the same time, it protects its clients from those components that, intentionally or not, attempt to provide less than a reasonable or quality level of sales and service or who extract a higher than acceptable profit for what is provided. Given this dual responsibility of representing the interests of both the buyer and the seller, a bureau must hold a high degree of autonomy to survive as an effective organization. This critical role is justified in part by the high turnover of hotel management teams and their pressure to generate every possible dollar from each and every customer. However, the total product, the city and its reputation, will be around well beyond any individual or management team; it is therefore the role of the convention and visitor bureau to serve as a stabilizing long-term influence through which conventions are solicited and serviced.[4]

Bureaus help pleasure visitors to their cities through information centers and by responding to travel inquiries. Bureaus can efficiently provide city visitors with an array of information that addresses a multitude of questions about hotels, restaurants, attractions, shopping, recreation and entertainment opportunities. The bureau essentially serves as a visitor's one-stop shopping center for ideas and information.

As noted earlier, "bureaus sell cities." Convention and visitor bureaus have one fundamental mission: *to solicit and service conventions and other related group business and to engage in visitor promotions, which generate overnight stays for a destination, thereby enhancing and developing the economic fabric of the community.* This mission can be realized through a variety of responsibilities delineated within a bureau's marketing program. Such programs tend to cluster around the following broad goals:

- to prospect, nurture, encourage, and invite associations and corporations to hold meetings and conventions in their city;
- to assist associations and corporations with the coordination of their conventions, seminars and trade shows while in that city, including housing, transportation, registration or other mutually agreed upon services;
- to work with the component elements of the visitor industry, coordinating their resources in support of bidding for conventions, seminars and trade shows;
- to provide an array of services to tour planners in developing tours into a city, including suggested itineraries and overnight accommodations;
- to provide leadership for the visitor industry, coordinating activities, encouraging marketing activities and providing a wholistic image on behalf of the city.

Bureaus have a sensitive and important role to play in the leadership of the travel and tourism industry within a community. Without the dynamic and professional role of a bureau, a city is less likely to have an image in the marketplace among meeting and tour planners, and as a result, will not gain the benefits that accrue from having convention and trade show delegates spending time and money in their communities. Bureaus are destination marketing organizations, operating within very fluid political arenas, providing stability for a city and confidence to the planner.[5]

The IACVB

In 1915, the International Association of Convention & Visitor Bureaus was founded; its purpose then was essentially two-fold: to exchange information about the convention industry among its membership and to encourage sound professional practices within the industry. This networking among bureau professionals became the cornerstone of the association. When the association held its first meeting in 1920, there were 28 member cities; it was at that time that the membership agreed to submit reports on all conventions hosted in their cities and to allow this information to be shared by one another. Though conducted in a rather sporadic manner for a number of years, it was not until a central office was developed in Cincinnati that the exchange of information became a methodical and essential program of the association. In 1970, the board of directors approved the process of handling these reports through a computer. Today, the IACVB has developed the INET system, which allows for the rapid reporting and exchange of convention reports among participating cities. In fact, the INET data bank represents data on more than 7,700 associations and more than 15,500 meetings. Their entries conform to the following criteria in order to be considered for the exchange of information program;

- they must be transient and solicitable conventions, open to bidding from any city in the world;
- they must include 50 or more rooms to qualify for a listing;
- they must be recognizable associations or organizations, either regional, national or international in scope.

These computerized convention reports have become an essential part of a bureau's marketing endeavors since it is possible to isolate specific groups or specific meetings that are held at specific times of the year. Each report provided to a bureau gives it comprehensive information that allows for effective client prospecting and convention targeting.

Because of the professional networking found in the IACVB, its growth over its history has been dramatic. Today, the association represents a membership in excess of 300 convention and visitor bureaus, representing 22 countries. New bureaus formed in recent years have been the mid- to small-sized cities, which have taken advantage of the financial resources of transient hotel room tax legislation to form a marketing entity for their destinations.

But even from its earliest days, the IACVB has been a strong advocate of sound professional practices in the soliciting and servicing of conventions and trade shows. For example, in 1938, less than 25% of all conventions held charged any kind of a registration fee. As a result, the IACVB published a pamphlet entitled *Sound Convention Financing* to encourage individual convention registration as a means for associations to pay for the costs of a convention.

It was also in the 1930's that the IACVB published another pamphlet entitled *Selection of the Convention City*. This publication strongly recommended site selection by a board of directors, an executive committee or a site selection committee over a delegate vote on such issues. The IACVB argument was that such delegate votes could lead to emotional voting behaviors and would not necessarily take into consideration the pertinent issues that require thoughtful review in order to select a site that will make an effective meeting. At the same time, the IACVB published another pamphlet entitled *Convention Planning,* which recommended the methodical steps for planning a successful convention.

In 1943, these pamphlets were combined into a single publication entitled *Conventions: An American Institution.*[6] In 1958, the IACVB released an enlarged and revised 136 page edition of this publication covering topics such as expositions, group business, convention financing, convention management, city selection, date selection and registration.

These were only some of the early steps taken by the association to provide professional guidance to a rapidly developing industry. In 1948, the association undertook its first "Convention Delegate Expenditure" survey with the cooperation of its 29 members. For the first time, conventions were elevated from their nebulous position as to their value and importance, to make cities more aware of their significant economic importance. The second survey was undertaken in 1957 with 37 member cities participating; and ever since those early days, the IACVB has made it a practice to assess the economic impact of conventions on cities through a periodic "Convention Delegate Expenditure" survey.

The IACVB has become a critically important information resource center or clearinghouse of information for convention and visitor bureaus, including the following kinds of information for its member bureaus:

- sample personnel contracts
- sample by-laws and articles of incorporation
- results of surveys on such varied topics as bureau funding, compensation and delegate expenditure
- sample personnel policy for bureau organizations
- code of professional ethics

Even more than information, the IACVB provides two critical programs which are open and accessible to both member and non-member bureaus: consulting team visits and the annual educational program. If a city wants a team of consultants to visit their destination to assess its potential for a bureau or to assist with refinements to an existing operation, the IACVB upon request and mutual agreement, will select a team of bureau executives who have had some similar consulting experience. The team will then visit that community for a number of days and meet with key representatives of the travel and hospitality industry, political and governmental officials, and representatives from the professional, commercial, educational and industrial segments of the community. Following the visit, a detailed report will be provided with the team's analysis and recommendations. Such team visits have been found extremely useful in establishing a new bureau and bringing an existing bureau into a stronger organizational character.

The IACVB also has developed a comprehensive educational program. More than 60 courses have been outlined in a comprehensive course catalog; these courses are offered on a rotational and periodic basis at the annual educational program and the annual summer convention. These three-hour intensive courses explore an array of topics that include convention and tourism sales, convention servicing, convention center management, bureau administration, housing bureau operations, bureau funding and marketing strategies. This program was a first for the association in that it established a body of knowledge that relates directly to the sales, marketing, administration and operation of convention and visitor bureaus. The acceptance of professional certificate programs has given even greater recognition to the importance of bureaus as destination marketing organizations and to the need for professional leadership.

The IACVB has joined with many other allied associations over the years to ensure the professional development of the convention industry. In 1948, the Convention Liaison Council (CLC) was formed and the IACVB was among its charter members. Today, the CLC includes 14 member organizations determined to establish and practice sound convention management. Toward this end, the CLC has published a *Manual of Convention Planning* and developed a "Certified Meeting Planner" educational program. Other associations to which the IACVB has closely allied itself include (see Appendix D): American Society of Association Executives (ASAE); American Hotel and Motel Association (AH&ME); Hotel Sales Marketing Association (HSMA); Professional Convention Management Association (PCMA); National Association of Exhibition Managers (NAEM); Trade Show Bureau (TSB); and the National Tour Associaton (NTA). It has been this kind of commitment to excellence that has provided the travel and tourism industry with strong leadership, revealing economic indicators and trends, and dynamic marketing organizations that represent an industry valued in excess of $30 billion annually.

Summary

The strength of a bureau is found in the unity of its parts; the intertwined relationships that bureaus have with members of the travel and tourism industry are based on integrity and respect for the mission that must be accomplished. What began as a small industry in 1896 is today a significant contributor to the economic vitality of communities. The nature of the competitive marketplace spurs bureaus to heighten their marketing endeavors to attract visitors to their cities. In fact, bureaus are the catalysts for action on behalf of a city's travel and tourism industry. Destination marketing is not simply a promotional effort but a sophisticated, well-developed plan of action executed by knowledgeable professionals. Today, whether conventions and meetings are small or large, or whether visitor promotions are aimed towards groups or individuals, investments are being made to ensure a city's economic strength for tomorrow.[7]

Discussion Questions

1. In what way does the concept of destination marketing differ from the general concept of marketing?

2. What factors make convention and visitor bureaus unique marketing entities?

3. Should a convention and visitor bureau be formed by a city?

4. In general terms, describe at least three (3) operations that are common to convention and visitor bureaus?

5. Bureaus are often called "brokers". What is meant by this term and why is this significant?

6. Name and describe at least three (3) primary programs of the International Association of Convention & Visitor Bureaus. Why are these significant programs?

Bibliographic Resources

1. Gillett, Charles, "Conventions and the City", Speech before the International Marketplace for Convention Cities and Facilities, Cannes, France, 1975.

2. Trafton, Warren L., "Conventions as an Industry," Unpublished Manuscript, 1977, 15 pgs.

3. Gillett, Charles, "The Long-Term Impact of Conventions in a Downbeat Economic Environment," speech before the Annual Meeting of the San Juan-Puerto Rico Convention Bureau, May 1982.

4. International Association of Convention & Visitor Bureaus, "Convention Bureaus: What They Are and Do" (Pamphlet, no date).

5. See Also: Kirkland, George, Diane Claytor, Shirley Long and Richard Gartrell, "The Convention and Visitors Bureau", pages 19–28 in Nichols, Barbara C. (ed.), *Professional Meeting Management* (Birmingham, Alabama: PCMA, 1985).

6. Turner, J. S. (ed.), *Conventions: An American Institution* (IACVB, 1958).

7. Gillett, Charles, "The Economics of Urban Tourism," Speech before the United States Conference of Mayors, Washington, D.C., January 1982.

VISITOR MARKETS AND THEIR ECONOMIC IMPORTANCE

2

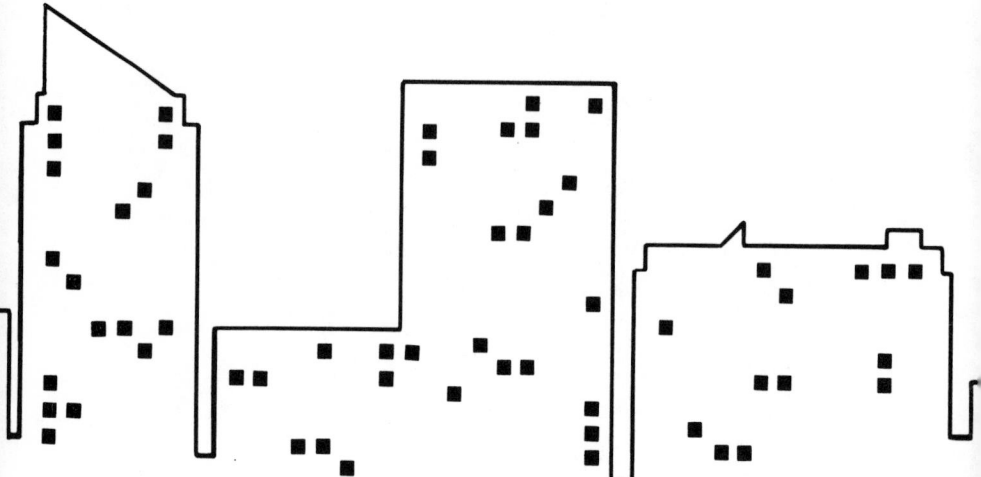

LEARNING OBJECTIVES

Upon reading this chapter, you will learn the
following:

- What composes the meetings and convention
  market segments;
- The economic significance of meetings and
  conventions;
- The diversity of tourism market segments;
- The economic importance of tourism
  domestically and internationally;
- And sources that can be consulted for
  information on various visitor markets.

Introduction

What is meant by visitor markets? What are the characteristics of those markets? What is their economic significance? Is the travel and tourism industry understood as to its importance in the economic vitality of communities?

Today, travel and tourism has become one of the most sought after means of economic development for destinations. Countries like New Zealand, Canada, India, Egypt, Indonesia, Singapore and Malaysia have discovered the significance of the travel and tourism industry as a source for new revenues and jobs. As a result, the stature of their national tourism offices has been raised, giving them greater visibility and importance. Within the United States, state travel offices also have seen increases in their overall marketing budgets as competition for visitors becomes even more sophisticated. In South Dakota, Alabama and Tennessee, state travel offices have been elevated to cabinet levels within state governments, signifying the importance of the travel and tourism industry to those states. Cities have now realized that they too can capture the economic benefits of conventions and tourism activities if they formulate and fund strong marketing programs through a convention and visitor bureau.

What does this all mean? Though many associate the word "tourism" with the romance of an exotic vacation, the reality is a rather cold, hard truth. Visitors are a critical source of revenue for destinations, necessitating a re-examination of priorities, attitudes and allocation of resources. Today international agreements allow visitors to purchase tickets and travel worldwide without the hassles of currency exchanges; this opens the potential for greater mobility as well as understanding amid the cultural diversities of this global village. With shifts in various economic markets, the travel and tourism industry has become the new clean industry which generates large revenues relative to the demand placed on the support structures of a destination.

Because of the diversity of this important industry, there is also a lack of total agreement as to what labels ought to be used when describing various market segments. For the purposes of this book, discussions will focus on "meetings and conventions" as one critical market segment, and "travel and tourism" comprising the other market segment. The latter is composed of "pleasure oriented travel" but also contains comparative information on what is termed as "business/convention travel."

Meetings and Convention Markets

The meetings and convention market segment is complex and diverse. In 1985, the U.S. Census Bureau estimated there were 500,000 associations at local, state and national levels, of which some 20,000 were national in scope.[1]

The industry held over 227,000 meetings and conventions attended by better than 31.6 million delegates.[2] More than 8,000 trade shows are also held annually with delegate attendance approaching 5 million.[3] Meetings and conventions may be small or they may be large. Regardless of their size, meetings and conventions have been recognized worldwide as a growing segment of the visitor markets and have, in recent years, been estimated as having more than a $30 billion impact on host destinations.

When discussing meetings and convention markets, it is important to know definitions and to understand how their application makes segmenting of those markets easier. One perspective to market segmentation would be an examination of the "type" of meeting or convention group being explored.

Conventions, for example, are formal meetings usually sponsored by an association for the purposes of exchanging knowledge and information with and between its members. Conventions usually require overnight accommodations; smaller conventions may be called conferences. Several examples of conventions include the Annual Management Conference of the American Society of Association Executives (attendance: 2,000); Annual Convention and Exchange for the National Tour Association (attendance: 3,000); American Dental Association (attendance: 30,000); and the International Fertilizer Industry Association (attendance: 169).

Trade Shows are exhibitions that are usually sponsored by an organization representing a specific industry group. They are open to members of that industry and may not be open to the general public. Trade shows are characterized by a gathering of "buyers" who view exhibits or see demonstrations by "sellers." Examples of trade shows might include the American Hardware Manufacturing Association (attendance: 72,000) or the Great Neck Premium Incentive Show (attendance: 30,000).

Corporate Meetings vary considerably in size depending on the sponsoring corporation. These meetings usually include overnight accommodations. They may be sales meetings, stockholder meetings, board meetings or small meetings of a similar type. An example might be a sales meeting for Ford Motor Company (attendance: 150).

Public Shows are similar to trade shows. Exhibitions are sponsored by an organization representing a specific industry. Such shows are always open to the public and as a result, attendees are not limited to a specific group of professionals. Generally, public shows require a paid admission. An example of a public show would be the Detroit Auto Show (attendance: 450,000).

Reunions are social gatherings organized exclusively for the purposes of bringing together family groups, alumni groups, military groups or similar groups. These activities usually include overnight accommodations and numerous social events and rarely involve business or educational programming. Examples of typical reunions might include the Class of '57 from Capuchino High School, San Bruno, California (attendance: 200), or the Military Order of the Purple Heart (attendance: 400).

Events are gatherings that involve entertainment-related activities; an event is usually open to the public and may require paid admission. Overnight accommodations may occur but are not usually the primary purpose of the event. Among examples of events would be the Gilroy, California Garlic Festival (attendance: 30,000), Portland, Oregon Rose Festival (attendance: 300,000) and the Ann Arbor, Michigan Street Art Fairs (attendance: 500,000).

Meetings and conventions also are looked at from the perspective of their "scope," or the geographic area from which their activities are drawn. The International Association of Convention & Visitor Bureaus has defined the scope of meetings and conventions in the following manner:

Intercontinental Meetings. These are international meetings that convene on more than one continent such as the Technical Association of the Pulp and Paper Industry (attendance: 725).

European meetings convene only in Europe and are not restricted by rules or practice to meeting in just one European country. The European Council for Rural Law is such an example.

Canadian Meetings. These organizations or associations meet only in Canada and might include the Royal College of Physicians and Surgeons (attendance: 875).

North American meetings are held in any two or more of the following: the United States, Canada, Mexico and the Caribbean. An example would be the Illuminating Engineering Society of North America (attendance: 400).

U.S. national meetings are held only in the United States and are not restricted by rules or practice as to any specific region or location within the United States. An example of such a group might be the National Business Education Association (attendance: 2000).

Regional meetings refer to a meeting held within a specifically defined group of U.S. states, usually ones from which the organization draws its membership. Occasionally a region will include Puerto Rico, U.S. Territories and Canadian Provinces. An example of a regional meeting might be the Central States Speech Association which is composed of a thirteen-state region, or a district meeting of the Rural Electric Cooperative Association.

State meetings are usually those sponsored by a state association or organization and restricted to a single state (usually the state in which that association's headquarters is located). State meetings seldom cross state boundaries into other states and usually rotate among cities within their own state boundaries. An example of a state association is the Alabama Dental Association.

Local meetings are usually generated by local organizations associations or corporations. Such meetings are held within the boundaries of a specific city and are usually for a specific membership or targeted audience. Overnight accommodations may be involved. Such meetings may be sponsored by banks, educational institutions, scientific corporations, businesses or the chamber of commerce.

Among the founding principles of the International Association of Convention & Visitor Bureaus was the idea that there should be some commonly accepted definitions of what constitutes a "group" and how one should document its movement. In addition to the above definitions, the IACVB agreed that the following criteria would apply to those groups being placed into its exchange of information program called INET. Groups which do not conform to these criteria, such as state or local groups, are not part of the IACVB reporting program.

- meetings must be held by a recognized association;
- meetings must be transient and solicitable;
- meetings must be held regularly;
- meetings must use 50 or more sleeping rooms (peak night);
- meetings must be regional or larger in scope.

These criteria have become particularly important to IACVB member bureaus not only for purposes of exchanging information on transient and solicitable groups but also for purposes of establishing a viable statistical data base for evaluating economic impact. The IACVB has been particularly significant in developing criteria and standards upon which industry members can agree.

However, there is considerably more to the meetings and convention market than simply segmenting by type of meeting or scope of representation. There are identifiable segments that represent particular groupings of associations, each of which has its own membership. The size, frequency and character of meetings will vary considerably from one association to another. Such classification of associations can provide some ease to a convention and visitor bureau when targeting a specific market segment for specific purposes (for example, medical groups). The following is a brief discussion of some of those groupings of associations and their potential for meetings and conventions.

There were, for example, more than 700,000 corporate meetings held during 1985.[4] Of these, some 163,500 were training seminars, 178,000 management seminars, and 113,000 regional sales seminars. The balance was composed of product introduction seminars, national sales seminars, incentive trips and stockholder meetings. Almost 40 million professionals attended these seminars. Seminars averaged 56 attendees and lasted an average of 2.6 days. Almost $8 million was spent by corporations for these meetings. Planning time for such meetings averaged 4½ months, ranging from nine months for incentive trips to less than three months for introduction of new product seminars. The top five factors influencing the selection of a meeting site were the quality of food service; the number, size and caliber of meeting rooms; the efficiency of billing procedures; the number, size and caliber of sleeping rooms; and the efficiency of check-in and check-out procedures. Among those criteria that would influence the selection of a destination were the availability of hotels and meeting space, ease of transportation for attendees, transportation costs, distance traveled and the availability of recreational facilities. In general, 31%

of the corporate meeting planners surveyed indicated an increase in the number of meetings held in 1985, while 59% indicated the same number of meetings as in previous years, and only 10% indicated a decrease.[5] Because of the generally small character of the corporate meeting, this market segment is usually vigorously sought after by individual hotels and resort facilities.

Whereas planning timelines for corporate meetings are relatively short, association meetings and conventions are planned further in advance and are more predictable. Depending on the size and character of the meeting or convention, associations may select sites two to five years or more in advance. In a recent survey, 31% of the planners indicated they book four years or more in advance, 33% indicated they book between three and four years in advance, and 26% indicated they book between one and two years in advance.[6] Rotation patterns also will affect site selection. Some associations will have an east-west, U.S. or outside-U.S. rotation pattern that will influence their planning timelines. For example, the Environmental Research Institute of Michigan alternates its annual meeting between an international destination and a U.S. location while the Travel and Tourism Research Association has an east-west U.S. rotational pattern, plus meeting in Canada every five years.

The association meetings and convention market continues to grow. In 1985, more than 227,700 meetings and conventions were held.[7] The International Congress Office of the United States Travel and Tourism Administration reported that 7,000 international congresses were held during 1986. In a related study, 19% of the meeting planners surveyed indicated an increase in the number of meetings held during the previous year.[8] Sixty-eight percent of the planners coordinate major annual conventions which are usually held between March and August. Average delegate attendance at these major conventions is about 1,100, involving more than 14 million delegates during 1985. Another 18 million are involved in smaller association meetings such as board meetings (22%), educational or training programs (30%), professional or technical meetings (47%), or meetings of a similar nature.[9]

For associations, the following general criteria are among those considered important when selecting a meeting or convention site: availability of hotels or convention facilities; ease of transportation to and from the meeting site; transportation costs; accessibility of the meeting site; and climate. For the hotel, association planners tend to rely on the same fundamental criteria used by corporate meeting planners. Most association meeting delegates rely on air transportation as their primary means of getting to and from a convention site; thus accessibility becomes a major concern when selecting the site.[10]

Unlike the corporate market, the association market can be subdivided into segments. For example, there are at least 35,000 medical or health-care professional meetings and conventions each year which involve any number of the more than 2.6 million professionals in medicine and related disciplines. Medical meetings use more than 23 million room-nights annually and account for expenditures in excess of $2.5 billion for food, beverage and lodging. Many of the medical meetings are small, involving an average of 200 delegates; however, there are several mega-meetings such as the American Medical Association. With the continuing education requirements for medical, dental and health care professionals, along with technological changes and growing medical needs of an aging population, medical meetings are seen as an excellent market segment to target.[11]

Educational meetings and conventions comprise another large market segment. The large number of educational institutions and their related programs contribute to this growth as does the increase of professional development programs within various professions. The average educational seminar has approximately 250 in attendance and may involve more than 4.5 million delegates in any given year. Many facilities find this a lucrative target market due to its size and growth potential.[12]

The insurance meetings market spends more than $2 billion annually on meetings. With the more than 5,000 companies that are said to comprise this industry, the number of meetings is substantial. On the average, insurance companies hold 20 meetings a year, with attendance ranging from 20–200. Major insurance conventions often draw as many as 2,000 delegates.[13]

International congresses have similar characteristics. For example, based on a recent survey, 63% of the associations hold their meetings in Europe, 19% in the United States, 12.6% in Asia and Australia, and less than 4% in Africa. Delegate attendance averages 500 per meeting for 70% of the associations. Seventy-seven percent of the meetings last five days or less. Thirty-nine percent use conference centers while 31% use hotel facilities. Fifty-eight percent of the associations make their decisions 1–2 years in advance while another 31% plan 3–4 years ahead. Only 37% indicated they hold exhibitions in conjunction with their meetings.[14]

Trade shows are another major segment of the market. More than 8,000 are held annually, generating in excess of $8 billion for the host cities. Trade shows, depending on their size and facility needs, may require space reservations from three to five years in advance. Delegate attendance averaged just under 20,000 in 1981 and is projected to exceed 30,000 by 1991. In 1981, the average net square feet of exhibition space required was in excess of 173,000 and is expected to exceed 300,000 by 1991. On the average, a trade show involved more than 4,000 hotel rooms in 1981 and is expected to exceed 7,000 by 1991. Trade shows are a major source for selling products and services; they offer the seller and the buyer a forum in which to discuss new products and services, renew business acquaintances or explore the latest in technological developments.[15]

As reflected above, there are many ways to segment the meetings and convention market. Market characteristics are important and a thorough understanding of these variables is necessary when prospecting or bidding on a meeting, convention or trade show.[16] Chapter 5 explores in more detail the sales and marketing procedures utilized by a convention and visitor bureau.

EXPENDITURE COMPARISONS

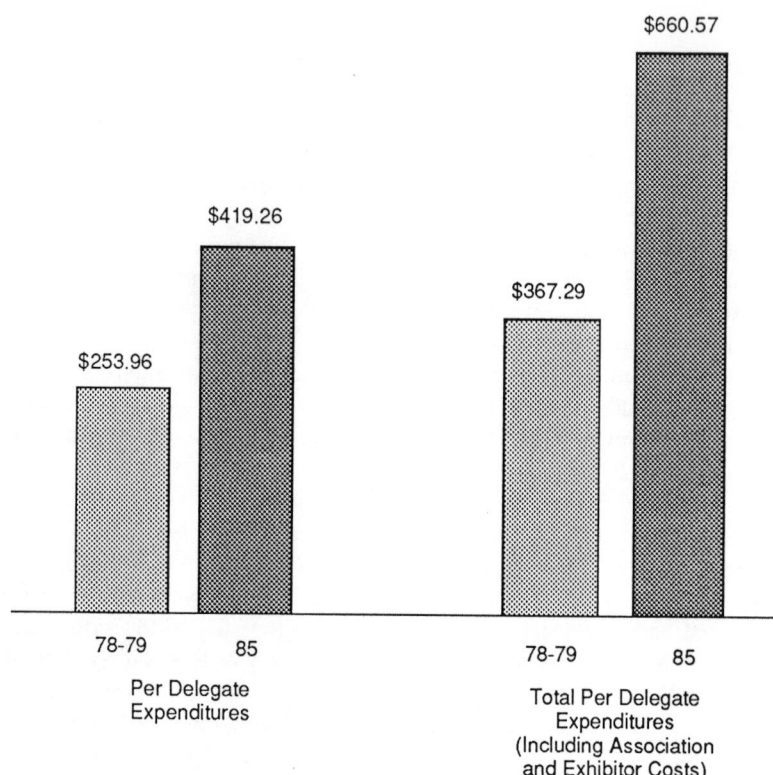

Source: International Association of Convention & Visitor Bureaus.

Figure 2.1

Economic Importance: Meetings and Conventions

Over the past years, the International Association of Convention & Visitor Bureaus has undertaken the challenge of assessing the economic impact of meetings. The most recent in a series of studies is the international survey completed in 1985 and updated in 1986. The 1985 study involved 1,314 conventions in both U.S. and non-U.S. cities. Conventions classified as international or national in scope numbered 639 while 675 were state or regional. The results confirmed the continuing growth and importance of the meetings and convention markets. For example, out-of-town convention delegates spent an average of $419 per trip, up from the $254 total spent by a delegate in the 1978–1979 study. A delegate typically stayed 4 nights, for an average of $105

DISTRIBUTION OF DELEGATE EXPENDITURES

1978-1979 Results   1985 Results

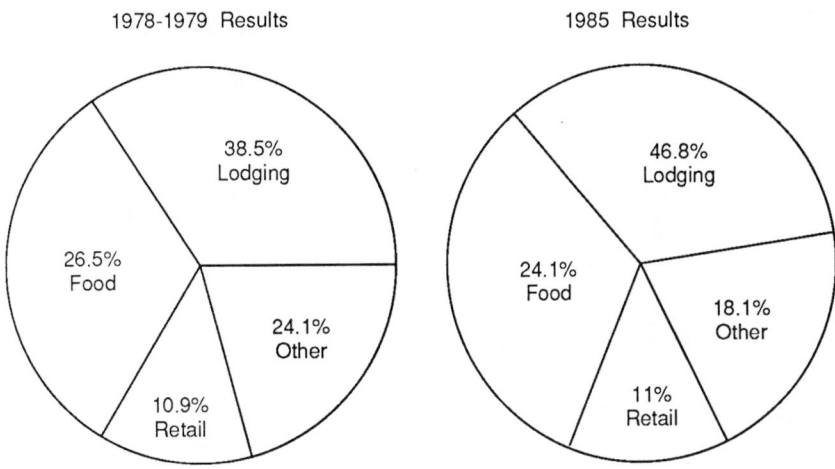

Source: International Association of Convention & Visitor Bureaus.

Figure 2.2

per day. When expenditures by associations, trade show exhibitors and exposition service contractors were added to delegate expenditures, the average figure rose to over $660 per delegate for the four-day period, compared to $367 total found in the 1978–1979 study. This represents a 79.9% increase in convention-related spending. During the same time period, the consumer price index (CPI) increased 56.1% while the travel price index (TPI) increased 74.2%. The travel price index measures changes in travel-related goods and services including food, lodging and transportation. Growth in excess of the TPI and CPI reflects the importance of meetings and conventions to the economic fabric of cities.

Lodging costs represented an estimated 46.8% of a delegate's expenditures in 1985, compared to 38.5% in 1978–79. Other expenditures included 24.1% for food, 11.0% for retail, and 18.1% for other expenses (including hospitality suites, entertainment, and local transportation).

In 1986, the International Association of Convention & Visitor Bureaus completed a validation study involving just U.S. cities. The study found a 9.73% increase in the overall spending by convention delegates. The study also showed that an estimated 65 million delegates attended over 135,000 meetings compared to 59 million delegates attending 126,000 meetings as noted in the previous year's study. This increase in delegates and the number of meetings and conventions being held indicated that the direct economic impact on U.S. cities would exceed $30.3 billion, compared to $27.7 billion the previous year.[17]

COMPARISON OF U.S. DELEGATE SPENDING 1985 AND 1986

Summary of Results

	1985*	U.S. CITIES ONLY		PERCENTAGE INCREASE
		1985	1986	
Average total expenditure per delegate	$419.26	$453.46	$477.49	5.3%
Average daily expenditure per delegate	$105.05	$122.56	$125.66	2.6%
Average length of stay per delegate	4.0	3.7	3.8	2.7%
Average travel party size	2.5	1.80	1.65	(8.3%)
Association expenditures per delegate	$44.90	$45.55	$49.43	8.5%
Exhibitor expenditures per delegate	$183.84	$201.36	$243.31	20.8%
Exposition service contractor expenditures per delegate	$12.57	$17.31	$17.31	0%
TOTAL	$660.57	$717.68	$787.54	9.7%

*includes international data.

Source: International Association of Convention & Visitor Bureaus.

Figure 2.3

The impact of meetings, conventions and trade shows on a destination is based on the total volume, length of stay, per-delegate expenditures, type of meetings and conventions and other related economic factors. Such information is usually gathered and released through the local convention and visitor bureau. However, for national and international studies, the International Association of Convention & Visitor Bureaus has established baseline information against which a convention and visitor bureau can evaluate and assess its own information.

Travel and Tourism Markets

Travel and tourism markets are not as easily defined as the meetings and convention market, yet they have a significant impact on the economic fabric of cities. Travel and tourism markets have traditionally been divided into pleasure travelers and business/convention travelers. Bureaus have been even more specific in segmenting travel and tourism markets. Chapter 4 reflects some of those divisions.

Depending on the character of the destination, convention and visitor bureaus have formed partnerships with airlines, cruise lines, hotels, rental car companies, attractions and many other industry components in order to take advantage of various visitor markets. Establishing a market presence and image is critical to being successful in attracting visitors. The more unique an attraction or destination, the more likely it is to be successful. The majestic beauty of Lake Louise draws thousands of groups and pleasure visitors to Banff (Alberta, Canada) as does the diversity of fantasies at Disney World in Florida. On a different scale, the attraction may be a unique tradition such as the changing of the guard at Buckingham Palace in London or the operation of cable cars in San Francisco.

Convention and visitor bureaus are not alone in these marketing efforts. In fact, there is a partnership among many promotional agencies that brings attention to a specific region, state, province or nation. These promotional agencies, whether state, provincial, territorial or national tourism offices, establish images for a destination, thus making visitors more aware of the attractions and resources of that destination. In many cases, the funds that are allocated for such marketing programs exceed the capabilities of a convention and visitor bureau. Equally important is the fact that these promotional efforts usually cover a geographic area that exceeds the responsibilities of a single convention and visitor bureau. For example, a state travel office will establish an image for a state and will enhance the efforts of a convention and visitor bureau when attracting tourism markets. Today, billions of dollars are spent worldwide on the marketing of geographic areas as destinations. Simply looking at an issue of *Travel and Leisure* magazine or an auto club magazine will reveal the competitiveness that exists among destinations such as Hong Kong, Australia, Ireland, Jamaica, Ontario or Texas. All are vying to establish recognizable and favorable market images that will influence the attitudes and buying patterns of potential visitors. Similarly, suppliers such as airlines, rental car companies, cruise lines, hotel chains and major attractions are supplementing these broader promotional campaigns in order to maintain and increase their own market share by influencing the buying patterns of potential visitors.

What are these visitor markets? How does one identify visitors and their needs and interests? These two questions are fundamental to a continuing research process that attempts to better understand visitor market segments, motivations and behaviors. Studies have explored segmentation of visitor markets based on seasonal benefits,[18] distance traveled,[19] vacation preferences and magazine readership,[20] vacation patterns,[21] decision making processes,[22] age,[23] and motivation.[24] Other studies have attempted to apply specific market research techniques as a means for gathering information for more effective travel marketing.[25]

Travel literature also suggests other ways of looking at visitor markets and travel behaviors. For example, travelers have been described psychologically as being either allocentric or psychocentric. Allocentric travelers seek unique travel experiences that allow them to explore new areas; they enjoy the novel and like to stay at "non-tourist type" lodging facilities. Psychocentric travelers seek the familiar. They prefer commonplace activities, familiar destinations, and tourist accommodations. They do not wish to be surprised or to experience an unsettling feeling. They want psychological security.[26]

Attempts at explaining the attitudes and behaviors of travelers also have been made by applying accepted psychological and sociological theories. One such study suggested that there is a consistency-complexity continuum along which decisions are made. People may wish balance, harmony or consistency in their lives and thus, when traveling, tend to select those destinations and services offering a high degree of predictability. Those who seek complexity are seeking new experiences; when applied to travel, they tend to drive back roads, wish to avoid heavy tourist areas, prefer to stay at independent lodging facilities and patronize local eating spots.[27]

Other studies have generally explored reasons why people travel. For example, some have suggested a "push-pull" theory for travel motivation. "Push" factors are those needs, motivations and patterns of thinking that come from within us. Such intangibles might include the need for self-discovery, rest, relaxation, prestige, recognition, adventure or challenge. "Pull" factors are those influences that draw people toward them; such factors would include scenic areas, historic areas, cultural events, educational meetings, spectator and participation sports or social attractions.[28]

The U.S. Travel Data Center annually conducts a National Travel Survey to measure domestic travel in the United States.[29] This survey found that 76% of all travel in 1986 was taken for pleasure purposes, while 17% was for business/convention purposes. Pleasure travelers often include children in their traveling party, while business/convention travelers rarely do. In addition, 51% of pleasure travel was found to include visits to friends or relatives.

In a study conducted by Tourism Canada, U.S. pleasure travel markets were divided into eight vacation segments.[30]

- Visit friends and relatives   44%
- Touring   14%
- Close to home   13%
- Outdoors   10%
- Resort   8%
- City   7%
- Theme Park   3%
- Cruise   1%

For international travelers, the reasons why people traveled to and from the United States were similar to other studies.[31]

Trip Purpose	To U.S.	From U.S.
• Business/Convention	44%	31%
• Vacation/Holiday	46%	59%
• Visit Friends/Relatives	31%	28%

Many of the national, state/provincial or regional promotional efforts are primarily addressed to the pleasure travel market segment. Traditionally, however, convention and visitor bureaus have looked at this segment in a more focused manner. Bureaus tend to focus their efforts, as discussed in Chapter 4, on the group travel, incentive and urban-bound visitor markets.

To discover why people travel, there must be a constant vigilance of interests and motivations, how decisions are made, criteria for selecting a trip direction or vacation destination, and the types of resources used while considering a decision. Understanding the character of visitor markets is not a single endeavor but a constant monitoring of trends, research findings, buying patterns and economic environments. What is understood today by marketers will influence sales and marketing successes tomorrow.

Economic Importance: Travel and Tourism

The U.S. Travel Data Center and the Travel and Tourism Government Affairs Council, both affiliates of the Travel Industry Association of America, have stated that the travel industry is the third largest retail or service industry in the United States, with domestic travel producing $234.5 billion in business receipts in 1985. This comprises 6.1% of the U.S. gross national product. In 1985, the travel and tourism industry contributed 3.8% of the combined tax revenues of federal, state and local governments. In 39 of the 50 U.S. states, travel and tourism is the first, second or third largest employer; for 13 states, it is the largest employer. The industry is the second largest private employer in the United States employing more than 4.95 million people. It also generated more than 460,600 new jobs in the U.S. during 1985 and has provided more than 3.2 million new jobs since 1975. International visitors alone contributed more than $11.7 billion to the U.S. economy in 1985.[32]

The growth of travel and tourism internationally can be seen in its economic significance. In 1985, tourism reached an estimated $1.8 trillion, comprising 12% of the world's gross national product.[33] International tourist arrivals exceeded 330 million, and more than 1.2 million new rooms were added to the world's accommodation capacity.[34] In recent years, the fastest growth for tourism has been seen in Asia and Europe.

Specific market segments also reflect the growing economic significance of tourism. The cruise industry had revenues that exceeded $4 billion in 1986, an 18% increase over the previous year. The fastest growing segment is the 3–4-day cruise. Distribution of ships to new locations plus the production of new ships are positive indications of the anticipated growth of the cruise line industry.

The group travel industry has grown from a $9 to $10 billion business since 1985. More than 85% of the National Tour Association tour operators incorporate some kind of intermodal transportation such as air, ship or rail. It has been estimated that this industry segment will experience significant growth over the coming years as population demographics change.[35]

The number of travel agencies continues to grow with nearly 29,000 operating today. Travel agents remain the primary distributor of some of the major tourism products including cruises (95%), package tours (90%), international air travel (80%), international hotels (85%) and car rentals (50%).[36]

Attractions are also a major beneficiary of visitor spending; 250 million people visited theme parks and attractions in the U.S., spending an estimated $4 billion at these facilities. An estimated 600–700 theme parks and attractions from small, family-owned businesses to large corporate operations exist within the U.S. The 45 parks with top attendance account for nearly half of the 250 million annual visitors.[37]

The economic significance of the travel and tourism industry cannot be underestimated. In 34 U.S. states, travel and tourism generates more receipts than agriculture. Italy spends $99.8 million, United Kingdom $42.5 million, France $26.7 million and Canada $26 million for promotion of tourism. The increase of international travel, the growth of destination marketing budgets, and the actual economic impact travel and tourism has on destinations have all contributed to the growth and recognition of this industry. Herman Kahn's futuristic prediction that tourism would be the largest industry in the world by the year 2000 has today become a reality.

Summary

This has been an overview of very diverse and growing visitor markets. The meetings and convention markets continue to expand and play a significant role in the development of hotel rooms, meeting and convention facilities, and the emergence of convention and visitor bureaus. The economic impact of meetings and conventions is monitored by the International Association of Convention & Visitor Bureaus as well as assessed by such publications as *Meetings and Conventions, Successful Meetings* and *Meeting News*. While there is a diversity within the meetings and convention market, there is some homogeneity in tracking and assessing its impact.

Unlike the meetings and convention markets, travel and tourism markets are diverse and often require different tracking and assessment criteria. Annually, numerous reports of economic impact are developed through the U.S. Travel Data Center as well as the World Tourism Organization. The statistical information appears in a variety of reports, such as the *National Travel Survey* (for the U.S.) or the *Travel Industry World Yearbook—The Big Picture*. American Express also publishes an annual analysis of world tourism. The United States Travel and Tourism Administration monitors world tourism as well as international tourism to and from the U.S.

The bottomline is that the industry is economically vital to countries, states/provinces, regions and cities. How the many markets are segmented is the challenge that awaits a convention and visitor bureau.

Discussion Questions

1. What is meant by "visitor markets"?

2. Why has the word "travel" generated negative feelings among some people? How would you positively overcome those perceptions?

3. What factors have contributed to the growth of the "travel and tourism" industry?

4. How would you define and describe the meetings and conventions markets?

5. How does a convention differ from a trade show?

6. What is an intercontinental convention?

7. Segment the association market and describe each segment. How would you market to each?

8. How would you define and describe "tourism markets"? How would you segment those markets into identifiable markets? What marketing strategies would you use for each market segment?

9. Economically how significant is the "tourism market"? How would you communicate that importance to locally elected officials, members of the board of directors, or the bureau's membership?

10. Name at least four sources that can be consulted for statistical information on various visitor markets?

Bibliographic Resources

1. American Society of Association Executives, "Association Factbook," 1986, p. 12.

2. Ibid., p. 19.

3. Trade Show Bureau, "Trade Shows in Black and White: A Guide for Marketers," 1986, pp. 2–3.

4. Shaw, Margaret, *The Group Market: What It Is and How To Sell To It* (Washington, D.C.: Foundation of the Hotel Sales and Marketing Association International, 1986), pp. 33–38.

5. Meetings and Conventions, "The Meetings Market 1985," March 1986, Tables, 5, 6, 9, 18, 20, 22.

6. Ehrenman, Gayle, "51% of Association Planners Make Meeting Site Inspections," *Meeting News,* August 1986, p. 24.

7. ASAE, "Association Factbook," 1986, p. 19.

8. Meetings and Conventions, Ibid., Table 45.

9. "Small Meetings," *Meeting News,* November 15, 1987, p. 5.

10. Meetings and Conventions, Ibid., Tables 66, 67, 70.

11. Shaw, Margaret, Ibid., pp. 39–44.

12. Shaw, Margaret, Ibid., pp. 55–60.

13. Shaw, Margaret, Ibid., pp. 50–54.

14. Union of International Associations, "International Association Meetings: 1985 Statistics."

15. Trade Show Bureau, "Trade Shows in Black and White: A Guide for Marketers," 1986 and Trade Show Bureau Report #14, January 1983.

16. Abbey, James, "The Convention and Meetings Sector: Its Operation and Research Needs," in J. R. Brent Ritchie and Charles R. Goeldner, *Travel, Tourism and Hospitality Research* (New York: John Wily Publishers, 1987), pp. 265–274.

17. International Association of Convention & Visitor Bureaus, "1985 Convention Income Survey" and "1986 Convention Income Survey."

18. See Calantone, Roger, Jotindas Johas, "Seasonal Segmentation of the Tourism Market Using a Benefit Segmentation Framework," *Journal of Travel Research,* Fall 1984, pp. 14–24.

19. See Etzel, Michael, and Arch Woodside, "Segmenting Vacation Markets: The Case of the Distant and Near-Home Traveler," *Journal of Travel Research,* Spring 1982, pp. 10–14.

20. See Crask, Melvin, "Segmenting the Vacationer Market: Identifying the Vacation Preferences, Demographics and Magazine Readership of Each Group," *Journal of Travel Research,* Fall 1981, pp. 29–34.

21. See Oppedijk van Veen, Walle M. and Theo W. M. Verhallen, "Vacation Market Segmentation: A Domain-Specific Value Approach," *Annals of Tourism Research,* Volume 13, 1986, pp. 37–58; Richard Gitelson and John Crompton, "Insights Into the Repeat Vacation Phenomenon," *Annals of Tourism Research,* Volume 11, 1984, pp. 199–217; and Alm Gottlieb, "American's Vacations," *Annals of Tourism Research,* Volume 9, 1982, pp. 165–187.

22. See van Raaij, W. Fred and Dick A. Francken, "Vacation Decisions, Activities, and Satisfactions," *Annals of Tourism Research,* Volume 2, 1984, pp. 101–112; C. K. Walter and Hsin-Min Tong, "A Local Study of Consumer Vacation Travel Decisions," *Journal of Travel Research,* September 1977, pp. 30–34; Roger Jenkins, "Family Vacation Decision-Making," *Journal of Travel Research,* September 1978, pp. 2–7; and Robert Gosenza and Duane Davis, "Family Vacation Decision Making Over the Family Life Cycle: A Decision and Influence Structure Analysis," *Journal of Travel Research,* Fall 1981, pp. 17–23.

23. See Jobes, Patrick, "Old Timers and New Mobile Lifestyles," *Annals of Tourism Research,* Volume 2, 1984, pp. 181–198; Hale Tongren, "Travel Plans of the Over 65 Market Pre and Post Retirement," *Journal of Travel Research,* Fall 1980, pp. 7–11; Beverlee Anderson and Lynn Langmeyer, "The Under-50 and Over-50 Travelers: A Profile of Similarities and Differences," *Journal of Travel Research,* Spring 1982, pp. 20–24; and Pamela Weaver and Ken McCleary, "A Market Segmentation Study to Determine the Appropriate Ad/Model Format for Travel Advertising," *Journal of Travel Research,* Summer 1984, pp. 12–16.

24. See Dann, Graham, "Tourist Motivation: An Appraisal," *Annals of Tourism Research,* Volume 3, 1981, pp. 187–219; David Snepenger, "Segmenting the Vacation Market by Novelty-Seeking Role," *Journal of Travel Research,* Fall 1987, pp. 8–14; Philip Pearce and Marie Caltabiano, "Inferring Travel Motivation from Traveler Experiences," *Journal of Travel Research,* Fall 1983, pp. 16–20; and Barbara Bryant and Andrew Morrison, "Travel Market Segmentation and the Implementation of Marketing Strategies," *Journal of Travel Research,* Winter 1980, pp. 2–8.

25. See Shih, David, "VALS as a Tool of Tourism Market Research: The Pennsylvania Experience," *Pennsylvania Travel Review,* Volume 6, Number 1, January 1985.

26. Plog, Stanley, "Why Destinations Areas Rise and Fall in Popularity," *Cornell Quarterly,* November 1973, pp. 13–16.

27. Mayo, Edward and Lance Jarvis, *The Psychology of Leisure Travel* (Massachusetts: CBI Publishing, 1981), pp. 161–175.

28. Epperson, Arlin, "Why People Travel," *Journal of Physical Education, Recreation and Dance,* April 1983, pp. 53–54.

29. U.S. Travel Data Center, *1986 National Travel Survey: Full Year Report* (Washington, D.C.: U.S. Travel Data Center, 1987).

30. "The American Tourist: Different Types for Different Trips," *Travel and Tourism Executive Newsletter,* August 1986.

31. Waters, Somerset, *Travel Industry World Yearbook: The Big Picture— 1986* (New York: Childs and Waters, 1986), pp. 62–65.

32. Travel and Tourism Government Affairs Council, "Tourism Facts: A Resource Kit," 1987; *The Impact of Travel on State Economies* (U.S. Travel Data Center, 1985).

33. Waters, Somerset, Ibid., p. 7.

34. Tuttle, Donna, "Whether Your Business Is Tourism or Not, Tourism Is Your Business," *Business America,* February 16, 1987, p. 3.

35. *Travel and Tourism Executive Newsletter,* April 1987, pp. 5–6.

36. "Travel Agencies Dominate Industry Distribution System," *ASTASTAT,* 1987.

37. Lyon, Richard, "Visitors Spend Estimated $4 Billion at Theme Parks," *Tour and Travel News,* November 30, 1987, p. 42.

THE ORGANIZATION AND MANAGEMENT OF A CONVENTION AND VISITOR BUREAU

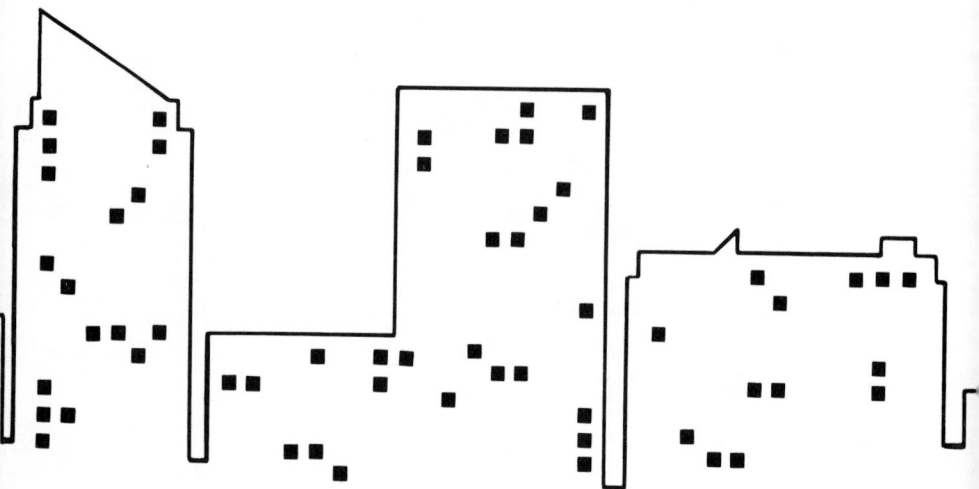

3

LEARNING OBJECTIVES

Upon reading this chapter, you will learn the following:

- A general understanding about organizational structures and relationships of bureaus;

- About the funding sources for bureaus;

- The leadership role of bureau boards and committees;

- An overview of the marketing activities which compose bureau programs;

- About personnel issues and job descriptions;

- About the reporting requirements for bureaus and the utilization of computers;

- About bureau functions as they relate to facility management and events sponsorships.

Introduction

The growth in the number of convention and visitor bureaus over the past years has been an exciting development in destination marketing. Yet this growth has not been without its concerns as well. Bureaus have emerged as a result of the competitive nature of the marketplace; tourism is being seen as a legitimate source of economic development for a community. But more importantly, the availability of funds through a transient hotel room tax has given this growth its impetus. Convention and vistor bureaus, therefore, are distinctive organizations which represent and market their communities in a very competitive marketplace which involves meetings and conventions, group tours and visitors. This chapter intends to provide you with an overview that will better acquaint you with the management and marketing activities of a convention and visitor bureau. Bureaus differ from city to city in part due to the character of the destination, the quality of its product and the funding level of the bureau. However, bureaus operate around fundamental, industry-accepted principles and guidelines which will be explored in this chapter and throughout the book.

Bureau Organization

According to the International Association of Convention & Visitor Bureaus, a majority of bureaus tend to be classified as independent 501(c)6 organizations under the Internal Revenue Codes. A 501(c)6 organization is described as a "business league", which is an association of persons having a defined common business interest which is generally promoted. Such "business leagues" do not engage in a regular business ordinarily conducted on a "for profit" basis. 501(c)6 organizations are therefore considered "not-for-profit" associations. Associations, convention bureaus, chambers of commerce, real estate boards and boards of trade are among those qualifying organizations. To qualify, a convention bureau must engage primarily in activities and programs constituting the basis for its exemption status, such as the marketing of a destination.

Bureaus are associations, and as associations, they are governed by boards of directors. In the organization's "articles of incorporation," it is classified as a "nonstock" organization governed on a "directorship" basis. The articles will further outline the fundamental purpose of the bureau, its location, term of existence, and the names of the incorporators and initial directors. Each state will have available through the Secretary of State, the Department of Commerce or a related office specific requirements for filing articles of incorporation. Once a legal entity, it is up to the new board of directors to implement bylaws (see Appendix E) that outline the following organizational items: qualifications for membership; membership expulsion process; resignation process; voting process; election of directors and officers; process for filling board and officer vacancies; responsibilities and authority of the directors and officers; standing committees; board meetings; quorum requirements; fiscal year; audit; and amendment procedures.

Some bureaus are not independent entities but parts of city or county government or the local chamber of commerce. Such a bureau is then governed by its parent organization and must abide by its governing structure and by-laws. These arrangements were initially established for convenience and political expediency when the bureaus were small; but as bureaus grow, such relationships tend to become proprietary. Among bureaus which are part of a governmental unit are Arlington, Texas; and Virginia Beach, Virginia. Bureaus which are part of local chambers of commerce are Dallas, Texas; Nashville, Tennessee; and Rapid City, South Dakota. Several other bureaus have special legal authority due to their structure and management of facilities; i.e. the Reno-Sparks Convention and Visitors Authority and the Las Vegas Convention and Visitors Authority.

Most large bureaus are independent organizations. Much like children who grow up and venture out on their own, many bureaus have become independent of their parents. Bureaus that have recently emerged from under a parent organization include: Tampa, Florida; Fort Worth, Texas; Buffalo, New York; San Jose, California; Augusta, Georgia; Charlotte, North Carolina; and Saginaw, Michigan. For each bureau, the evolutionary process takes time and thought. Among the many reasons that have influenced such separations are the following:

1. Bureaus need to develop their own identity if they are to be effective in marketing a destination. This is particularly critical when developing rapport with clients such as meeting planners, for it is essential that a bureau not only be recognizable but also able to pull together efficiently the necessary resources required to meet planners' needs. The bureau's identity also is important in developing an awareness of its economic importance to a community. Being credited for marketing programs that generate visibility for a destination, in turn, adds to the stature of that bureau.

2. A bureau has the challenging task of generating an image for its destination that will attract meetings, conventions, group tours and visitors, thereby increasing overnight stays and spending within the community. While these objectives are often confused with those of other organizations, the crucial and often misunderstood nature of the bureau's mission is that it must reach outside the community to bring group and individual business into the community through a variety of selected marketing strategies. Frequently, bureaus are faulted for not doing enough within their communities; however, their marketing objective is to generate new sources of revenue for their

communities through destination marketing activities. Anything less than that is not fulfilling the mission. To divert bureau energies and resources in other directions only diminishes the potential strength of marketing efforts.

3. Bureaus must have the flexibility to develop their financial resources. As part of a parent organization, for example, bureaus are frequently restricted from developing a membership program. New bureaus, funded through the transient hotel room tax, need to develop additional funding sources through membership programs and other non-dues sources of income if they are to continue to grow and remain competitive. Strong private sector involvement not only helps financially but also places the bureau in a strong industry position in the city and helps ensure against unwanted involvement from outside segments of the community and the unwarranted involvement of the political sector. Though bureau budgets range from very small to very large, an average bureau budget is generally $1.7 million, composed of a diverse number of revenue sources.

4. A bureau is engaged in marketing a destination and cannot afford to be involved in partisan politics. However, a bureau should play an active role regarding issues that would impact the travel and tourism industry. But overall, bureaus must be an apolitical marketing organization. Often parent organizations will become actively involved in the political process and take positions on a variety of issues that would limit the bureau's flexibility and potentially place the effectiveness of its marketing mission in jeopardy. A convention and visitor bureau must be able to work with and maintain effective and cooperative communications with all political leadership if it is to accomplish its mission.

5. Because of the competitive nature of the industry and the growing strength of bureaus, it is important that bureaus select strong executives who as leaders can select and pull together a sales and management team that will effectively attain the bureau's goals. Strong bureau executives with knowledge and experience in the industry may not be eager to direct a bureau that is a part of a parent organization, which may have diffused management responsibilities or restricted financial resources. The sophistication of the marketplace requires that a bureau retain the best possible leadership available.[1]

6. Bureaus that are part of a governmental unit find themselves subject to its governing administrative and personnel practices. For example, compensation may be tied to established salary scales; bureau personnel might be treated like personnel in any other departmental unit, subject to rotation and/or economic reductions. Purchasing might require bidding procedures; and personnel selection may be limited by governing policies that restrict hiring flexibility. One of the key issues

a bureau confronts when it is part of a governmental unit is the perception that it holds within the community. It may be seen as a bureaucracy, not to be trusted because it is a governmental unit, or a political organization. Gaining the support of the community may be complicated by such perceptions. But equally important is the management flexibility available to the bureau to carry out its sales and marketing efforts. Without such flexibility, the bureau may not be able to efficiently and effectively carry out its primary mission.

Bureaus which are a part of a parent organization do also benefit from those relationships. Having the strength of the business community behind a bureau that is part of a chamber of commerce is important, particularly when it is new, in its infancy or part of a smaller community. Credibility is an important commodity for a bureau. Bureaus which are a part of a governmental unit may benefit through stabilized financial resources including the availability of personnel benefit packages and governmental travel rates. As long as the structural relationships between bureaus and their parent organizations are functional, the bureau is able to fulfill its primary mission. When the focus of that mission becomes confused, it is essential that bureaus be structured in such a manner that they can reach their primary goals and objectives.

Periodically, the International Association of Convention & Visitor Bureaus is asked to assist in providing consulting services to an existing or emerging bureau; such services are mutually defined and arranged with the hopes that by having industry professionals share their expertise, the requesting bureau will benefit from those insights provided.

As mentioned earlier, many new bureaus have emerged in recent years as a result of the transient hotel room tax. Destinations that at one time had not been given serious consideration as potential meeting sites are today competing in the marketplace as a result of these new resources. The character of their locations, the accessibility of their destinations and the quality and quantity of their meeting facilities and attractions have expanded the potential market. Whereas for decades larger cities with bureaus tended to occupy the meetings market, smaller bureaus have now broadened those markets and given the planner a smorgasbord from which to select.

In order to effectively accomplish their marketing objectives, bureaus tend to be organized into two or three departments. An organizational chart is a graphic way of showing the general relationships among the various units. The following reflects generally the relationships between these units: Sales and Marketing, Operations and Communications. The complexity of a bureau's organization will depend on its budget and scope of responsibilities. The Huntsville Convention and Visitors Bureau (Alabama) will have a different organizational structure than the Metropolitan Toronto Convention and Visitors Association (Canada) or the Reno-Sparks Convention and Visitors Authority (Nevada) (see Appendix I). However, a bureau's mission remains the same: to sell and market its destination.

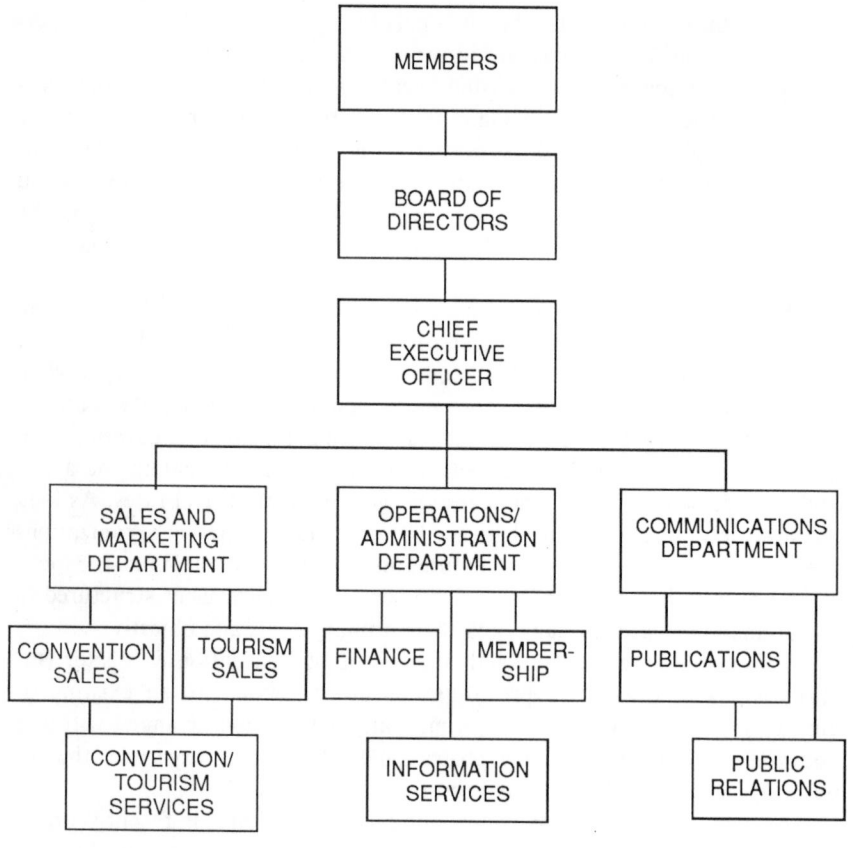

Figure 3.1

Sales and Marketing

Bureau sales executives have primary responsibility for identifying potential clients; qualifying their trade show, convention or meeting requirements; issuing bids and invitations; obtaining a commitment to host their trade show, convention or meeting; and following up with appropriate communications that will support that client and assure him/her of the bureau's continued interest. Sales executives develop their sales accounts, maintaining a thorough written record of communications and agreements in order to reduce any potential for misunderstandings. Such sales accounts are retrieved on a scheduled basis for review and update. These clients are an important investment on the part of the bureau and represent the economic stability of the industry for that destination. They are the lifeline of the bureau and require careful handling and monitoring.

Sales personnel are supported by the servicing staff. Among their many services that are available to planners are: housing assistance by accepting reservation requests from convention delegates; registration personnel to assist with on-site registration of convention delegates; assistance with the formulation of pre and post convention tours for delegates; assistance with the development of a spouse program during the convention; and as a source for promotional brochures and audiovisual materials about that destination. The degree of services provided by a bureau will vary considerably depending on the size and resources of the bureau and the kinds of meeting facilities and attractions in the area.

Operations

The operational or administrative aspects of a bureau are many and require the same attention as sales and marketing. Among the operational elements are activities related to finances and membership development. The former is concerned with the maintenance of financial records, income sources and the general financial welfare of the bureau. The latter is responsible for securing new members as well as retaining current members. Membership is a key program for any bureau and serves as a means of enlisting commitment and involvement from the community for bureau programs. Information services are associated with mailroom operations and/or the operations of a welcome center for visitors.

Communications

The communications department has a multitude of responsibilities directly related to the development of bureau publications, the writing of news stories and press releases and the coordination of events. This department is important in telling the bureau's story not only to its own community, but also to the trade and consumer markets. There is an enormous amount of effort spent in developing a marketing theme and destination image and then translating the theme into the publication and promotional materials. This department also is responsible for writing, scripting and producing media materials such as slide shows which can be used before large audiences to sell the amenities and resources of a destination.

The primary activities of a convention and visitor bureau look beyond the daily occupancy rates of local hotels, protecting the destination for the future by developing an image in the marketplace that will attract trade shows, conventions, group tours and visitors to its area. The bureau is fundamentally a marketing organization and what it does today will impact its destination's tomorrows.

Bureau Foundations

Organizationally, bureaus may establish a foundation or a 501(c)3 entity. To qualify for such a classification, the organization must be operated exclusively for charitable or educational purposes. In other words, if a bureau wished to form an educational foundation, it could file with the Internal Revenue for a 501(c)3 classification. The Flint Convention and Visitors Bureau (Michigan) has formed such an entity for educational purposes. Of course, forming such an entity is easier for an independent 501(c)6 organization than for a bureau which is part of a parent organization.[2]

Bureau Funding Sources[3]

The competitive nature of the convention and tourism industry has brought economic vitality to communities that have invested in the programming of their convention and visitor bureau. To accomplish this, bureau budgets have increased through a variety of sources that include the hotel room tax; general city, county, state and province tax; state matching funds and program grants; membership dues and cooperative investments; publication revenues, trade shows, convention services, sponsored events, sale of trademarks, and other creative sources of revenue.

Every two years, the International Association of Convention & Visitor Bureaus monitors bureau funding sources and levels of support. In 1987, the IACVB's Bureau Funding Survey[4] revealed that the total annual budgets of participating bureaus increased by 35.6% between 1985 and 1987; the average bureau budget was $1,755,899. Of the bureaus responding to the survey, 87.8% reported a budget increase, while only 9.6% reported a budget decrease. Major revenue sources for bureaus include the following:

Hotel Room Tax Revenues

In the U.S., the room tax remains the largest revenue source for bureaus according to the funding survey. It accounted for 60.7% of the total annual budgets. According to survey findings, communities charge an average room tax of 5.15%. The average total tax that is charged for a room, including city, county and state taxes, comes to 8.8%. The highest total room tax reported in the survey was 17%.

A majority of the survey respondents reported that local enabling legislation allows a major portion of their room tax to go directly or indirectly to the convention and visitor bureau. The system for receiving room tax revenues varies greatly among cities and states. Some state legislation mandates that entire receipts from a hotel room tax must be allocated to the local convention and visitor bureaus. There is, however, other legislation that allows flexibility as to the allocation of those revenues. In some instances, the state code clearly indicates that a certain percentage of the room tax is to be allocated to visitor promotion, facilities and/or services. When it comes to local interpretation, though, rulings have allowed these funds to support a variety of civic projects and arts and cultural projects. Bureaus often have found themselves lobbying for funds in competition with the leaders of the community. Room tax legislation also may be earmarked revenues for construction and operation of convention centers.

When bureaus rely on the room tax as a funding source and the tax is also used to fund other projects, an annual presentation may be necessary before funds are allocated; this process makes long term marketing planning difficult. When a bureau relies totally on the room tax as its source of funding, that bureau also finds itself facing fluctuations that affect its income monthly, quarterly or annually. Declining room tax revenues are an indication that a city has to invest more funds into its bureau to regain its share of the market; and when a bureau relies solely on the room tax, it may find itself in a budget cycle that negates an ability to market itself out of a slump. The use of room tax revenues to support bureau programming is a critical matter that needs serious consideration.

Membership Investments

Membership programs provide a wide variety of funding sources. In addition to an annual membership investment (see Chapter 7), bureaus offer opportunities for their members to participate in cooperative advertising programs and trade shows, advertise in bureau publications and sponsor special events. The Bureau will act as the coordinator of these programs or projects with member contributions covering the costs. In some instances, the bureau will charge a commission, thereby creating an additional source of revenue.

The 1987 Bureau Funding Survey showed that an average of 7.19% of a bureau's annual budget is derived from membership dues. Monies provided by memberships increased 11.8% over the 1985 survey. In past funding surveys, membership dues as a revenue source for bureaus was the second largest source of dollars; but in 1987, it dropped to third place, surpassed by "other revenue sources."

The value of membership investments goes well beyond just dues; many businesses do not have a large source of funds set aside for dues and contributions but have larger line items that are related to advertising and marketing. Bureau members are often approached for participation in advertising or special promotional programs. In some communities, bureau members have contributed resources toward the development of a multi-media presentation, hosting of familiarization tours, printing of publications, or the development of visitor information facilities. The value of these programs goes well beyond their immediate financial significance and builds community awareness and support for bureau programs.

Matching Funds and Grants

State or province matching funds or grants are another source of bureau revenues. Some states match a local bureau's expenditures for out-of-state marketing; other states have established grant programs based on applications submitted for expanding convention and visitor services. These programs differ considerably among states as to the criteria for obtaining such funds and the level of funding available.

General City, County or State Tax

A convention and visitor bureau also may receive funds from general city, county or state tax revenues. These funds are not always stable and usually require an annual presentation to an appropriate governing body before such funds are granted or released. Such dependency impacts the long term marketing efforts of a bureau and its flexibility in planning and making commitments.

Non-Traditional Sources of Income[5]

Non-traditional sources of income provide today's convention and visitor bureaus a new challenge. There is a need to be more creative and innovative in ways traditional funding sources can be supplemented with non-traditional sources. Not only is there a need to supplement budgets but there is a need for diversification so more than one or two sources of revenue are available for bureau programming. Traditional sources tend to be revenues usually generated through a hotel room tax or other public sources or membership dues. Non-traditional sources might include revenues generated through cooperative programs, advertising, sales leads, special events, educational programs, in-house services, merchandising or numerous other possibilities.[6] Creative ideas need to be explored, developed and replaced as needed. Each idea needs to be thoroughly researched to insure that the revenue it might generate will offset expenses and risk. Non-traditional revenue-producing programs require time, effort and financial commitment.

As the IACVB Funding Survey has indicated, bureaus have sustained an increase in their funding through a variety of sources. As the competitive nature of the industry sharpens and the value of tourism dollars to a community increases, funding resources for the convention and visitor bureau's programming will be even more crucial. Creativity, endurance, perseverance, aggressiveness, determination and fiscal integrity will establish the bureau's credibility and ensure future financial resources.

Bureau Boards and Committee Relationships[7]

Though bureaus have professional staffs to implement sales and marketing programs, they depend on volunteer leadership to provide them with program insights and support. Bureaus are "directorships" and rely on their Boards of Directors for support and direction. The bureau's Board of Directors traditionally has five primary functions:

1. To set bureau policies.
2. To hire and evaluate the chief executive officer.
3. To approve programs and budgets for the organization.
4. To provide community access and political clout for the programs of the bureau.
5. And to serve as advisors and disciples of bureau programs and initiatives.

In selecting board members, bureaus seek to identify those individuals within the community who are interested in the bureau, understand the bureau's objectives, are willing to financially support or influence support for those programs, and who personally and professionally support the bureau and its chief executive officer. Other desired characteristics of board members include a willingness to do their homework and to become familiar with all pertinent reading materials, issues and legal documents (e.g., bylaws, Roberts Rules of Order); to approach issues with an open mind and a desire to accomplish the best for the organization; to share their opinions and insights even if doing such would show them to be in the minority against their more influential peers; and to undertake assignments, seek a diversity of input from the membership, and submit any substantial report in writing with recommendations that clearly define a course of action. Assisting in the identification of board leadership is one aspect of effective bureau management. In developing volunteer involvement, effective and frequent communications with board members, volunteers, and community organizations is essential in keeping them fully aware of bureau programs and activities. The development of close communication between and among board members will generate an espirit de corps and make them feel they are valued contributors to the bureau's marketing efforts. When it comes to reviewing and approving bureau programs and budgets, board members should feel a part of the process; if the bureau seeks the investment of their time and talents, it must actively include board members in the developmental processes. The frequency of board meetings varies from bureau to bureau; in fact, the Metropolitan Detroit Convention and Visitors Bureau (Michigan) holds only two board meetings a year but more frequent executive committee meetings. On the other hand, the Las Vegas

Convention and Visitors Authority (Nevada) holds board meetings twice a month in order to ensure effective communication between the board and the bureau. Other bureaus may hold board meetings four or five times each year with more frequent executive committee meetings. Whatever the pattern, the Board of Directors is the bureau's governing policy body, composed of important and influential supporters for the bureau and its programs.

Committees oftentimes involve more than just board members. In some associations, each committee must be chaired by a member of the board; others vary this practice, seeking a highly qualified and interested individual to chair a given committee. That which committees undertake as agenda items varies among bureaus. For example, bureaus frequently will have the following committees exploring some of the issues indicated:

1. Marketing Committee. This committee will usually assist bureau personnel in identifying markets, assessing market trends, analyzing market competition, exploring marketing strategies and setting program goals. The committee also may be involved in the coordination and hosting of familiarization tours and site inspections. Such a committee becomes an excellent resource for "brainstorming" marketing ideas and strategies.

2. Finance Committee. This tends to be an oversight committee charged with the responsibility of monitoring the financial operations of the bureau, from monthly statements to the annual audit. Its concern is the general financial welfare and fiscal integrity of the bureau.

3. Membership Committee. This committee assists the membership department in identifying prospective members, calling on current members and working on member retention. The membership committee can play an important role in communicating to the at-large membership the value of bureau programs and the need for member involvement and investment. It also can be invaluable in monitoring membership perceptions and concerns.

4. Long Range Planning Committee. This committee takes on the more serious task of exploring issues and concerns that might impact the bureau and its programs over the coming years. It seeks to explore the "what if" scenario and to sort out action options that will allow the bureau to remain effective. Such meaningful issues can impact bureau funding, staffing and programming in light of perceived social, economic or political trends.

Bureau professionals have a challenge in making volunteers feel a vital part of their dynamic organization. The chief executive officer must convey a vision of what the bureau's goals and aspirations are and how important it is that volunteers feel a part of them and committed to their attainment. In communicating these aspirations, the chief executive officer shares an agenda that will excite and attract involvement. If volunteers feel that they have made a legitimate contribution, it will make a significant difference in their attitudes, their degree of commitment and their willingness to be advocates of the program. Volunteers can give the bureau added clout in the community. They can help the bureau make program goals a reality through their influence and financial networking. The talent that exists among volunteers is amazing; and it is that talent that can help a bureau, or any organization, function more effectively.

Bureau Marketing Programs

The internal organization of a bureau's marketing activities varies greatly depending on the size, budget and overall goals of the bureau. Historically, bureaus have concentrated on convention sales; this department tends then to be the largest and as the oldest, the most advanced in systems. But with the emergence of medium and smaller bureaus, there has developed a recognition and growing interest in the importance and impact of travel and tourism activities and the development of the resources of a destination. This trend also was recognized and acknowledged when in 1974, the International Association of Convention Bureaus inserted into its name the word "Visitor" to represent a more balanced approach to destination marketing.

The bureau also may retain and establish a relationship with an independent advertising agency. In some bureaus, the advertising agency is an integrated part of the marketing team while in others, the agency is simply contracted for specific jobs. The following explains in some detail the dimensions of the various marketing efforts that are undertaken by a convention and visitor bureau.

Convention Sales and Marketing

Because of its overall importance to the mission of the convention and visitor bureau, the Convention Sales and Marketing department (or division) is generally the largest within a bureau; the head of that division, again depending on the size of the bureau, is generally given the title of "Vice President" and is usually the second in command at a bureau.

It is this person's responsibility to plan and implement, with the support and approval of the chief executive officer, the entire convention sales and marketing program. This includes the creation of a marketing plan, supervision of the convention sales staff, supervision of convention services and housing bureau staff, creation and supervision of the convention trade advertising program and cooperation with the other bureau departments in order to create an overall marketing image for that destination. In a larger bureau, due to the number of supervisory responsibilities involved, this person is generally not actively engaged in direct convention sales. However, in smaller bureaus, this person will handle a full load of client accounts in addition to administrative responsibilities. In all cases, this person will be actively involved in major bid presentations for city-wide conventions.

Most people in this position have backgrounds as convention sales managers for bureaus or directors of sales for hotels or resorts. The position requires the creativity to design a complete marketing plan; supervise, direct and motivate a sales team; and maintain effective tracking systems for results. This person also will work closely with volunteers, city officials, hoteliers, and the convention center and serve as the bureau's representative at most industry trade shows.

Director of Sales

The director of sales executes the marketing plan and tends to the details and changes that convention sales managers may encounter. It is the director of sale's responsibility to ensure that sales quotas are met, the sales staff is completing the proper number of call reports, marketing programs are on schedule, and the sales staff is fully informed about the resources of its destination. The director of sales usually coordinates and supervises inbound "familiarization tours" and outbound "sales missions" and participates in industry trade shows.

Perhaps the director of sales' most important responsibility is to maintain enthusiasm and high morale among the sales team, encouraging, supporting and challenging them to attain higher levels of professional performance.

In addition to these supervisory responsibilities, the director of sales usually will carry a full load of convention clients; these tend to be the bureau's larger or more important clients. The director of sales will work closely with the vice president of convention marketing in the preparation of the annual marketing plan and sales objectives and on all bid presentations.

A director of sales should have a convention sales background with a bureau or a hotel; strong communication skills; good organizational and management skills; a flexible personality; self-confidence and high self esteem; high stamina; and a willingness to travel and work long hours.

Convention Sales Manager

The convention sales manager is the "front line" of a bureau's sales efforts. Depending on its size, a bureau may have from one to eight or more convention sales managers. Each convention sales manager has access to lists of associations and organizations that regularly hold meetings. It is the job of the convention sales manager to research the meeting requirements of each of these groups; determine how these requirements can "fit" their destination; initiate interest in the association's local chapter to host a meeting in the city; identify the meeting planner's needs and respond or "sell" them on the various resources and amenities in that city that can meet their needs and provide them with a positive experience; conduct site tours of hotels and public meeting facilities (e.g. convention center); coordinate the final arrangements for shuttle transportation for convention delegates and other related services; and to arrange and finalize all pertinent details and information which will result in a signed contract between an association, the hotels and the selected meeting space. This is no simple task since every association, organization or corporation has its own meeting and facility needs, decision-making requirements and processes, and sequence for locating its meetings and conventions (e.g. west, east; north, south; North America, overseas). Depending on the destination under consideration and the meeting planner's requirements, the process of securing or "booking" a meeting or convention may take on the average of two or more years. There are always exceptions, and one may find that a few telephone calls result in an immediate booking of a meeting. The length of time also may vary depending on whether the group is a corporation or an association.

Convention sales managers perform a variety of sales related functions. Through phone calls, sales calls, industry trade shows, correspondence and direct mail, the sales manager must maintain contact with hundreds of meeting planners, constantly updating information about their meeting requirements while at the same time bringing the meeting planner up-to-date with the developments in that city.

The sales manager also must maintain contact with local chapters of associations and work with them to help make an invitation or bid for a meeting of their regional or national affiliates. In addition, the sales manager must be familiar with every aspect of his/her city; must know all the destination's hotels and meeting facilities and their staffs; must be familiar with restaurants, service firms, transportation and other services that a meeting planner may require. The sales manager is the local contact or "legs" for a meeting planner and, therefore, must be able to answer any question a meeting planner may have about that city.

Assignment of accounts to sales managers varies among bureaus. In some bureaus, convention sales managers are assigned accounts on a regional basis. One sales manager, for example, may be assigned associations headquartered in the northeast, including such cities as New York, Boston, Hartford and Philadelphia. Another sales manager may be assigned the Washington, D.C. area; and yet another sales manager may be assigned Chicago, the West Coast or Texas and the South. This method makes it convenient for the sales manager when making sales trips. On such trips, sales calls can be arranged geographically to accommodate efficient use of time and to keep travel costs at a minimum. There are some problems, though, with this kind of an arrangement; not all associations are evenly distributed across North America or in other countries. In developing a geographic region, therefore, it is imperative that the bureau be sensitive to these geographic distributions.

Another system that is used to assign sales clients is based on the type of meeting or association. One convention sales manager, for example, may be assigned to those organizations that specialize in medical and health care services; this also may mean that that particular sales manager is assigned to a specific trade show such as the annual PCMA (Professional Convention Managers Association) show which is composed of predominately medical and health care specialists. Another sales manager may be assigned educational associations, while another is assigned religious, fraternal, scientific or governmental groups. This method has a distinct advantage of allowing a sales manager to learn the individual meeting requirements of one type of association; on the other hand, it also may require considerable travel due to the geographic distribution of those associations and organizations.

A third means of assigning sales clients is based on the size of the prospects. For example, one or more sales managers may handle groups that have large convention and meeting requirements such as exhibition space, room-nights that exceed a specific minimum, and/or the number of hotel rooms involved. Other sales managers may be assigned groups with smaller meeting space or room-night requirements. Because of the number of groups that do hold meetings and the diversity of that marketplace, this third method may prove to be rather complex for a bureau.

Some bureaus have sales managers who handle all types of accounts, large, small, medical, fraternal, with no regard for geographical location or type of account. The advantage to this is that each sales manager is equally experienced in all types of accounts and can better serve the bureau in case of a prolonged absence or vacancy in a sales position on the part of a colleague. In other words, no one sales person is an expert on a particular market segment. In addition, there is no differentiation in titles thus clients do not feel they are being handled by a second- or third-level person.

In some bureaus, there is a differentiation made between association and corporate meetings. Corporations tend to have smaller meetings and shorter lead times for planning such meetings. Still other bureaus have defined sales client assignments on the basis of state, regional, national or international characteristics of the association or meeting. The actual assignment method selected by a bureau must be a local option yet sensitive to the effective handling of sales clients by sales managers.

Since convention sales managers must perform a variety of tasks, they need a variety of skills. They must be talented salespeople with strong oral and written communication skills, good public speaking skills and effective human relations skills. They must be organized and detail oriented, flexible in their thinking and able to generate ideas as well as respond creatively to the needs of meeting planners. They must like to work long hours, travel and socialize professionally with their clients and colleagues. Most sales managers have a college education and extensive sales experience with hotels or bureaus.

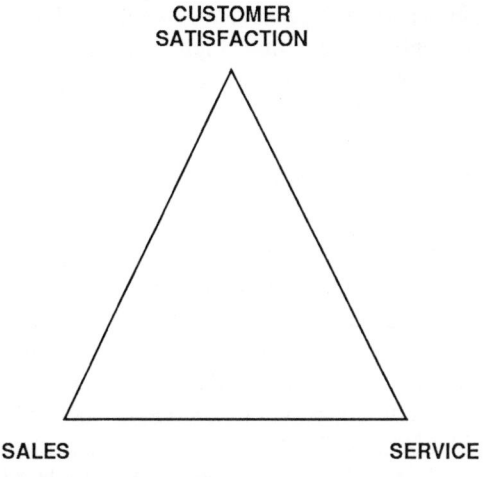

Source: © Richard B. Gartrell

Figure 3.2

Convention Services Manager

The primary job of the convention sales manager is to sell the city as a meetings destination. However there is more to sales than simply closing the deal. Customer satisfaction is predicated on effective sales and quality service.

In an effort to complement the sales manager's endeavors, most bureaus have created a convention services department. The responsibility of this department is to assume control of a convention or meeting once it has been booked into that city. Since conventions can be booked as far in advance as five, six or more years, it is imperative that effective communications be established between the bureau and the meeting planner. The responsibilities of a convention services department would include updating the meeting planner regarding changes in that city; arranging a site tour; conducting on-site visits by the meeting planner (the sales person handling that account may wish to host the on-site visit); acting as a liaison between local service firms and the meeting planner; arranging for local transportation; supervising and handling convention registrations and housing assignments; arranging for on-site registration personnel; and a hundred other possible meeting needs and details involved in planning and executing a successful meeting, convention or trade show.

Depending on the size of a bureau, it may have a one- or two-member services department or a considerably larger staff. The convention services manager must be able to supervise this staff; be flexible and able to work with and respond to the needs of diverse groups and associations; be creative in handling questions and problems that might arise; have excellent communication skills; be familiar with the resources of the community; and have knowledge of wordprocessing and/or computers.[8]

File Research and Maintenance Personnel

Smaller bureaus usually do not have the budget for a person on staff to exclusively handle the research and maintenance of sales files. This responsibility may be divided among the sales managers and the convention services personnel. However in larger bureaus, file research departments have been established to complement the bureau's sales and servicing efforts. Their employees research and maintain bureau sales files on potential group meetings. Large bureaus may maintain between 4,000 and 8,000 sales files on groups that regularly hold meetings. Smaller bureaus may have from 1,000 to 2,000 sales account files. The file researcher's job is to trace sales files so they rotate annually out of the filing system onto their desks in order that information may be updated, corrected or expanded. It is particularly important to check their specific meeting requirements for the year a meeting has been booked for that destination in order to determine if there have been any changes. It also is important to maintain current names of the organization's leadership including officers, board members and meeting planning staff. Other data that may be sought would relate to meeting histories, decision-making criteria, decision-making timelines and key decision makers.

File Research positions are usually entry level jobs and require strong clerical skills, including good oral and written communication skills, good telephone presentation, efficient filing skills and strong organizational skills. In some bureaus, these responsibilities may be assigned to qualified interns who are seeking to fulfill internship credits in such academic programs as clerical training, travel and tourism, hotel sales or sales management.

Tourism Sales and Marketing

This department varies considerably from bureau to bureau depending on the character of the destination. For some bureaus, this department is essential in its marketing endeavors and is therefore well staffed and well funded to meet those objectives. For other bureaus, leisure sales is not an important element of the marketing program and thus staff and funds tend to be limited. With the increase in smaller bureaus, there is a third perspective; for those bureaus, tourism sales may be all a destination has and as a result, the bureau may have only that department and no convention sales efforts to speak of. This latter example, however, is not the norm; today, bureaus carry both programs reflecting their balanced marketing endeavors for "conventions and visitors" alike. A tourism sales and marketing department tends to be composed of the following positions.

Vice President of Tourism Marketing

The head of the tourism sales and marketing initiative usually carries the title of Vice President; this tends to be the case more with larger bureaus than with the medium or smaller ones. Due to budgeting, small bureaus may call this person a "Director of Tourism Marketing" or "Tourism Sales Manager." Whatever the title, the person heading this department is responsible for assessing viable markets, selecting marketing strategies and implementing agreed upon marketing programs promoting that city as a desirable vacation and leisure destination. In developing such programs, this individual will work with the following industry resources:

- travel wholesalers
- group tour planners
- travel agents
- incentive travel planners
- motorcoach operators
- international travel packagers
- attractions/events
- airlines
- rental car companies
- hotels
- cruise lines
- travel writers

For example, if one of the targeted markets for a bureau is vacationing families, a marketing plan will be devised to assess and develop the attitudes and decision making criteria for that market segment, timelines for considering possible destinations and the most effective marketing strategies for reaching that market segment. Among the many that might be undertaken are the following:

- responding to mail and telephone inquiries
- developing an advertising program
- providing information to state operated information centers
- attending consumer travel shows such as boat and sports shows
- working with travel writers in order to obtain features on the destination.

In marketing to the "group" market, strategies tend to be significantly different. For example, in addressing the domestic group tour market, the tourism sales and marketing activities would be focused on direct sales calls to tour operators, direct-mail programs and attendance at key trade shows such as those sponsored by the National Tour Association and the American Bus Association. Numerous group tour planners also sponsor their own trade shows in order to attract clients and give them an opportunity to see destinations first hand. Depending on budget size, trade shows offer bureaus an interesting marketing option. A private association of interested destinations and suppliers also may market collectively to the group tour planner. Circle Michigan, Inc. targets key cities and annually sponsors its own "road show" of Michigan destinations and suppliers. Invitations are extended to group tour planners and their clients to visit the trade show and have lunch. Familiarization tours are another critical marketing tool for soliciting interest from group tour operators.

If, on the other hand, the target is international groups, the strategies might include familiarization tours, trade missions to targeted countries and attendance at key trade shows such as the annual Pow Wow sponsored by the Travel Industry Association of America, ITB-Berlin, World Travel Mart, United States Tour Operators Association, or Rendevous Canada.

Regardless of whether aimed at domestic or international tour operators, the purpose of any marketing plan is to bring group tours into the area, either as a part of a planned itinerary or as a destination in and of itself, and to increase the number of tour groups of any one operator coming into an area as well as lengthen their stay.

But one of the frustrations confronting tourism sales and marketing endeavors is the fact that unlike convention sales efforts, tourism sales do not end in signed contracts. Consequently, it is difficult to monitor the results of these many sales efforts. Efforts continue toward universally accepted standards for tracking and establishing the economic importance of tourism sales. Regardless, depending on the size and character of the destination, business the tourism department brings into a community can be just as vital, and in some cases even more so, to the city's economy than the business brought in by the convention department.

Generally, bureaus will have one to three people in the department working with the group markets. These individuals, similar to convention sales personnel, require excellent sales and communication skills, detailed knowledge of their cities, creativity, stamina and enthusiasm. Considerable travel is involved, particularly as it relates to trade shows, travel missions and direct sales endeavors. Their public speaking skills must be excellent as well since they are frequently called upon to welcome groups and make group presentations. Most leisure sales and marketing personnel have sales backgrounds related to attractions, hotels or bureaus.

Advertising Liaison

When there is an advertising budget, larger-budgeted bureaus tend to have a liaison to work closely with the advertising agency. This person monitors the creative development of ads and their placement to insure that the bureau is getting full value for the investment. Frequently, the advertising liaison person is part of the communications department and also is involved in the production of visitor information brochures and other related bureau publications. Sometimes this person is actually involved in the creative processes of generating ads. The position can be one of control where the person monitors agency production costs and works in communicating bureau desires to agency staff. In all cases, the position requires a detailed understanding of advertising.

Advertising and Related Marketing Mix

The role that an independent advertising agency has with a bureau depends to a large extent on the personalities and experience of the bureau executives and the size of the budget. In some bureaus, the advertising agency is crucial to the entire marketing plan and is involved in every stage of the creation and implementation of that plan. When a bureau includes an advertising agency in this kind of a dynamic relationship, it develops a close working relationship between the bureau and the agency, but more importantly, it allows for the integration of the creative efforts with the usual and expected sales and servicing activities. The advertising agency can provide recommendations regarding marketing and advertising strategies, provide useful cost analyses and, if not otherwise available, provide the bureau with needed market research. This kind of a relationship between a bureau and an advertising agency calls for greater understanding of a bureau's mission and what must be accomplished on behalf of its destination and in turn, more efficient use of agency personnel in the development and implementation of bureau programs.

Some bureaus, however, cannot afford an agency as a full partner in the development of their marketing programs. Under such circumstances, a variety of relationships can be established, the most common being the selection and hiring of an advertising agency to perform specific tasks or projects. The key in this kind of a relationship is to ensure that the advertising agency fully understands the bureau's marketing goals and the kind of creative image the bureau desires. Once creative materials are developed, the bureau will frequently wish to amortize those costs over a period of time before embarking on another creative strategy. This means that initial costs are offset by the benefits of having a creative strategy used long enough in the marketplace to gain consumer and trade recognition before it is changed and production costs again incurred by the bureau.

Today, more and more bureaus are developing their own in-house agencies, placing their own ads and therefore benefiting from the commissions, and hiring their own artists and writers on a freelance basis to create those ads. This management strategy has benefits for a bureau with its own in-house capabilities or communications department. Those departmental personnel are then charged with the responsibility of overseeing freelance contracts and ensuring that the bureau receives appropriate discounts for ad placements. Just as a word of explanation, when an ad is placed with a media source, the agency placing the ad receives a discount on that placement; the difference between the actual costs and the discounted cost comprises the "commission." If an advertising agency is involved, they receive that discount from the media source, though they charge their client the full rate. If a bureau has an in-house agency, then the bureau benefits by paying the discounted rate to the media source, thus "saving" the commission. If an extensive program is involved, the in-house arrangement can allow a bureau to extend its program even further than might have been the case had it contracted with an advertising agency.

Some bureaus employ two or more advertising agencies, depending on the nature of the task that must be accomplished. For example, a local agency may be selected to do most of the work, particularly as it applies to creative development and placement of local, regional, national or international advertising. However, a bureau may select another agency to assist with its marketing endeavors if they involve some kind of specialty, such as direct mail or overseas marketing. The latter is particularly important in ensuring that bureau efforts in another country relate to the standards of that country. If the message is translated into another language, using a local resource in the targeted country insures proper linguistic phrasing. The last thing any bureau needs is a misunderstanding caused by poor or unacceptable linguistic translations.

Payment to an agency also differs considerably among bureaus. Some agencies are paid on the basis of a monthly retainer fee or a predetermined hourly wage for copywriters, artists or account executives. In these cases, the usual commission an agency derives from placement of ads in publications is returned to the bureau. Still another payment format involves an agency working for the commission only or for the commission with additional hourly charges. Whatever the final payment schedule, each bureau assesses the kind of relationship it wishes with an advertising agency and then reaches a mutually acceptable agreement as to a fees schedule.

Politically, a bureau finds it very difficult to hire an advertising agency that is not from its own destination. Not only is it a matter of keeping revenues within the city and among its own membership, but also it seems odd to have an agency in city A designing and implementing creative programs that sell city B. At the same time, many bureaus find it difficult and sometimes impossible to locate and hire a local advertising agency with the necessary experience in the convention and travel markets and an understanding of market segments that also is capable of creating effective ads. As a result of these frustrations, many bureaus bring these functions in-house.

Developing a unified creative theme and campaign, whether it be in advertising, direct mail or a combination of marketing strategies, is the cornerstone for any successful marketing endeavor. Whether such a theme is developed by an outside advertising agency or in-house is not the overwhelming issue; what is important is that the bureau's marketing programs have undergone a thorough examination as to their competition, target markets, preferred marketing strategies and related costs and timelines for implementation and evaluation of effectiveness.

Bureau Annual Reports and Financial Statements[9]

There are numerous reports that a bureau utilizes to display its marketing and financial activities. Two of those specific activities include the annual report and financial statements.

Annual Reports

The annual report provides an accounting of the bureau's program activities for the past year. The exact information depends on the presentation format desired by a bureau. The most common types of information that usually comprise an annual report include an overview of the program of work (or what is often called the marketing plan), program results, market profile statistics and the financial audit.

The *program of work* (see Appendix F) provides the bureau's membership, funding sources, board, staff and other interested parties with relevant information on how the bureau plans to utilize its resources to market the destination. Some of the common elements which comprise that portion of the report include: identification of key staff and members of the board of directors; overall marketing thrust and goals for each department; description of the bureau's policy on member participation; trip schedules and trade shows selected to attend along with description of target markets; familiarization tours scheduled; and advertising media schedule. The program of work may be a separate report to the membership or included as part of the bureau's annual report.

Whereas the program of work addresses the bureau's current and future plans, *program results* measure the success of the previous year's efforts. Some of those criteria that would be included in such an analysis include the following: convention bookings and leads including information on delegates, room nights and economic impact; conventions serviced and registration hours provided; tour operators, travel agents and other travel industry bookings, leads and contacts; travel writer contacts and actual free publicity generated; visitor services statistics such as mail requests, visitor center activity and brochure distribution; and membership solicitation results. The results of these programs are usually shown in the annual report as graphs and tables which make it easy for the reader to grasp and understand the information. Information is usually compared to previous years' performances and carries explanatory notes.

Every destination receives inquiries regarding local industry trends. These inquiries generally are made by local or national media, developers, real estate agents, financial institutions or other community sources. The bureau has a responsibility to respond to such inquiries whether the information has been obtained through bureau research efforts or through secondary sources.

Without such information, it is difficult to make an accurate situational analysis or assess future trends. Including this information in an annual report may be useful to the reader in understanding the setting in which the bureau operates, or it may be included in the annual marketing plan. Some of the *visitor impact data* that would be of interest includes: tourism economic impact including airlines and highway totals; convention economic impact; visitor spending patterns including food and beverage, entertainment and shopping; average expenditures per person per day per stay; number of visitors to the area; transient occupancy/room tax collections; hotel occupancy percentages; average daily rates; inbound airline traffic; convention center bookings; and future trends projected. Some of the *visitor profile data* might include the following: trip purposes (business, convention, family, leisure); mode of transportation; type of accommodations; attractions visited; leisure activities; reasons for selecting the destination; source of information about the destination; frequency of visits; levels of satisfaction or dissatisfaction with destination; permanent residential location or point of origin; group size and composition such as number of children or convention size; demographic profile including age, income level, sex and spending pattern.

The challenge a bureau has is in the development of reliable monitoring systems that will capture the information outlined above; the methodologies used must, for comparative purposes, be reasonable and consistent over time.

The bureau also may wish to include in the annual report information from the annual financial *audit*. The decision to include or not include such information should be determined by the bureau on the basis of how it plans to design and use the annual report and what it considers to be appropriate information for the community.

Financial Statements[10]

The need for accurate and meaningful financial statements for a bureau is no less essential than that required by any company. It is particularly important given the fact that most bureaus have a policy of limiting the build-up of reserves and expending as much of the resources as prudent for programming. Without timely accounting, the scenario could lead to financial confusion. The following, therefore, is intended to provide basic information on fundamental accounting issues and principles which bureaus must address. The way they are addressed will depend on the bureau's varying reporting requirements.

There are two ways of monitoring the bureau's finances, cash and accrual. Cash accounting provides that income is recorded when received and expenses are recorded when paid. Accrual accounting provides that income is recorded when earned and expenses are recorded when the obligation is established. The difference between the two procedures is one of timing and not amount.

Over a long period of time, the resulting cumulative net fund increase or decrease is the same under either procedure. How, for example, the bureau profiles its financial information for the board of directors will depend on the need of the financial statement reader. For the most part, most bureaus have adopted a policy of recognizing everything except membership dues on a full accrual basis, stipulating that membership dues are somewhat voluntary in nature and therefore not actually earned until received. With regards to the year-end audited financial statements, the American Institute of Certified Public Accountants have taken the position that financial statements should be presented on an accrual basis.

Fund accounting may also be required by specific sources of funding. Such accounting provides that money or other resources which are earmarked for specific purposes be collected and accounted for as a separate independent fiscal and accounting entity. Under this system the bureau may have several bank accounts, each one appropriated for different purposes. Unless specifically stipulated by the funding source, keeping detailed records on the cost of specific projects can be accomplished without tying them to specific revenue sources or funds.

The bureau also establishes its chart of accounts; these are accounts to which all accounting entries are made and then are reflected on the financial statements. Appendix J is a sample bureau budget and chart of accounts.

Many of the account categories have accepted commonality among bureaus such as advertising, personnel costs and travel. These are generally easy to identify and assigned as direct expenses. Other accounts such as rent, insurance and depreciation are known as indirect expenses and not specifically identifiable to any one department. The procedures for departmental allocations will depend on the financial reporting procedures adopted by the bureau. Smaller bureaus may not make a division of the bureau's expenditures by department and may simply have one account classification. For bureaus with more sophisticated division of accounts, expenses on the year-end audited financials should be allocated to the various departments. It would not appear appropriate to charge rent entirely to administration since it would overstate administration and understate one of the other departments. The most common way of allocating rent, for example, is on the basis of the floor space occupied by each department. There are other techniques for the allocation of indirect costs, too, including such criteria as the number of employees, copier usage or number of mail pieces.

At a minimum, a balance sheet and income statement should be prepared on a monthly basis. The format of such statements will vary again among bureaus. Boards of directors are usually concerned with the larger scope of financial commitments whereas bureau management will want detailed information. With this in mind, some bureaus prepare two sets of financials to meet the needs of each group. Even though detail may vary, the balances provide comparisons of actual versus budgeted for current month and year-to-date.

Bureaus must be aware of other financial issues that relate to programming and the need for thorough documentation. Among such issues are the following: unrelated business income tax (Sec. 511–515 of the IRS Code); information returns requirement such as 990 [Sec. 1.6033–2(a)] and 990T (if unrelated income received); returns for payment of services to third parties such as 1099 return (Sec. 6041); and taxability of employer provided automobiles (Sec. 1.61–2T). The tax laws are very complicated and dynamic and must be carefully monitored annually to insure that bureau reporting requirements are in compliance.

Some bureaus recognize the effect of complimentary goods and services which are provided to the bureau or its clients by members. For example, when a hotel member provides free lodging for a bureau client invited into the area, no money is exchanged but a real ascertainable value has been provided to the bureau. In many instances, bureaus have recognized this support on their financial statements either through a footnote or an actual gross-up of revenue and expense based on the value of the service. Whatever the reporting technique used, it is important that a bureau track and document such in-kind services.

These are just a few of the many reporting requirements that a bureau may have; but these are the fundamental ones, assuring responsible handling of funds and sharing with the community the dynamic impact of bureau programming.

Bureau Personnel Administration

Not unlike any other major business, the administration of bureau personnel is concerned with the identification and selection of talented professionals who are motivated toward excellence and committed to the mission and programs of the bureau. Simply having job descriptions and organizational manuals will not ensure that a bureau has the most effective persons performing the most important tasks. However, this text cannot explore that which is already well developed in other resources as to the selection and motivation of personnel. General area responsibilities have been outlined throughout the chapters of this text, and Appendix K contains several sample job descriptions for key bureau positions.

Developing an effective team of professionals who are willing to commit themselves to the fulfillment of bureau objectives is one of the primary leadership responsibilities of the bureau's chief executive. Working with each staff member to identify his/her talent strengths is important as it relates to the undertaking of various job assignments. Nurturing staff growth through continued professional development also is necessary if staff are to feel a valued part of the bureau and professionally competent in the dynamically changing marketplace. Supporting their ideas and efforts is another important aspect of personnel administration and carries with it tremendous leadership responsibilities; asking staff associates to share their insights and suggestions, for example, as it may apply to the development of an annual marketing plan requires active listening skills, sincere and meaningful dialogue and an open mind. This kind of interaction can produce strong feelings of loyalty and commitment by staff associates toward bureau programs and can ensure their success as a result of each feeling a personal role in the development of goals and programs.

There is one formal activity related to personnel administration that plays a significant role in the smooth operation of a bureau. Whether small or large, bureaus have personnel policy manuals that orient personnel to the organization and clarify procedures that impact personnel performance and expectations. A personnel policy manual should define key terms and conditions of employment, outline standards for performance and conduct in and out of the office while on the job, clarify employee benefits and services, insure the quality and consistency of personnel decisions, reduce the risk of litigation on personnel-related issues and preserve appropriate management perogatives. The personnel policy is not an employment contract nor is it a replacement for sound personnel and management practices. Each bureau has to develop its own manual format and have it validated through legal counsel as to the pertinent state or federal laws that govern personnel matters. Regardless, the manual should be carefully written and easy to read.

The contents for such a personnel policy manual should include basic employment information such as office hours, pay periods, benefits, and employee conduct and safety. Some of the other items that might be included in a personnel manual, depending on the desires of the bureau or recommendations of legal counsel, include the following:

Introduction
- History and Current Profile of the Bureau

Organizational Structure
- Organization Relationships Among Staff
- Job Descriptions/Employee Classifications

Employment
- Equal Opportunity/Affirmative Action
- Promotions and Transfers

Office Hours and Pay Periods
- Regular Office Hours
- Pay Periods
- Overtime and Compensatory Time

Employee Benefits

- Holidays
- Vacation, Sick Leave, Maternity Leave
- Leaves of Absence
- Bereavement Leave
- Jury Duty
- Time Off to Vote
- Group Insurance Benefits
- Retirement Plan
- Memberships in Service Clubs and Trade Associations

Employee Relations

- Compensation Administration
- Performance Appraisals
- Grievance Procedures
- Garnishments
- Terminations

Employee Conduct and Safety

- Standards of Conduct
- Outside Business and Related Activities
- Safety
- Evacuation Procedures (i.e. fire)

Office Administration

- Business and Travel Expense Reporting
- Forms and General Office Procedures

Needless to say, the foregoing is only a sample of what might be included in a personnel manual. Depending on the bureau and its location, considerations might be given to other items such as military leave, merit increases, tuition aid programs and probationary periods for new employees. It is important that a well developed personnel policy manual exist to insure consistency in dealing with personnel matters.[11]

Bureau Computerization[12]

Over the past few years, there has been a significant increase in computerization of bureaus as a result of the need for greater efficiency. As a part of this trend, bureau personnel are becoming knowledgeable about the automated office, techniques for retrieving and storing information, and the creative uses of computers. Bureau management, however, cannot simply snap its fingers and expect to modernize the bureau overnight; some basic understanding of computerization is necessary, particularly the need to identify the desired end product. Once it is known what a bureau wishes, then it is possible to explore the many software and hardware options available within the constraints of the bureau's budget. Preparation for the growth that is to occur is vital; therefore, it may be useful to explore several applications being used by various convention and visitor bureaus.

Financial Records

Perhaps one of the most beneficial aspects to management is the computerization of accounting procedures. The most standard uses of computer-driven programs cover such financial items as general ledgers, accounts receivable, accounts payable and payroll.

The general ledger retains month-end balances for the past and current year. It also may include cash disbursements, cash receipts, general journal entries, balance sheets, income statements, annual summaries and journal reports. Accounts receivable retains customers' names and addresses and prints invoices; depending on the system selected, formating options are available. The accounts payable programs handle vendor invoices on a monthly basis. The capability should be there to record invoices and handle hand-written checks as well as print computer checks on any pre-printed form. Payroll could be handled as well depending on the sophistication of the program and hardware. Many bureaus, however, opt for a low-cost contract with a payroll service to cut payroll checks, monitor monthly tax payments and compile end-of-year tax information for employees (W-2 forms).

Housing Programs

The single most important application of computers to bureau operations has been the development of housing programs. This allows the bureau to handle more easily incoming hotel reservations for numerous conventions. Such programs should allow the operator to enter names and assign hotel rooms; update listings both by general alphabetical order and by date of arrival and hotel assigned and modify or cancel reservations. The program should be able to produce a series of reports including a reservation acknowledgement, roster by arrival dates, roster by assigned hotel and an alphabetical listing of all attendees. The capabilities of these programs will depend on the size and flexibility of the hardware and the sophistication of the software programs.

Membership Records

Computers also allow the bureau to computerize its membership records. This enables bureau management to know who is a member, date joined and at what level of membership investment, date usually billed and date payments are usually received. Such information assists the membership and the accounting departments in analyzing the monthly cash income and receivables as well as project, based on aged reports of receivables, the bureau's cash flow.

Again, depending on the size of the computerized system, membership records may include the ability to delete and add members; provide descriptive information to include in membership directories; merge names and addresses into documents or letters; classify members into categories; produce mailing labels or an abundance of other potential creative uses. The intent of any program should be to support the membership department in its search for and retention of members.

Sales Files

Computer systems are very well suited for the permanent storage of the vast array of information associated with bureau sales files. Depending again on the size of the bureau and its sales efforts, anywhere from 1,000 to 5,000 sales files on the average are being handled, each file having the capability of multiple meetings. Once it is recognized and understood that sales personnel are handling millions of pieces of information, computerizing such systems becomes a more reasonable way for handling such volume. Once the types of end products are determined, then the systems can be developed. If, for example, mailings are an important part of the sales effort, sales files need to be designed in such a manner that they can easily be sorted by the desired criteria and address labels generated. In developing and managing a computerized sales system, allowances must be made for the time needed for data input, update and access. Depending on the desires of a bureau, a well-designed computerized sales system can generate a multitude of reports and useful information including the following: a list of conventions and meetings scheduled for a specific period of time, along with related information such as dates, size, scope of the meeting, whether exhibits are involved, the association contact and the local contact; booking reports that can reflect, depending on the format, monthly sales activity including tentative and definite convention bookings, size of groups, room-nights generated, and by which sales person; a monthly booking bulletin that provides bureau members with information as to which groups will be coming to that city; an annual convention and meetings calendar which lists bookings for that and subsequent years; and the ability to search dates to determine whether there are convention bookings or clear dates.

Tracking Systems

Every bureau is seeking a means for more effective monitoring of its sales and servicing activities. The creative use of computers allows for the development of systems that support various convention and tourism programs. For example, a system has been developed for microcomputers that allows telephone call-in or write-in inquiries to be entered into the system and held on disk until labels are printed. Before labels are printed, various reports can be generated such as from which state the inquiry originated, what publications or information was requested, and whether it was a call-in or write-in inquiry.

Such systems support the needs of the bureau in analyzing the flow of information and the dedication of its resources. What is ultimately developed depends on the goals of the bureau.

The potential for computerization of bureau operations boggles the mind. Such capabilities, in essence, depend on the bureau, its resources, management goals and creativity. For example, there are some twelve convention and visitor bureaus, at this writing, that have made major investments in large systems with custom-designed programs for sales tracking. The investment for application of software and hardware begins in the $60,000 price range. However, there are many others which have invested in microcomputer installations which have cost between $8,000–$15,000, depending on the complexity of the systems. A large number of bureaus also have invested in tying into the International Association of Convention & Visitor Bureau's INET system for sales tracking and exchange of information via telephone lines (modem) between their respective offices and the international headquarters.

The competitive nature of the marketplace and the sophistication of computer systems have led bureaus to perform similar to any other major corporation, utilizing the technology of the day to insure the quality of sales and service performances for tomorrow.

Bureaus and Facility Management

Many convention and visitor bureaus have become involved in management of related facilities in addition to their primary destination marketing responsibilities. Such facilities may include:

- visitor information centers
- convention centers
- public golf courses and related civic facilities

Whether the visitor information center is free standing or a part of the bureau's office facilities will differ considerably; for example, the San Jose Convention and Visitors Bureau (California) supports a visitor information center at their international airport. This facility is managed by a person from their tourism department and involves a large number of volunteers who staff the facility throughout the week. The Houston Convention and Visitors Bureau (Texas) operates an in-house visitor center where individuals can literally drive-up for information; its offices are located in an old bank building, allowing use of the drive-up teller stations as information outlets. Some bureaus manage detached information centers which are free-standing buildings, while others use their front offices as visitor centers. The Denver Convention and Visitors Bureau (Colorado) operates a static or non-manned information center at its international airport; still others have developed interactive systems for visitor information. These television-like terminals are located at key visitor points throughout the city and provide the visitor with a menu of options offering vital information about area attractions, lodging facilities, events and restaurants. The key is that the visitor center be easily accessible.

Bureaus also have become involved in the management of convention centers. Charged with developing, through visitors and convention groups, the economic viability of a destination, bureaus can provide insight and direction regarding the development of a convention center, the marketing of a convention center and, in some cases, the management of such facilities. In managing a convention center, it must be remembered that the operational function differs considerably from the marketing of such a facility. Management of the operations and maintenance of the facility must be separated from the marketing responsibilities that a bureau must fulfill for its destination. Facility management would include supervision of personnel; union contracts and contracts with renters; operations, including utilities, concession outlets, maintenance and repairs; and outside services such as exhibition decorators, and related functions.

Some bureaus have marketing responsibilities for a convention center. Such agreements make the bureau responsible for creating an awareness for that facility among meeting planners by developing a comprehensive marketing program. While this represents a specific contract between a convention center and convention bureau, most bureaus integrate their convention center facilities into their marketing programs. In fact, it is imperative that the convention center work closely with the convention bureau in developing a unified marketing image for that destination.[13]

Closely related to any management or marketing agreement with the convention center is the establishment of a booking policy for that center. The Washington, D.C., Convention Center has defined and prioritized events requesting space. For example, it is more beneficial for a convention center to book a week-long trade exhibition than to book a one-day show. Which function has a priority over the other is defined by the convention center in cooperation with the convention bureau and relates to the economic impact shows have on that destination. An example of such levels of priority, from highest to lowest, is suggested by the Washington, D.C., Convention Center as follows:[14]

1. The *first priority level* is given to those conventions and trade shows which are international, national or regional in scope and which will have a significant economic impact on the hotel community in terms of room-nights and patronage. These groups must agree to sign a contract eighteen (18) months or more out from their scheduled exhibition and meeting dates.

2. The *second priority level* shall be given to multiple day annual public shows such as sports and boat shows or automotive shows. Such shows shall not be booked more than eighteen (18) months ahead of their event.
3. The *third priority level* are multiple day local events such as graduations and related functions. These events shall not be booked until the first priority level dates have elapsed.
4. The *fourth priority level* are single day events; such requests are not honored sooner than six (6) months prior to the scheduled event and on a space available basis. Such events might include hobby shows, special banquets or civic club activities.

When considering these priority levels, the Washington Convention Center takes into consideration, as do most convention centers, the following factors:

a. projected overall economic impact on the city;
b. total number of hotel rooms required and room-nights;
c. projected revenues for the convention center in terms of rental revenues, concessions and related building services;
d. time of the year;
e. potential for repeat bookings; and
f. previous history and experience of the potential user with respect to use of similar facilities.

This important relationship between the convention center and the convention bureau is fundamental to a destination's ability not only to project a unified marketing image and program but to acquire sufficiently large conventions and trade shows that will generate a significant economic impact for the community in terms of hotel room-nights and delegate expenditures. It is important, therefore, that centers and bureaus develop a mutually acceptable communication and marketing liaison as it applies to the convention center's reservation books and procedures. The bureau's marketing flexibility is dependent on this relationship. Equally important will be the convention center's ability to efficiently fill its rental space and, in turn, provide adequately for its debt retirement.

Several other bureaus have become involved in the management and marketing of additional public facilities. The Reno-Sparks Convention and Visitors Authority is responsible for management of several public golf courses as well as convention facilities. Such management relationships are the exception and not the norm among bureaus internationally.

Bureaus and Events Sponsorships

Thousands of events are sponsored worldwide annually with the hopes of drawing attention to a destination. Among those events are:

Alaska State Fair, Palmer, Alaska

Albuquerque International Balloon Fiesta, Albuquerque, New Mexico

Aloha Week Festivals, Honolulu, Hawaii

Arbor Day Celebration, Nebraska City, Nebraska

Calgary Stampede, Calgary, Alberta, Canada

Cheyenne Frontier Days, Cheyenne, Wyoming

The Fiesta Bowl, Phoenix, Arizona

Gilroy Garlic Festival, Gilroy, California

Indianapolis 500, Indianapolis, Indiana

Kentucky Derby, Louisville, Kentucky

Pro Football Hall of Fame Festival, Canton, Ohio

Street Art Fairs, Ann Arbor, Michigan

These events not only draw attention to a destination, but also have an economic impact on that destination, depending on the length of the event, the use of hotel rooms and restaurants and the number of outside visitors attending. Convention and visitor bureaus work closely with the events in their area. They incorporate those activities into their total marketing scheme and capitalize on the images such events portray for the destination. They provide technical assistance and/or serve on boards and committees to assist those events to be successful in their own right. To a limited extent, they even may be the catalyst for the development of seasonal events and/or sponsors for an event. Again, relationships that a bureau has with events is directly dependent on the size of the bureau and its budget. Events may generate significant local involvement and participation and not draw visitors and *new revenues* into an area. However, it still may be very important to that destination for community spirit. Equally important is the reality that a bureau must remain focused on its primary mission of developing the economic viability of an area through visitor development, whether individuals or groups. Each destination has its own character that in part dictates a marketing strategy that will benefit that destination.

Bureau structures vary as do their marketing endeavors; however, the primary mission of any convention and visitor bureau is that of marketing and promoting its destination. How this task is undertaken in detail for tourism sales as well as convention sales will be the focus of the remaining chapters of this book.

Summary

Convention and visitor bureaus are versatile marketing organizations. In fact, they are a city's experts on its convention and tourism resources. The bureau knows what its facilities can handle. It knows about the events and activities that are going on. And its staff knows the people behind the scene and can serve as a knowledgeable liaison between buyers and sellers. Bureaus have the challenging job of selling the city as a destination through a variety of marketing strategies. And it can pull together the diverse components of the industry in order to present a unified image.[15] The organizational structures of a convention and visitors bureau are complex yet efficient; their dynamic growth is, in part, a response to the growth of the marketplace. Knowledgeable professionals who are talented, creative, motivated and skilled are required to meet the competitive demands of the industry. And today's convention and visitor bureaus reflect that sophistication.

Discussion Questions

1. Several observations are provided as to why a majority of convention and visitor bureaus are independent; discuss the merit of the arguments, both pro and con for being a part or not a part of a parent organization.

2. What is the difference between a 501(c)6 and 501(c)3 organization?

3. Outline the responsibilities for each of the three fundamental departments within a bureau.

4. Why has the convention sales and marketing department usually been considered the most important of the departments within a bureau?

5. What are the primary responsibilities of a board of directors?

6. Why are committees important to a bureau's program?

7. List and define the responsibilities of four committees identified within this chapter.

8. List the professional talents and characteristics desired in the sales and servicing personnel of a bureau?

9. What are several ways of defining sales territories?

10. Discuss the concept "service" and why it is important in today's sales environments.

11. Define and discuss several of the target markets for the tourism sales and marketing department; how can these markets be efficiently and effectively sold and are there other markets that need to be considered?

12. What are several possible relationships for advertising agencies and convention bureaus? Which role might provide the best input for bureaus when developing the annual marketing plan?

13. Describe various funding sources for bureaus. What are some other ways to generate revenues for a bureau?

14. Why are annual reports and financial statements important?

15. Why is personnel administration a leadership responsibility? Discuss why a personnel policy manual should contain the items listed in this chapter.

16. Should bureaus computerize?

17. Bureaus have become involved with facility management and marketing of those resources; outline and discuss the advantages and liabilities of such relationships.

18. Why should bureaus become involved with events in their local area? What are the strengths and possible pitfalls of such involvements?

Bibliographic Resources

1. Economic Research Associates, "Convention Marketing Analysis," unpublished research report prepared for the San Jose Convention and Visitors Bureau (California), February 1984.

2. *How to Establish and Fund An Association Foundation* (Washington, D.C.: American Society of Association Executives, 1985).

3. Adapted from materials written by Marlyce Heidt, "Bureau Funding Sources" (Unpublished, No Date).

4. *1987 Bureau Funding Survey,* Unpublished Report Prepared for the International Association of Convention and Visitors Bureaus, June 1987.

5. Sprague, Ted, "Non-Traditional Funding Sources," Professional Notes for the IACVB Newsletter (No Date).

6. Milner, Neil, "100 Ways to Generate Non-Dues Income," *Association Management,* August 1987, pp. 127–129.

7. Cumings, Robert E., "Developing Effective Board Relations," Professional Notes from the IACVB Newsletter (no date); and Cyril O. Houle, *The Effective Board* (New York: Association Press, 1960).

8. Gartrell, Richard B., "Convention Bureaus: One-Stop Convention Shopping," *Association Management,* November 1984, pp. 101 and 103.

9. Adapted from materials written by John Marks and Barry Shemer entitled "Bureau Research and Reporting Requirements" (Unpublished, No Date).

10. For more information see Barry Joseph and Charles Mundt, *Financial Management Handbook for Associations* (Washington, D.C.: Chamber of Commerce of the U.S., 1973).

11. See McManis, Gerald L. and Jerrie A. Stewart, *Personnel Management in Associations* (Washington D.C.: American Society of Association Executives, 1980).

12. Adapted from materials written by Charles (Sonny) Mares, "Computerization of Bureau Functions" (Unpublished, No Date).

13. Marks, John, "Convention Center Marketing," Speech before members of the travel industry, Sydney, Australia, April 22, 1987.

14. Washington Convention Center, "Booking Policy" (Unpublished, No Date).

15. Gillett, Charles, "Professionalism: The Success Force in Convention Marketing," Speech before a Graduate Seminar of the International Congress, and Convention Association, Yale University, July 22, 1980.

TOURISM SALES AND MARKETING

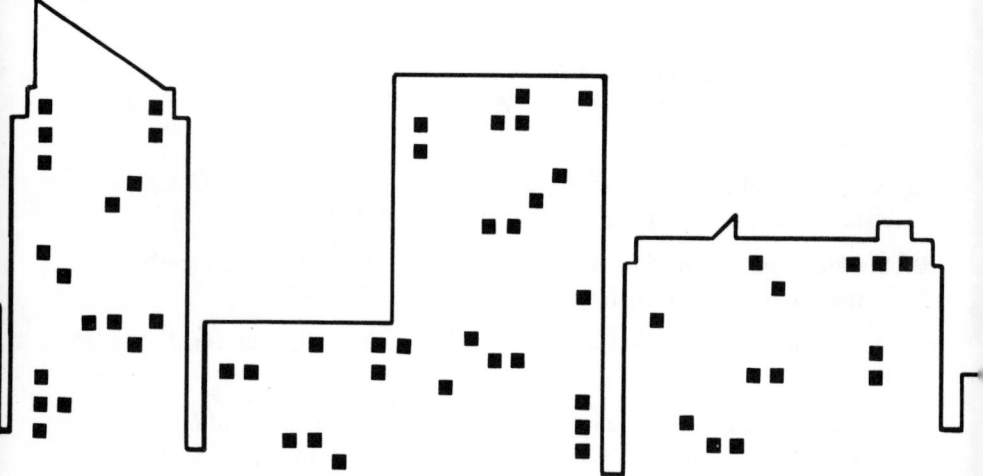

4

LEARNING OBJECTIVES

Upon reading this chapter, you will learn the following:

- About the diversity of market segments which constitute the "tourism industry" for convention bureau marketing;

- The seven divisions of a marketing plan for a convention and visitor bureau tourism program;

- How to identify and define tourism markets;

- About the vacationing family market and relevant marketing strategies;

- About the Incentive Travel market;

- About the Group Travel Market and relevant marketing strategies;

- Ways of evaluating the impact of various tourism markets;

- How to develop tourism sales accounts;

- How to develop tourism sales leads;

- The value of hospitality training programs for a community.

Introduction

When you mention the term "travel," it is usually perceived as something that is glamorous, romantic or even exotic; but for those who are involved in this diverse industry, whether it is called "travel," "tourism" or "leisure," it is a business which, like any other business, responds to market needs and demands. The complex entities which comprise the tourism market pose a challenge to those who work within it and confuse, for the most part, the disinterested consumer. Because the marketplace is composed of "small businesses," it does not always receive the attention or credit it deserves for influencing the economic fabric of a community.[1]

This attitude toward tourism sales efforts has been complicated by the lack of systematic tracking techniques which reflect accurately the economic impact of tourism sales endeavors on the community. Because of the ease in tracking the impact of convention sales through such variables as conventions booked, delegates attending, room nights used, and therefore economic impact, the assumption has been that these sales efforts are more valued than tourism efforts. The results have been that tourism is not given the same credibility as convention sales though, for many bureaus, these functions are considerably more important than convention sales. Tourism markets are diverse and for the most part must be tracked individually to determine their economic impact. But there is a maturation occurring within the tourism industry that will bring about a resolution to some of these discrepancies. It is not convention sales versus tourism sales; it is sales and marketing programs that bring visitors to a destination, whether part of a convention, group tour or as individual visitors. These programs are not in competition but are the primary functions of bureaus and need to be supported.

Convention and visitor bureaus represent their destinations, and as such, develop comprehensive programs that will attract those who are involved in delivering a travel product to the consumer. Such markets may include group tour planners, international wholesalers and retail agents, travel agents, travel writers and visitor information outlets. Other activities may be aimed at the consumer directly, though this can be a very costly and time consuming endeavor. Assessing preferred and profitable markets and identifying efficient and productive marketing strategies are among the responsibilities of a convention and visitor bureau as it develops its various tourism markets.

This chapter will explore the specific marketing activities undertaken by convention and visitor bureaus as they pertain to identifying tourism markets that will have a significant impact on the economic fabric of their communities.

Goals for a Tourism Sales and Marketing Department

Marketing plans among convention and visitor bureaus define goals for their tourism sales and marketing activities in different ways, but with the same bottom line: to increase sales and the economic impact of those tourism markets on their destinations. Below are some examples of how these goals and objectives have been defined.

Atlanta

The purpose is to increase tourist visitation and spending in the area through strategic marketing plans, service and information programs, and direct sales efforts focusing on the target markets of group travel, individual traffic and motorcoach tours.

Objectives

To strengthen and increase existing sales efforts in travel trade and consumer market segments, complementing and augmenting marketing efforts of area hotels and attractions.

To increase awareness of the area as a tourist destination through effective visitor service programs, familiarization tours and consumer/trade advertising campaign.

Baton Rouge

To establish Baton Rouge as a prime destination for motorcoach travellers and to attract a larger percentage of the overnight business.

> *Action 1. Participate in the following travel industry trade shows:*
> *a. National Tour Association*
> *b. American Bus Association*
> *c. Travel South Showcase*
> *d. Travel Industry of America's International Pow Wow*
> *2. Create a Group Tour Operator's Manual which highlights the resources available to the group tour market.*
> *3. Follow a daily sales effort for soliciting new group tour business, accomplished through maintaining and updating a file system on current and potential tour planners. Work 25 new files per week.*

Tulsa

International Marketing:

Project A: *Alliance of Canadian Travel Association*
Western Regional Conference
Winnipeg, Manitoba

Performance Criteria: We will reach a minimum of 75 tour operators/agents selling Tulsa and the State.

Project B: *Ontario Motor Coach Association Annual Convention*

Performance Criteria: Presentation of Tulsa and Oklahoma as a destination to 50 tour operators.

Project C: *World Travel Market, London, England*

Performance Criteria: Presentation of Tulsa and Oklahoma as a destination to a minimum of 100 tour operators, retail agents and media representatives.

San Francisco

The primary focus (of San Francisco's marketing division or tourism sales efforts) is directed toward developing and servicing the pleasure travel segment of the area's visitor audience. The division also is involved in the development and implementation of advertising, promotions, and a variety of collateral materials supporting tourism programs. Implementation of strategies recommended in the long-range marketing plan also will occur.

The overall objective of the five year plan is to return the area to 1979 levels of visitor activity:

- *Increase annual visitations to the area by 16% over 1983 levels to 2.7 million visitors by end of year five of the plan;*
- *Increase annual visitor-generated revenues to $1,139 million by end of the year five of the plan, an increase of $157 million over 1983 levels;*
- *Increase annual visitor tax revenues to $83 million by year five of the plan, an increase of $12 million over 1983 levels;*
- *And increase employment in the city's travel and tourism related industries by 9,200 jobs over the five years of the plan.*

The goals and objectives are fairly explicit; sales efforts are to increase the economic impact of travel-related revenues generated within a destination. Department personnel therefore develop their sales efforts in such a manner as to maximize the investment of their time with clients that are the most productive for their destination. Activities are assessed in light of their value in reaching stipulated goals. Planning is dependent on priorities; and though many activities may appear to be "worthwhile" or "tourism oriented," a convention and visitor bureau must evaluate the impact those activities will have on its destination in generating new and long-term revenues as well as on the time commitments required of bureau staff.

What are those programs in which a tourism sales and marketing department should become involved? And how does one outline them in a marketing plan?

Developing a Marketing Plan

The nature of the marketplace requires a sophistication on the part of a convention and visitor bureau if it is to remain competitive and have an impact. Too often, marketing has been practiced without a clear sense of direction or an understanding of markets, market segments or the effectiveness of marketing techniques. A convention and visitors bureau cannot survive without the development of a marketing plan that places into focus its competition, resources, goals and program strategies.

Marketing plans may be long or short, and they will vary among convention and visitor bureaus. Whatever their length or character, they are valued as a tool for effective planning and assessment of productivity. The following are some general guidelines for developing a marketing plan.

First, a bureau needs to assess its present situation. This assessment will explore the realities of the industry, the community, the travel product, the economic environment and the potential or present visitors. For Tourism Sales and Marketing, some of the following questions should be asked, the answers to which will give a bureau a better understanding of its current situation.

1. What is the present demand for tourism activities and attractions in your community?
2. What facilities and resources do you have to market to visitors?
3. What is your community known for? What kind of image does the destination have to outsiders? And to people who live there?
4. What are your strengths and weaknesses as a community and how do they impact your tourism markets?
5. What changes do you anticipate in the next five years, and will they impact your ability to attract visitors to your destination?
6. What other trends might impact your community/destination?
7. How responsive is your community to having visitors?

Developing a "situational analysis" is fundamental to better understanding the capabilities, potential and interest that may exist for visitors within
a destination. For example, the following appeared in a recent marketing plan
for the Albuquerque Convention and Visitors Bureau (New Mexico) reflecting
its assessment of various markets.

> Positioning Albuquerque as the "Gateway to Enchantment" for the past two
> years has stimulated thinking on the part of both the travel planner and the
> "trip-takers," that this city and area offer an immense opportunity for the
> curious traveler.
>
> The response to the advertising campaign in both trade and consumer
> publications has been incredible: 19,093 responses in the 18 months of
> advertising. . . .
>
> Automobile travel remains the predominant mode of visitor traffic. But for the
> first time, we are able to evaluate the impact of motorcoach business in
> Albuquerque. The National Tour Association SEA report shows 59,000
> motorcoach visitors in 1984 representing a total direct economic impact of
> $5.1 million dollars.

The second element in developing a marketing plan is the establishment
of measurable goals. This can be accomplished only after carefully considering
the demand and supply potential of visitors to a destination. Questions that
address this issue are as follows:

1. What kinds of goals should be established? Should they be short and/
   or long-term? Is there a baseline against which such goals are being
   set?
2. What kinds of tourism markets should be targeted and what are the
   goals for each market segment?
3. How will the bureau assess the attainment of these goals?
4. Are the goals realistic in terms of the bureau's resources, timelines
   and travel products?

Upon an assessment of its market potential, the Reno-Sparks Convention
and Visitors Authority (Nevada) states some of its marketing goals for its
tourism sales efforts in the following manner.

> *Domestic Markets:* To strengthen the Reno/Tahoe presence in top priority
> markets by means of expanded "Reno Night" travel agent promotions, backed
> by trade advertising: and to educate travel agents in selected markets through
> participation in trade shows and by hosting local familiarization tours. To
> establish two new wholesale tour programs and host 12 fam tours, resulting in
> 20,000 new visitors.
>
> *Motorcoach/Rail:* To establish Reno/Tahoe as a prime destination for
> motorcoach travelers with a goal of definite motorcoach tour programs with a
> minimum of 50 companies resulting in 75,000 arrivals of motorcoach
> travelers.

These goals not only take into account Reno's geographic location but also give serious consideration to the quality travel products it has to offer. Strategies supported by adequate funding and personnel, are then developed to bring these goals into reality.

The third essential element in a marketing plan is that of identifying and selecting the target markets. This is usually called market segmentation. No bureau is equipped with financial resources to simply "market," "sell," "advertise" or "promote." In fact, the competition has become so sophisticated that bureaus must identify and carefully define their target markets. For tourism sales and marketing efforts, some of those markets may be defined as follows:

1. Vacationing Families/Pleasure Travelers
2. Incentive Travel/Business Travelers
3. Domestic Group Tour Planners
4. International Wholesalers
5. Travel Agents
6. Travel Writers-Media

There are additional means for dividing market segments. For example, when examining the general "pleasure traveler" market segment, a bureau, depending on its location and possible seasons, may wish to target its efforts to specific, identifiable subgroups. For example, Colorado Springs may wish to target hunters or skiers, whereas Valley Forge may wish to target history buffs. San Juan may target the resort market while Las Vegas, the gambling clientele. Each market segment potentially requires a different set of strategies and may require different vehicles for communicating a messge. It is fundamental that a bureau know and understand the characteristics of various market segments. There are several ways of examining market segments through demographics, psychographics and geographic analysis.

Demographic variables most commonly used to identify groups include age, sex, income, expenditure patterns, occupation, education, household size, marital status and ethnic background. A resort destination such as Tucson may find it caters to "empty-nesters." These are couples who have no children or have raised their children and who enjoy resort activities such as golfing, swimming, horseback riding, dining and dancing. A destination such as Elko, Nevada, may find among its market segments vacationers who are enroute to or from a destination, driving an automobile or camper, and usually involving children. The "enroute" or "transient" market is approached considerably differently than a resort market.

Psychographics pertains to an individual's underlying motivations for travel. We have talked about hunters and skiers, which is a means of defining market segments on the basis of behaviors. Psychographic research (or personality research) goes beyond demographics and asks why people behave or select travel products in a certain way. It wants to get at the root of their decision making process; it wants to find out why some select one destination over another or one mode of transportation over another and why different people travel. Plog[2] asserts that psychographic research can measure which population segments will travel, what motives can be identified to increase their potential to travel, what kinds of destinations are preferred, what activities they wish to engage in upon arrival, and what kinds of marketing themes need to be creatively developed to focus on their motives and needs. Mitchell[3] and Shih[4] also have examined the "values and lifestyles" (or VALS) of Americans to better identify and understand the behavioral patterns of market segments. For example, the VALS typology divides Americans into nine lifestyles grouped into four categories. These categories are: (a) Need-Driven Groups (survivors and sustainers) whose lives are driven on the basis of needs more than by choice; (b) Outer-Directed Groups (belongers, emulators and achievers) comprise two-thirds of the population, are concerned about how they appear to others and conduct their lives influenced by others' perceptions of them; (c) Inner-Directed Groups (I-am-me's, experientials and societally conscious) are self-directed who base their lives on internal and emotional rewards rather than external and materialistic things; and the (d) Combined Outer-Inner Directed Group, which reflects an Integrated Lifestyle where people tend to be self-assured, self-actualizing, self-expressive, aware of issues and possessing a world perspective. What VALS has found, as it relates to the travel industry, is that certain groups prefer certain types of travel experiences. For example, achievers and societally conscious tend to stay in hotels while on business while emulators do not; achievers are not heavy television watchers but are interested in magazines and newspapers whereas survivors tend to be heavy viewers. These findings influence marketing strategies that are most likely to be effective in reaching target markets.

Geography is another means of defining a market segment; for example, a convention and visitor bureau may find that it has a potential market for daytime or overnight tours from group operators within a five-hour drive of that destination. Specific events or activities, such as antique fairs, cultural events or special pageants may be of interest to those tour operators who have groups that wish to spend only a day away from their homes. Geographically, this opens a new market segment for a convention and visitor bureau.

The fourth element in a marketing plan is that of identifying and selecting the appropriate and most productive marketing strategies for the targeted market. There are an abundance of techniques available to a bureau; asking some of these questions will provide guidelines for selecting the best techniques for each market segment.

1. Which selected marketing strategies will be the most effective for an identified market segment? What are the strengths and weaknesses of a strategy? Who are affected by a selected strategy?

2. What combination of strategies might be most productive in reaching a selected market segment?

For example, in a 1984 survey of domestic group tour planners regarding marketing techniques that might be employed by convention and visitor bureaus, the tour planners indicated first a preference for familiarization tours, followed in priority by resource manuals, appointments at an annual trade show, direct mail, personal sales calls and rapport with the bureau representative. Advertising, for example, was not a high priority, though advertising might stimulate their attention with new ideas that might be developed into a tour or added to an existing tour. Planners also indicated a preference for appointments and considered cold sales calls an infringement on their time. Such an informal study enlightens a bureau as to a preferred set of marketing strategies that might be undertaken to influence an identified market segment.[5]

Fifth, a bureau needs to allocate its resources adequately to support the programs outlined for attaining desired goals. Without funding and personnel, programs will simply not be productive.

1. To what extent will personnel and money be dedicated for a specific program?
2. Will the allocation be sufficient to reach the desired program goal?
3. Does the bureau have other community resources that might be employed toward a specific program to ensure its success?

The issue of funds and staff time becomes a critical element in planning, particularly for smaller bureaus. But with planning and some creativity, programs can be implemented and a level of success attained.

Sixth, a marketing plan needs to be implemented. When do you do the things you have outlined in a plan? Timing has a lot to do with how successful a marketing plan will be. It affects the placement of advertising and its impact on the targeted market segment; it also will affect how successful one might be in reaching planners during or prior to their planning time. Questions that might direct the implementation of a plan include:

1. When is the best time to launch a specific marketing strategy for a specific market segment?
2. What kinds of lead times applicable to various market segments would impact goal attainment?
3. In what sequence should various marketing elements be implemented? Does one strategy need to follow another to maximize impact?

4. And far from least, who is doing what, when, how and with whom? In implementing a program, is it coordinated for maximum bureau efficiency?

Convention and visitor bureaus always face pressures to implement programs that will provide immediate return on investments. This may not always be the case; for example, in responding to the oil embargo crisis of 1979, bureaus had to take some quick steps to overcome the negative publicity about the availability of fuel if they were to keep visitors coming to their destinations during those summer months. However, when dealing with other market segments, implementation of strategies requires careful planning, timing and execution if they are to be effective in creating an image for a destination and/or generating travel-related revenues.

Last, a bureau has to be able to assess the effectiveness of its marketing programs. This does not always mean change; in fact, if a program continues to prove of value, then there may be little reason to change it. On the other hand, if a marketing effort seems to fizzle, being able to make an evaluation then is imperative.

1. What kinds of results are being sought in a specific marketing effort? Are the results quantified?
2. What kinds of criteria have been established against which to assess a marketing program?
3. What kinds of contingencies have been developed for a program that may prove less effective than intended?

Because of the diversity of market segments which compose the tourism industry, a marketing plan is much like a navigational chart. The marketing plan requires a look at all the relevant activities, defines goals, identifies markets, selects strategies, makes assessments and determines results. Navigation likewise plots courses, charts status and aims for the final destination. The development of a marketing plan does not require intensive scholarly work; it is an attitude that will govern and influence the directions a bureau intends to go. The investment of time is critical to the most efficient use of a bureau's resources.

But now that we have reviewed some of the thinking that must go into the development of a marketing plan, it seems appropriate to explore some of the tourism market segments and the kinds of marketing strategies that might be employed by a convention and visitor bureau.[6]

Figure 4.1

Tourism Markets

For years, writers such as McIntosh and Goeldner, Davidoff and Davidoff, Mayo and Jarvis, Hodgson, Lundberg, Pearce, and Mill and Morrison[7] among others have attempted to define and describe motivations for travel, selecting a travel destination, sources for information gathering, purchasing behaviors of the traveler, characteristics of various market segments and many other aspects of the tourism market. The diversity of information continues to provide insights into market characteristics, market behaviors and market trends. What was understood about a market segment yesterday may not be applicable today or tomorrow; thus it is important that research continue to explore these changing frontiers of an industry that has such dramatic economic significance to communities.

Vacationing Families/Pleasure Travelers

Annually, bureaus embark on advertising programs that will generate visitor inquiries about their areas. Such a program involves the development of a thematically consistent advertising program that includes a coupon for requesting information or a toll-free telephone number in ads placed, for example, in consumer-oriented publications. Among publications selected, depending on the bureau and its geographic location, are: *Travel South, Sunset,*

Figure 4.2

Better Homes and Garden, Family Circle, National Geographic and AAA publications. Usually ads are placed for the months of February through May; and it is hoped that during that four-month timeline, they will generate sufficient inquiries indicating an interest in visiting a given destination.

A research article by van Raaij and Francken[8] indicates there is a series of steps through which vacationers proceed. First is the decision to go or not to go; once the decision is made to go on a vacation, they begin to gather information from a series of sources. The decision to travel is usually predicated on the selection of a destination, then the selection of lodging and service facilitites. The information that is gathered also seems to begin with general knowledge gleaned from advertising (both print and non-print media), catalogs and references, followed by information sought specifically from such resources as bureaus, state or national travel offices and AAA offices. Throughout their considerations, vacationers tend to bounce their ideas and intentions off family and friends to gain their input as well. In a related study by Jenkins,[9] it was discovered that planning usually began from one to three months in advance for about 50% of the vacationers, for 35% from three months to one year, and for 15%, plans were made in less than a week. Thus, to be effective in reaching the largest potential audience during months in which they are the most receptive, summer destination advertising usually takes place during the late winter and spring months of each year.

Simply having a large number of travel inquiries does not indicate that they actually generated visits to the area. To make such an assessment, an "Inquiry Conversion Study" or a "Coupon Conversion Study" is done. The intent of such studies is to determine, based on a sampling of the inquiries received, how many visitors actually visited the area, what they visited, how long they stayed, and how much they spent.[10] The fact that one source over another might have drawn a larger number of inquiries (or coupons) does not necessarily mean it is a more effective channel for generating visitors; the conversion study can, in essence, assess the performance of advertising campaigns and the selected media. The data gathered will indicate the number of visitors coming to a destination, their economic impact, and the most effective advertising medium for generating actual visitor-days (visitors coming to a destination).

Included in the marketing strategies potentially available for use with various tourism markets are:

1. Print Advertising. This technique has already been addressed but deals with both magazines and newspapers. Magazines, such as *Travel South* or *Sunset,* are often seen as highly geographic, credible, consisting of high quality reproductions, and having a long shelf or pass along life. In placing ads, however, there is a long lead time with no guarantee of position, and they are expensive. Newspapers, on the other hand, have tremendous flexibility as it applies to position of an ad, good local market coverage, broad acceptance and credibility, relatively low cost, and are a high public mode of communication. Newspapers, however, have a short life, poor reproduction quality, small pass along audience, and competition from surrounding ads. The VALS research suggests that the targeted audience has to be carefully examined to determine which media selection can be the most effective.

   There are also directories which fall into print advertising which must be maintained; such directories include automobile club directories and the Mobil Travel Guides.

2. Non-Print Advertising. Television and radio comprise these marketing strategies. Television combines sight and sounds thereby teasing the senses and providing animation for a message; it tends to target different age groups depending on the types of shows being watched. Ads, however, can be expensive depending on the time slot and frequency selected, and can be fleeting exposures (depending on who gets up during the commercial to go to the kitchen). Radio seems to be a pervasive medium; it can be selectively used based on the time slots selected. It is strictly an audio presentation and is vulnerable as well to the fleeting exposure.

Figure 4.3. The greater Houston Convention and Visitors Bureau operates a drive-through visitor information center.

3. Travel Shows. These are consumer-oriented programs which are usually held in major cities, offering those who attend information on vacation destinations, sporting activities and sometimes recreational equipment such as campers and boats. Travel shows must be selectively chosen based on what a destination wishes to accomplish; consumers attending will also make a heavy demand on printed materials.

4. Visitor Information Centers. In many cities, visitor information or welcome centers have been developed to serve the transient public. These centers usually are staffed with vacation information for that city and its surrounding area; the intent for having such a facility is to meet the needs of visitors to a community, with the hope of extending their length of stay and/or bringing them back for another visit at a future date. These centers may be located in the front office of a convention and visitor bureau, a static display of information at an airport, a manned booth at an airport, or a separate building.

5. Information Distribution. This involves the mailing of bureau informational flyers and booklets to major visitor information outlets such as AAA offices and regional and state operated visitor information centers. The goal of this strategy is to get materials about a destination into other hands for public dissemination. The audience that is primarily targeted tends to be automotive oriented, vacationing and transient. Information also may be distributed through local hotels, restaurants, attractions and other travel-related enterprises.

Figure 4.4. The Wichita Convention and Visitors Bureau developed a guest card for visitors which served as one means for attracting and tracking visitors to their community.

The strategies selected by a convention and visitor bureau for marketing to this or any other market segment are limited only by the resources and creativity of a bureau.

Measuring Visitor Impact

Unlike convention sales, tracking the impact of visitors to a community can be cumbersome; whatever the marketing strategy employed by a convention and visitor bureau, it is essential to determine an effective means for tracking the effectiveness of a marketing technique as well as its productivity in generating new revenues for the destination.

For example, as previously noted, the "Inquiry Conversion Studies" can make an assessment as to the economic impact visitors have on a community based on those who requested specific travel or visitor information.

Such studies could be augmented by intercept studies; these studies are designed to capture information from visitors by intercepting them while they are actually in the community at such facilities as hotels, restaurants, attractions and service stations. Such a study may be predicated on locating those with out-of-state or out-of-county license plates and having them respond to a set of questions, including economic impact questions. Of course, this kind of technique requires personnel to perform the intercept, a brief but effective questionnaire instrument and a statistical ratio of where to draw the sample (how many at hotels, restaurants, attractions and service stations). Survey forms also can be employed during festivals and other major events to glean information about the attendees (see Appendix L for sample form).

Tourism sales and marketing efforts are not that different from convention sales efforts. The fundamental difference is that convention sales has different markets but one type of tracking that identifies economic impact (number of groups, number of delegates, room-nights, economic impact) whereas in tourism, there are diverse market segments, and each segment requires a different technique to evaluate its economic impact. Acquiring an understanding of these diverse techniques often overwhelms a bureau unless it has a research team who can track and monitor each and every diverse tourism undertaking.

Incentive Travel

Many companies are involved in providing some form of incentives to their sales and marketing personnel. Travel is sometimes an option used in incentive programs. Among the types of companies that use travel as an incentive are: insurance (the first industry group to exceed $300 million spent on incentive travel); electronic, radio and television; auto parts and accessories; auto and truck; farm equipment; heating and air conditioning; office equipment; electric appliances; toiletries and cosmetics; building materials; petroleum; pharmaceuticals; books; housewares; sporting goods; and mail order. The incentive program is simple; it consists of a contest designed to increase sales, improve morale or increase productivity, and a prize or reward. The contest usually runs from a few months to a year. Prizes awarded reflect the level of attainment achieved during that contest. Prizes may consist of money, merchandise or travel; extraordinary travel awards are seen as the most beneficial to a company with residual value from the pleasure spoken about upon the winners' return. With roughly $2 billion spent annually on incentive travel, the average expenditures per person is in excess of $1,600, the average length of stay at least five nights, and the average number of participants 140,[11] little wonder there is interest among convention and visitor bureaus in addressing this market segment. Not only are the expenditures greater than those of individual visitors, but incentive groups represent the corporation's finest, including their executives who also may have an influence on other corporate business.

In another related study, additional profile data about incentive travel were ascertained including the following:[12]

- those responsible for planning incentive programs plan an average of 2.5 trips per year;

- corporate officers and upper management are responsible for the final decisions regarding incentive programs (56.8%) followed by middle managers (25%);
- the average lead time for planning an incentive program is 15 months;
- 75.7% of the respondents use incentive travel houses or travel agents for planning and execution of their incentive programs;
- and 84% of the respondents indicated a preference for domestic destinations followed by Hawaii (50.7%), Mexico (48.6%), other off-shore destinations such as Asia and the Pacific rim (47.3%), Caribbean (44.6%) and Europe (37.1%).

Understanding the nature of the incentive travel market is critical for a convention and visitor bureau. For example, when a convention and visitor bureau undertakes a marketing strategy for this market segment, it is essential to identify first those motivational companies or incentive houses that include travel among their incentives, corporations that promote their own incentive programs and travel agents who are involved in incentive efforts. With a majority of corporations using professional incentive houses, it is important that a bureau develop rapport with the users to keep them fully knowledgeable about a destination and its potential for incentive travel. A bureau will need to know about the kinds of incentives planned by the incentive house, the history of its incentive endeavors including successes and failures, the background of incentive planners, and why a group is coming to a particular destination. In turn, the incentive planner is seeking a partnership with the bureau that will include open communications and trust. Incentive planners are seeking destinations that are promotable over a period of time as well as destinations that are accessible. The incentive planner is seeking to develop a first-class experience by providing an exciting destination to his/her clients. Whatever a bureau selects in the form of marketing strategies, it is fundamental that there be a high level of communication between the incentive planner and the bureau if programs are to be developed and executed effectively.

One organization that specializes in incentives is the Society of Incentive Travel Executives (SITE). (See Appendix D.) Annually, they conduct a "University of Incentive Travel" which helps suppliers such as bureaus, hotels, airlines, cruise lines, travel agents and ground operators better understand their interactive roles in the planning and delivery of an incentive trip. Obviously, some destinations have a distinct advantage over others as to their attractiveness for incentive packages; each convention and visitor bureau needs to assess its travel product and destination to determine the degree of involvement and commitment it wishes to make to incentive travel.

Group Travel[13]

Travel is an activity that lends itself to a group experience, not only for its enriching quality but also for the economic benefits that can be shared by participants. As a result of the growth of the group travel market, it is not surprising that many convention and visitor bureaus spend a good deal of their marketing energies on this segment of travel. Indeed, those who have been successful in attracting group business can testify to the return on investment in terms of both profitability and repeat business.

Like most marketing efforts, attracting group business is the result of careful planning by the convention and visitor bureau. There are a variety of ways to reach the group market, some of which are more productive than others. In simple terms, the group market can be broken into "per capita" and "pre-formed."

"Per capita" describes a group tour product which is sold to individuals. The tour operator designs a tour itinerary that will interest a particular segment of his/her clientele; each tour component is carefully selected, from destinations to attractions to lodging, food and related travel services, with the clientele's needs and interests in mind. Such itinerary planning may average from 12 to 18 months for development. Shorter tour itineraries, for example, two day/one overnight trips or daytime tours may require considerably less time to develop. Each component is carefully costed and a final tour price determined. Once the tour is finalized, the work just begins for the tour operator, who must sell that product in anticipation that enough individuals will want to participate and purchase the product. In other words, the tour is presented to the public on a speculative basis. Tour operators will use a variety of distribution channels to market tour products, including newsletters, direct mail, tour catalogs, advertising and travel agents. The tour operator is not only trying to sell the products but also attempting to respond to the particular interests of potential clients by offering a variety of travel destinations that consider activities, cost and length of tour.

"Pre-formed" groups are those usually associated with clubs and organizations whose members enjoy traveling together. A list obtained from the local chamber of commerce or public library will begin to identify the enormous potential of pre-formed groups as a market segment. Usually tour operators work with such groups through a group leader; this group leader communicates with the tour operator the interests of the pre-formed group and in turn, the tour operator packages a tour that will meet its needs and interests. For the most part, however, tour operators have a mixed clientele and undertake a variety of marketing techniques to "sell" their tour packages.

In developing the strategies[14] for this market segment, a convention and visitor bureau must give thoughtful consideration to at least six techniques that have the potential for exposing group business to its destination. It also must be remembered that these techniques need to be monitored carefully and assessed as to their effectiveness and productivity, particularly in terms of reaching per capita tour planners and/or pre-formed groups.

Trade shows and industry conventions are among the primary ways of meeting a maximum number of decision-makers in a minimum amount of time. There is an abundance of trade shows from which to choose; understanding the nature of a trade show and its target audience is necessary in planning the marketing mix. These questions might assist a convention and visitor bureau in identifying which shows to attend:

1. Who attend the trade show? If they are per capita tour operators, are they decision-makers who determine tour itineraries and the components that will be included? If they are pre-formed group operators, do they recommend destinations and specific inclusions to their group leaders or are they merely order takers?
2. What is the schedule of events for the trade show? Does the program allow for ample time to meet with prospective clients? Under what format will a bureau have the opportunity to meet tour operators? Does the program allow for getting to know the client on a social level?
3. To what geographic markets do the clients in attendance direct their products? Are these products sold domestically, internationally or both? Do the users of their products come from a bureau's targeted geographic market?
4. How does the timing of the trade show relate to the decision-making cycle of the tour planner? Most per capita tour planners make decisions about their tour itineraries and components roughly the same time of year, whereas pre-formed tour planners tend to be less married to a predictable cycle.
5. Does the cost of the show make sense according to the number of potential clients a bureau will be able to see and the quality of the time spent with each tour planner?

The cost effectiveness of a trade show must be determined by each individual convention and visitor bureau; it is impossible, depending on the size of the bureau's budget, to attend all the available trade show "opportunities." Assessing and prioritizing those that are the most productive is essential. In part, this assessment of a trade show might include not only the number of contacts reached during the show, but also the quality of those contacts. Prior to attending a trade show, a bureau should prioritize its client and potential client lists in order to make the most effective use of trade show time. This can be most useful, particularly when planning to attend a domestic tour operator's

Figure 4.5. Courtesy: National Tour Association

show such as the National Tour Association's Annual Fall Convention or Spring Tour and Travel Exchange or an international show like the Travel Industry Association of America's Pow Wow, all of which provide suppliers scheduled one-on-one appointments with targeted tour operators.

Another marketing strategy that has proven its value in the group travel market is offering familiarization tours. No trade show can compare with the first-hand experience a tour operator gains by participating in a familiarization (fam) tour. It is definitely easier to sell operators on a destination if they have the opportunity to visit it. Some general guidelines for fam tours are:

1. A fam tour should be oriented to selling a destination and region. There are very few destinations that can be sold without the help of its neighbors, especially to the group tour market. Tour operators are looking at areas; and the group traveler is looking for a variety of experiences for his/her vacation investment.

2. Fam tour participants should be advised that the purpose of the trip is work; organizers should be business-like in their approach, from their initial invitations to the follow-up letters. These tours are designed to give tour operators a good look at a destination and its surrounding areas; their time is as important as the investment being made by a bureau.

3. Supplier participants should be cooperative with the bureau in respecting the needs of those involved in the tour. Suppliers should be well informed about the needs and interests of the tour planners so that time spent with them can be mutually beneficial.

Fam tours are an effective marketing tool for introducing a destination and region. When the bureau organizes such an event, it is imperative that the community be thoroughly briefed about the tour. Gaining publicity during such a tour is another way to highlight the bureau's important role in developing the economic fabric of a community. The effectiveness of a fam tour is not only found in the number of participants but also in the number of tours that may come into the area as a result of the visit. It must be remembered, though, that the type of tour that is developed also will have an affect on the timeline for seeing results. For example, a tour that is designed and sold to a pre-formed group may have a shorter timeline than a tour itinerary that relies on per capita clients.

Direct mail is another effective strategy for the group market. There is considerable debate as to its effectiveness but this has focused fundamentally on the failure of many to identify targeted tour planners selectively. Tour planners often complain about receiving too much unsolicited mail; but if bureaus were more selective in identifying priority tour operators who might benefit their destinations the most, this concern might be reduced. The concerns go well beyond bureaus; many suppliers, such as hotels and attractions, make massive mailings and, as a result, overwhelm the tour operator with materials that may not be solicited or wanted. For a convention and visitor bureau, it is important to narrow the targeted market and to maintain some consistency in the frequency of mailings in order to generate an acceptable level of awareness and exposure.

There are two ways of examining the effectiveness of direct mail. First, if direct mail is simply to generate an awareness of an area, there is little that might be used to assess its impact except a survey questionnaire to the tour operator. The survey should be designed to determine if a specific marketing program influenced the operator's development of tour itineraries. This technique can be cumbersome, costly and potentially irritating to tour planners if undertaken by all bureaus. The second technique for assessing the effectiveness of a direct mail program is through the use of a response mechansim. A simple reply card can afford useful information about the interest level of tour operators to the direct mail campaign.

A third marketing technique is that of the personal sales call. If prospecting is the single most important result of attending a trade show or industry convention, then making sales calls is perhaps the single most effective means to follow up on those prospects. The sales call can accomplish several objectives:

1. It can serve to build rapport between the client and the bureau.
2. It can provide both the client and the bureau with quality time in which to learn about each other's needs and concerns.

3. It is relatively time-efficient. The duration of an average sales call is approximately 30 minutes and, if pre-scheduled by bureau personnel, can be an efficient use of bureau time and an indication of the respect for the tour operator's time.

In designing sales trips, it is important to consider the following guidelines:

1. Identify those cities that have the most potential for producing appointments with the most important tour operators.
2. Once a destination has been selected, review the tour operators in that area, prioritize them in order of importance, arrange them geographically within the city (to make efficient use of time between appointments), and then make scheduled appointments with each tour operator.
3. Once a trip has been planned, carefully identify materials to take along; these might include tour planning resource manuals, attraction brochures, rate information and maps of the area and state. These support materials become critically important when working with international tour planners.

The results of a sales trip may not be measured immediately; however, there may be times when tour operators develop new itineraries, make last-minute tour adjustments into an area or literally sign contracts with suppliers (this may happen particularly with international operators). One of the key purposes behind the sales call is to develop rapport with the tour operator. This relationship between the tour planner and the bureau can, in turn, have an impact on that destination's ability to be included in future tour itineraries. But sales calls also can be evaluated on the basis of the number of contacts; though this is a superficial means for evaluating a sales trip, it is another step closer to the client "booking" a tour or tours into a destination.

Advertising is perhaps the most frequently used of all the marketing strategies. It can be used to develop an image, communicate information or generate sales leads.

It is a relatively simple task to determine which travel industry publications have tour operators as a target audience. Most of the major travel industry associations have a publication which is read by their memberships. The two most significant publications for this particular market are *Courier,* the publication of the National Tour Association, and *Destinations,* published by the American Bus Association. In addition, most tour operators read at least one of the major travel trade publications such as *Travel Weekly, Tour and Travel News, Travel Agent,* and the regional publication *TravelAge.* Most publications design their editorial calendars well in advance so that suppliers with a limited budget can place ads in special sections geared for their geographic region or specific business interests.

Advertising is the most expensive of the marketing strategies suggested. Depending on the intent of the ad, one means for measuring interest is based on using a response mechanism built into the ad in the form of a coupon, reply tip-in card or an 800 telephone number. Effectiveness of one publication against another can then be measured. Ad responses can be built into a sales call program to insure follow-up on each inquiry.

Other publicity and promotional techniques that might be developed by a convention and visitor bureau include:

1. Building a list of key media contacts, including editors and travel writers of newspapers, consumer publications, trade publications and radio and television stations. Using these contacts, a bureau can generate additional editorial coverage about its destination, creating a greater awareness of it. Hosting some media contacts on a fam tour also benefits a destination. Media kits should be frequently sent to targeted contacts. Measuring the effectiveness of this program involves tracking resulting column inches in print and the length and frequency of non-print media spots.

2. Developing a group tour resource manual. This publication should contain all the vital information on a destination, allowing a tour planner to make decisions from the data contained therein. Such information should include the following lists: lodging facilities, including guaranteed rate information; attractions, including group rates and suggested length for a visit of that facility; restaurants which will service group tours; other entertainment resources such as dinner-theaters; a detailed map of the destination and its surrounding areas; tour escort information; special events and activities in the area; ground operators and local bus companies; service facilities for motorcoaches; airlines serving the area; shopping malls and other retail/wholesale opportunities; and suggested itineraries.

   If a destination is seeking to host international groups, the group manual should also include information about qualified guides with linguistic capabilities; instructions on how to use telephones in other languages; current exchange information; climate information; time zone information; health and emergency services; passport/visa information; and whether menus, itineraries, maps and other resource materials can be obtained in other languages for inbound groups.

   The group tour planning manual is a convention and visitor bureau's primary sales tool for its destination to tour operators.

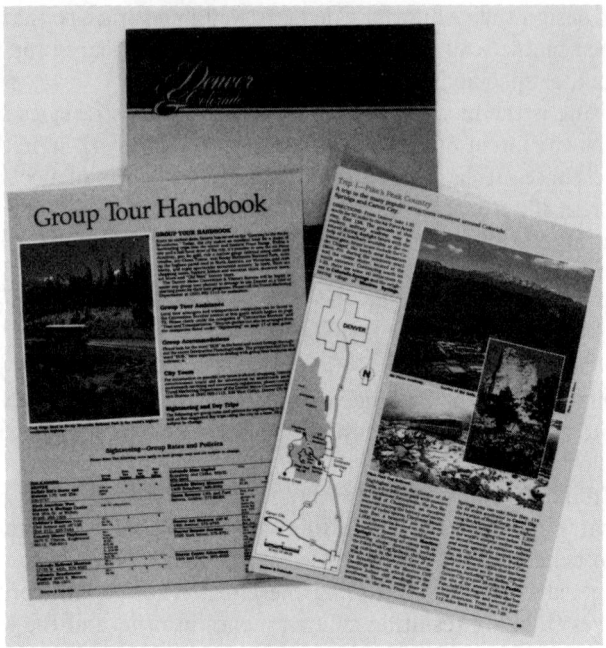

Figure 4.6

3. Providing tour planners with color slides and black and white photographs. These materials are used by the tour operator in developing his/her promotional catalogs and flyers and in making presentations before pre-formed groups. The partnership that is forged between the bureau and the operator is important in generating excitement about a destination to the consumer.

There are many other support services which a convention and visitor bureau may provide tour operators, including the development of special itineraries, escort notes (for the tour escort to use enroute to the destination), and the availability of step-on guide services (on arrival at a destination). These support services are an essential part of the "sales" efforts when targeting the group tour markets.

Measuring the impact of the group tour market still has a long way to go before it is fully mature. Not unlike the convention and meetings market, the group tour market is more easily assessible because of the size of the groups involved and the relative ease in documentation. Developing the economic impact of group tours has been a priority for convention and visitor bureaus which now can obtain statistical information based on data gathered from tour operators and motorcoach companies which belong to the National Tour Association, American Bus Association, United Bus Owners of America, Ontario

Motorcoach Association, unaffiliated tour and motorcoach companies and Greyhound Lines Inc. In 1986, for example, based on information from 14,000 individual itineraries representing some 275,000 tour departures, the economic impact of the group tour market in North America (based on the 50 states and ten Canadian provinces) exceeded $10 billion and was growing.[15]

Developing Tourism Sales Accounts

Regardless of the identified market segment, a Tourism Sales and Marketing Department can develop and track sales clients similar to the way convention sales are developed and tracked. Maintaining a list of active clients and prospects provides for a systematic means of monitoring and tracking. It also helps the department manager allocate staff and resources to the most productive market segments. Sales accounts, whether for tour operators, travel agents, international packagers or other tourism markets, should be composed of at least the following elements:

1. The *sales file* should consist of a folder which contains the latest specific information about that client; this includes name of appropriate contact, telephone number, address, description of product or service, decision making guidelines such as deadline dates for brochures or catalogues, copies of recent flyers and/or catalogues, types of programs (e.g., types of tours a tour operator prefers to develop), audio-visual and brochure needs, relevant correspondence and a tracking log of contacts with that client.
2. The system also should allow for a *geographic index card* and a *tickler card* for each client. The geographic index card allows a bureau to keep track of clients by geographic region; this is particularly useful information when planning a sales trip. The tickler or trace card schedules each client's file for review at least once annually if not more frequently, insuring that accounts are reviewed, updated and nurtured. Showing interest and maintaining contact with clients demonstrates that a bureau is attentive and serious about its sales efforts.

Developing Tourism Sales Leads

Not unlike convention sales efforts, the Tourism Sales and Marketing Department must also develop and qualify potential sales leads for its industry partners. Such leads take a form similar to convention sales leads; in fact, some convention and visitor bureaus talk about their red, blue, green and yellow bordered lead sheets, each color representing a different size or type group.

NO:
R/N:
MO/RPT:
NRR#:
BOOKED:

California's Site to Sea

TOURISM SALES LEAD

To: _____

From: _____

Date: _____

Subject: _____

Company: _____

Name of key contact: _____

Address: _____

_____

_____

_____

Telephone: _____ Telex:_____

Type of company: _____

Type of product: ___Tour Series ___Ad Hoc (Group) ___FIT

___Tariff ___Congress ___Incentive

Number of room nights anticipated: _____

Porterage requirements: _____

Food & Beverage requirements: _____

_____

_____

Remarks: _____

_____

_____

_____

LONG BEACH AREA CONVENTION AND VISITORS COUNCIL, INC.
180 E. Ocean Boulevard, Suite 150, Plaza Level, Long Beach, CA 90802, (213) 436-3645, Telex 650421

Figure 4.7

For some bureaus, such as Long Beach, yellow borders represent tourism sales leads while for other bureaus such as Ann Arbor, tourism leads are green bordered. Figure 4.7 is a sample of the kinds of information that should be included on such sales leads. Having a lead program can be of great value to a convention and visitor bureau. It enables sales leads to be forwarded to industry representatives such as attractions, ground operators, restaurants or other related travel services which may not otherwise receive bureau convention leads. Prospecting is one of the bureau's primary goals.

Hospitality Programs[16]

One of the other functions that might be undertaken by a Tourism Sales and Marketing Department is that of hospitality training, or training of the frontline industry personnel. Needless to say, every convention and visitor bureau wants providers of travel related services to be well-informed, enthusiastic ambassadors and hospitable hosts. While most visitors to a community do not meet bureau professionals, memories of their visit to that community definitely will be affected by their contact with front desk clerks, bellmen, maids, restaurant waiters and waitresses, cab drivers, tour guides and even store clerks. One significant leadership role for a convention and visitor bureau is to provide training for those who come in contact with the visitor.

An example of one bureau which has taken that dynamic role is Lincoln, Nebraska. There, the bureau has sponsored a training program on a regular basis for frontline personnel; included in the training is a 134-page "Front Desk Manual" which provides useful information on the community and its history and attractions. The manual contains newspaper articles on shopping, recreation, mini-tours, entertainment and special events. It even attempts to address critical questions that might be asked by visitors, ranging from after hours emergency information to local hours of attraction/operations.

In a similar vein, the Detroit Convention and Visitors Bureau (Michigan) sponsors an orientation program for new front line personnel which includes a several-hour tour of the community and its attractions. This first-hand experience of what the community has to offer helps them help visitors enjoy their stay.

San Diego developed another rather interesting hospitality program targeting members of its own community; in wanting to nurture a better community-wide attitude toward visitors, the San Diego Convention and Visitors Bureau (California) developed a "Host Survival Kit" (see figure 4.8) that includes a map, information on transportation and tours, information about the visitor hot line, general facts and information about San Diego and a wallet size card that explains the "dollars and sense" of tourism and the new convention center. The message was loud and clear: tourism is an important part of San Diego's economic fabric.

Figure 4.8

Other types of programs have been developed by various convention and visitor bureaus with the intent of raising awareness of the importance of tourism activities. While the industry is valued for its tradition of employing unskilled labor, that labor force is also known for its high turnover. The necessity, therefore, of implementing such hospitality training programs in our service-oriented society is an integral part of a convention and visitor bureau's leadership role in the community.

Summary

The complexities of tourism markets pose an exciting challenge to convention and visitor bureaus; the evolution of destinations which offer family attractions, resort facilities or special events provides a rich diversity of marketing opportunities. Because tourism has often been seen as a glamorous enterprise, there has been a general misunderstanding as to its significance and economic value. The influx of visitors, however, to a community has produced an awareness as to the importance and value of tourism. Although some destinations cater more to recognizable groups, such as conventions, it does not mean that visitors to a community may not have an equal importance. The character of destinations varies and what attracts visitors to one may not draw them to another. Tourism programming within a bureau therefore becomes an important bridge between diverse market segments and community resources. The effective marketing of tourism resources and facilities is not unlike any other marketing effort that requires thoughtful analysis, careful planning, astute execution and competent measurement. As reflected in this chapter, the tourism efforts of a convention and visitor bureau have matured and warrant careful considerations as they are integrated into the total destination marketing scheme.

Discussion Questions

1. Why is there a negative stereotype to such words as "travel," "tourism," and "leisure"? How can those perceptions be changed?

2. Define several marketing goals for a tourism sales and marketing department.

3. Should goals be general or explicit? Discuss the merits of each position.

4. Define the steps in developing a marketing plan. Which of the seven suggested steps is pivotal to an effective plan?

5. Define and discuss market segmentation based on demographics and psychographics. Why is psychographics considered a more viable way of segmenting a market?

6. What is meant by "the development of a marketing plan is an attitude"?

7. What are some effective marketing strategies for reaching vacationing families?

8. Why are travel advertisements placed in the spring for summer travel? Discuss related research and how it applies to tourism marketing.

9. What is an "Inquiry Conversion Study"? What does it demonstrate?

10. What is incentive travel? Why is it an important market segment for a convention and visitors bureau to consider?

11. What are group tours? How important are these in a market mix?

12. Discuss the most effective marketing strategies for reaching the group travel market.

13. What criteria might be used to assess the potential value of attending a trade show?

14. What value is there in making personal sales calls?

15. What kinds of "services" may be sought by tourism sales clients? How should a bureau respond?

16. What should be included in a client's sales file?

17. Why is hospitality training important to a community?

Bibliographic Resources

1. Bowden, Bill, "In Search of Respect for Tourism," *Courier,* August 1987, pp. 45–54.

2. Plog, Stanley C., "Understanding Psychographics in Tourism Research," in Ritchie, J. R. Brent and Charles R. Goeldner (eds), *Travel, Tourism and Hospitality Research* (New York: John Wiley and Sons, 1987), pp. 203–213.

3. Mitchell, Arnold, *The Nine American Lifestyles* (New York: Macmillan Publishing Co., 1983).

4. Shih, David, "VALS As a Tool of Tourism Market Research: The Pennsylvania Experience," *Pennsylvania Travel Review,* Vol. 6, No. 1, January 1985.

5. Gartrell, Richard B., "Survey of Marketing Strategies Employed by Tour Operators and Public Sector Members of the National Tour Association," Unpublished Seminar Paper, October 1984.

6. Gartrell, Richard B., "Developing A Marketing Plan," *Partners in Profit* 2nd edition (Lexington: NTA, 1987) pp. 10–13.

7. McIntosh, Robert W., and Charles R. Goeldner, *Tourism: Principles, Practices, Philosophies* (New York: John Wiley and Sons, 1986); Philip G. Davidoff and Doris S. Davidoff, *Sales and Marketing for Travel and Tourism* (South Dakota: National Publishers of the Black Hills, Inc., 1983); Edward Mayo and Lance P. Jarvis, *The Psychology of Leisure Travel* (Massachusetts: CBI Publishing Company, 1981); Adele Hodgson (ed), *The Travel and Tourism Industry: Strategies for the Future* (Oxford: Pergamon Press, 1987); Donald Lundberg, *International Travel and Tourism* (New York: John Wiley and Sons, 1985); Philip L. Pearce, *The Social Psychology of Tourist Behavior* (Oxford: Pergamon Press, 1982); and Robert Christie Mill and Alastair M. Morrison, *The Tourism System* (New Jersey: Prentice-Hall, Inc., 1985).

8. van Raaij, W. Fred and Dick A. Francken, "Vacation Decisions. Activities and Satisfaction," *Annals of Tourism Research,* Vol. 11, pp. 101–112, 1984.

9. Jenkins, R. L. "Family Vacation Decision-Making," *Journal of Travel Research,* 16(4), pp. 2–7, 1978.

10. Ronkainen, Ilkka A. and Arch G. Woodside, "Advertising Conversion Studies" in J. R. Brent Ritchie and Charles R. Goeldner (eds), *Travel, Tourism and Hospitality Research* (New York: John Wiley and Sons, 1987), pp. 481–488.

11. Stack, Brian, "Understanding the Role of Incentive Travel," *Corporate and Incentive Travel,* May 1986, pp. 30–33; Susan Edwards, "Marketing Incentive Travel: Make It Part of Your Marketing Plan," *Travelling on Business,* October 1985, pp. 7–8; Robert Lewis, "The Incentive-Travel Market," *Cornell H. R. A. Quarterly,* May 1983, pp. 19–27; Alderson, J. W., "The New World of Incentive Travel," *Meetings and Conventions,* August 1987, pp. 59–74.

12. "Incentive Travel Study," Conducted by *Corporate Meetings and Incentives,* November 1986.

13. Davidson, Pattie, "A Prototype Marketing Strategy for the Group Market," Unpublished Paper, 1986.

14. National Tour Association, *Partners in Profit: An Introduction to Group Travel Marketing* (Lexington, Kentucky: National Tour Association, 1987).

15. Bowden, Bill, "Tracking Tours: The NTA Report," *Courier,* November 1986, pp. 47–49.

16. "National Tour Association Hospitality Service Training Model," November 1987; See also: Knight, John B. and Charles A. Salter, "Some Considerations for Hospitality Training Programs," *Cornell Quarterly,* February 1985, pp. 38–43.

CONVENTION SALES AND MARKETING

5

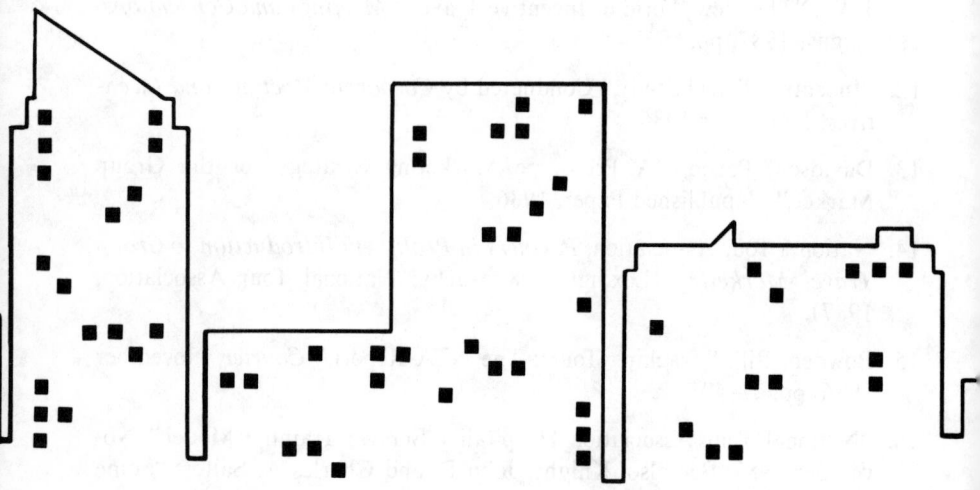

LEARNING OBJECTIVES

Upon reading this chapter, you will learn the following:

- About the roles and responsibilities of a Convention Sales Department;
- About the development of a marketing plan for convention sales;
- About evaluating the impact of convention sales on a community;
- About the strategies which compose a marketing mix;
- About the significance of sales leads and bid presentations;
- About the characteristics and importance of the international market;
- About the significance of the INET system for exchange of convention information.

Introduction

The selling of meetings, conventions and trade shows has been the foundation of convention bureau operations since their founding days. The primary objective of these sales and marketing efforts has been to enhance and increase the economic vitality of a city. Groups can be identified, meeting rotation patterns defined, space requirements known, and structured sales programs developed to influence decision makers that one city should be considered over another. Though the marketplace is composed of a kaleidoscope of associations and organizations (for example, social, fraternal, educational, medical, professional and scientific associations), understanding their meeting, convention and trade show requirements remains a relatively consistent effort for convention sales personnel. It has therefore been fairly easy to track their economic impact through the number of convention bookings, delegates attending, delegate expenditures, room nights, length of stay and total exhibition space. Assessment of convention sales efforts has become fairly sophisticated as a result of these criteria. Through their systems of sales leads and convention bookings, convention sales departments satisfy local expectations by providing their membership with client information that will produce room nights. Bureaus may have different methods and procedures for reporting and determining productivity; but whatever the process, the reporting is useful and necessary to reflect the quality of their sales efforts.

Bureau efforts are accomplished by skilled and knowledgable professionals who spend years becoming familiar with and developing rapport among association executives, meeting planners and exhibition managers. Bureaus have become the stabilizing influence in an industry that has a reputation for high turnover. This continuity of sales and marketing personnel provides a positive image for a city. In the competitive marketplace, bureaus have to be prepared to offer the highest level of sales and service to every client. Sales personnel must be sensitive to the needs of clients and flexible enough to respond reliably to those needs. They must demonstrate that the attention and service they provide will be present throughout a client's relationship with the bureau. Because services may vary among bureaus, it is important that a meeting planner understand the scope of services available through a bureau in order to develop a feeling of confidence in that bureau. Reciprocally, when working with clients, bureau sales personnel are establishing rapport, trust and an important relationship that can generate many productive benefits over the years.

Convention sales departments have many responsibilities. Among their sales and servicing activities are the development of opportunities for their members to participate with the bureau in various marketing endeavors. This may include cooperative advertising efforts, joint sales trips, familiarization tours or attending trade shows. These programs ensure that those who have the biggest investment in the hospitality program for that destination are encouraged to participate, thereby presenting a stronger and more unified marketing presence.

Convention sales departments are usually organized as described in Chapter Three. Sales managers and service personnel execute the annual marketing programs. Of course, the size of a convention sales department also will vary depending on the size of the bureau. Some bureaus have sales representatives in key cities to enhance their position among associations and trade organizations. This insures a constant presence for that bureau in those specific markets.

This chapter will explore these and other marketing activities and how they are accomplished through a convention sales department.

Goals for a Convention Sales and Marketing Department

Regardless of the size of the convention and visitor bureau, there are stipulated goals for convention sales. These goals can be simple or complex statements that influence the allocation of bureau resources toward their attainment. The following are some examples of goal statements for convention sales made by bureaus over the past few years.

Kansas City

- *To heighten Kansas City's name and image in the convention and meetings field;*
- *To promote Kansas City as a convention and meeting destination through special promotions to specific target audiences;*
- *To generate more meetings and convention business for Kansas City through personal sales contacts;*
- *To offer a comprehensive service package that will further enhance our ability to market Kansas City as a convention destination.*

Following each of these objectives, the marketing plan outlined specific goals that would attain these general goals. For example, more than 50 sales trips were planned and placement of advertisements were outlined for trade publications that would reach over 650,000 readers. Other bureaus have stated their convention sales goals as follows:

San Jose

- *Pursue convention bookings with an emphasis on weekends, state associations, corporations and educational seminars;*

- *Pursue trade shows that utilize our existing Exhibit Hall and Convention Center as well as surrounding hotel rooms;*
- *Increase qualified leads to all hotels and convention center;*
- *Improve our image locally and nationally through advertising and public relations;*
- *Promote San Jose as a national destination for meetings.*

San Francisco

The overall goal of the convention and meeting market segment is to contribute an increasing share of overnight visitor traffic to San Francisco.

The five-year objectives of the convention and meeting segment are:

- *increase the convention/meeting related percentage share of all overnight visitor by 2.8% from 15.5% to 18.3% by year five of the plan;*
- *this will represent a total of 501,000 convention/meeting overnight visitors in year five, or 18.3% of all overnight visitors;*
- *the total value of these visitors will be $209,418,000 in year five of this plan.*

Reno-Sparks

In the fiscal year, the booking goal is to initiate or assist in booking 400,000 room nights in future meeting business with an estimated economic impact of $165 million. This is based on the 1985 (IACVB) Convention Income Survey, with expenditures of $660.57 per delegate per meeting, exclusive of gaming.

From the general objective of the Kansas City program to the specific goals of the San Francisco and Reno-Sparks programs, the primary objective remains the same for all convention sales departments, to generate revenues through the booking of group business into the community represented by that bureau. Goal statements will vary considerably from bureau to bureau and from year to year, reflecting changes in the market, destination needs and program maturity. Convention sales departments have many audiences that need to be served, whether hotels, resorts, convention centers or other meeting facilities. An integral part of a department's effectiveness is the blending of these diverse destination needs and expectations into a comprehensive program that will bring about their fulfillment. The development of a marketing plan that outlines market competition, trends, goals, strategies and allocation of resources blends these resources into a coordinated program that will attain the goals and objectives outlined for a given fiscal year.

Convention Sales and the Marketing Plan

A marketing plan structures the sales and marketing approach that will be undertaken by a convention and visitor bureau. In Chapter Four, the development of a marketing plan is discussed. Those same principles apply equally to the convention sales efforts. Before marketing strategies can be implemented, it is necessary to assess and identify target markets, establish goals, allocate bureau resources, and identify and implement the most productive marketing mix that will yield the greatest return on the investment made by the bureau.

First, a bureau needs to assess its present situation. This includes an examination of the travel product, the bureau's resources, the competition and market trends. This situational analysis is fundamental in better understanding how to position or market one's travel product. Such an analysis might include the following considerations:

Product Considerations

1. What types of meeting, convention and trade show facilities does your destination have?
2. What are their capabilities in handling small groups? Large groups? Exhibitions?
3. What are the limitations of your meeting, convention and trade show facilities?
4. How many hotel rooms are within a block of your major convention center? Within five blocks of the center?
5. Is the convention center designed to be a profit center in and of itself or has it been designed to provide leverage in the marketplace in order to get groups booked into your city?
6. How accessible are convention facilities from the airport? By car?

Promotional Considerations

1. What is the image of your city in the marketplace? What is the image of your city among meeting planners?
2. What advertising media have been used in the past? How effective have these media been in generating interest in your city?
3. How does your bureau's advertising budget compare to that of the competition?
4. What sales materials are provided for the sales staff? What is the quality of these materials? How do they compare to the competition?

5. Does the bureau have a budget allocation adequate to sustain an image campaign?

6. How are the bureau's sales personnel allocated? Can they adequately cover the identified markets? Are their sales efforts the most cost-efficient in light of the targeted markets?

Market Considerations

1. What are the bureau's primary markets? How have these markets been defined (geographic, demographic, psychographic)?

2. What is the potential for demand in these markets?

3. Are the targeted markets users of all the potential facilities in your city, or are they potential users of only the convention center?

4. What are the criteria upon which these markets make their selection of future meeting, convention and trade show locations?

5. How does the competition address these markets? Are their programs any more successful than yours?

6. What market trends might impact future bureau programs? In what manner might the bureau anticipate and address these potential trends?

In its 1985 marketing plan, the Greater Palm Springs Convention and Visitors Bureau (California) made the following statement about the erosion of the market due to increased competition in their area:

> In 1984, Palm Springs generated 62 percent of the Valley-wide occupancy tax revenues and had 55% of the rooms in the Coachella Valley. In 1983, the comparisons were 65% of the Valley-wide transient occupancy tax revenues and 63% of the rooms. . . . The entry of new, large nationally-affiliated quality hotels, not within the City, will, until the construction of the Convention Center and of renovation of existing hotels and construction of new hotels within the City of Palm Springs, accelerate further erosion of the Palm Springs share of market and extend revenues disadvantages (into future years).

This analysis led Palm Springs to build a convention center and to propose a merger with others in their area in order to develop a mutually beneficial competitive marketing posture that offers diverse meeting, convention and trade show facilities to meeting planners.

The second step in developing a convention sales program is to identify goals and objectives. As previously indicated, goals can be general in nature or complex; they can be short or long statements. Goals usually are followed by very specific marketing behaviors that will be undertaken in order to attain what each goal states. For example, the Ann Arbor Convention and Visitors Bureau (Michigan) made the following goal statement supported by a specific objective and strategy:

Goal

To increase the awareness and selection of Ann Arbor as a viable small meetings destination for association, corporate and other group meetings.

Objective

To market Ann Arbor as a meetings destination, thereby generating at least 60 sales leads for prospective small group meetings to area hotels.

Strategy

Each convention sales manager will generate at least five qualified sales leads each month on groups that can meet within any one of the city's convention hotels.

Additional strategies would then be developed to support that goal and objective. These strategies become part of the total marketing mix developed by a bureau to help attain its objectives for the fiscal year.

In convention sales, many of the objectives established by a bureau focus on the need to fill hotel rooms. Along these lines, some other criteria upon which goals could be established might include the following:

- number of meetings, conventions and trade shows booked;
- meeting, convention and trade show types (state, regional, national, international);
- total number of delegates attending;
- total number of rooms used;
- total number of room nights;
- total number of bids made by bureau staff;
- total number of leads generated through advertising, direct mail, telemarketing or other marketing strategies;
- total number of familiarization tours and tour attendees;
- total number of client accounts opened by bureau sales personnel.

The third marketing consideration is identifying target markets. In part, those markets will be partially dependent on the nature of the destination's product, whether it is a small meetings market only, whether it has a convention center or is a combination of large and small facilities. The resources of a destination also will have an impact on the type of groups that are sought. A university community might be seeking those meetings which are professional, educational and scientific in nature, whereas a destination that has a major convention center might target groups that can comfortably fit into those facilities regardless of the type of group. This identification of markets is usually referred to as market segmentation; the assumption is that the market cannot be addressed as a whole and must therefore be divided into smaller units, each unit reflecting some type of homogeneity. With these classifications, groups can be targeted by the bureau utilizing an appropriate marketing mix. For example, bureaus may "package" their resources in various ways, selling whichever is appropriate to convention markets that demonstrate a preference for resort locations, downtown facilities, convention centers or airport locations. This differentiated marketing technique reflects the sensitivity and sophistication of bureaus to the diverse characteristics of market segments.

The fourth step is the selection of marketing strategies. Developing a marketing mix that will achieve a bureau's goals is not as simple as it might initially seem. Market segments may respond to one strategy or technique and not another. Finding the one that is most effective and cost efficient is important if a bureau is to attain established goals. In convention sales, some of the strategies that are used include the following:

- direct sales
- sales blitzes
- local organizations and contacts
- trade shows
- advertising
- familiarization tours/site inspections
- destination publications/brochures
- direct mail
- telemarketing
- bid presentations
- other marketing and promotional strategies

These strategies will be discussed in more detail later in this chapter. But it must be remembered that when exploring which strategies might be the most preferred, several questions arise which need to be considered in making a judgment.

1. In assessing the target market, what types of marketing techniques seem to be most effective in gaining their attention and interest?
2. Does the market segment respond to one type of marketing technique over another at different times of the year?
3. What is the most effective way of positioning the city compared to how the competition approaches it?
4. What are the strengths and weaknesses of each of the marketing strategies?

The fifth step in designing a marketing plan is the allocation of resources in order to accomplish established goals and objectives. This refers to both personnel and financial support. Convention sales departments many times tend to be the larger department within a bureau's structure because of their potential for bringing groups to a city and generating overnight stays. The issue then is to ensure that these dynamic sales endeavors are supported relative to their overall importance to the bureau's total program and their economic impact on the community. If, on the other hand, convention sales is not as important as tourism sales to a destination, that bureau must allocate its resources accordingly to reflect the character and strength of the destination. Concerns have arisen regarding the dependency of many smaller bureaus on the room tax revenues and the need to insure that such dependency is seen as an investment, in turn assuring a continuity of programs for an economic vitality that would not otherwise be present.

Sixth, the marketing plan needs to be implemented. This is the process that turns marketing plans into action assignments and ensures that such assignments are executed in a manner that accomplishes the plan's stated goals and objectives. The action calendar is one effective tool in coordinating a bureau's programs. The calendar should include dates and times of major trade show activities, the start and finish dates for major promotional programs including advertising campaigns, dates for familiarization tours, dates for completing new publications and brochures, scheduling of sales trips and any other related marketing activities. The action calendar also ensures that proper staff have been assigned to the various projects, distributing responsibilities as well as effectively utilizing talents and interests. The involvement of the staff in the development of the marketing plan, along with other members of the hospitality industry, is important and will influence their enthusiasm and commitment to the programs and the attainment of goals for that year.

The final area of a marketing plan is that of assessing the effectiveness of programs. A bureau must tenaciously monitor its marketing plan to ensure that it is accomplishing what it was intended to do. Monthly or quarterly goals should be established to serve as benchmarks for assessing the plan's effectiveness. Based on an evaluation of those benchmarks, required adjustments must be carried out in order to redirect marketing efforts toward more acceptable levels of performance. Though bureaus have different ways of tracking their marketing and sales efforts, there are several common measurement factors used in assessing the level of a program's performance. These include the following:

Convention/Trade Show Information

- total room nights for soft periods
- room nights booked monthly

- room nights booked year-to-date
- business booked from international, national, regional or state clients
- business booked for expositions
- business booked for special events
- business booked by each bureau sales staff
- business booked by hotel sales staff
- business booked by cooperating agencies
- number of delegates attending
- number of delegates attending according to international, national, regional, state, exposition or special event categories
- total number of conventions booked
- total number of conventions booked based on category: international, national, regional, state
- conventions booked via various marketing techniques (e.g. from trade shows, sales calls, direct mail, advertising, etc.)
- conventions booked with the assistance of local membership participation
- number of trade shows/expositions booked
- number of special events booked

Convention/Trade Show Information After Hosting the Event

- total number of convention/trade show delegates
- total number of convention/trade show room nights
- delegate expenditures
- local tax revenues generated by groups

Convention/Trade Show Servicing Requirements

- housing figures
- convention registration figures
- group transportation figures
- material distribution figures
- sponsorship figures
- housing bureau room nights for each hotel
- economic impact of conventions on the community

Of course, there may be other criteria or techniques used by a bureau to assess its program effectiveness. Such monitoring and evaluative techniques must have a reliable relationship with each element of the marketing program in order to adequately reflect the performance level of the marketing plan.

Marketing Strategies for Convention Sales

Marketing strategies will vary considerably among bureaus. As bureaus identify their target markets and assess their own travel product, strategies will be selected that best fit into their scheme and budget capabilities. However, among most convention and visitor bureaus, the following marketing strategies are those selected for the convention sales mix.

Direct Sales

The backbone of any effective convention bureau operation is that of direct sales. Prospecting and qualifying potential clients are essential to developing sales accounts that will generate meetings, conventions and trade shows. The value of direct sales is readily apparent; it provides immediate feedback regarding client needs. It is personal and transactional, allowing each individual to observe and respond accordingly within the context of the meeting. Direct sales allow for the establishment of rapport between the bureau representative and the meeting planner. This relationship is important for developing trust and confidence. And though the cost per call may be more expensive than the per-unit cost of other marketing techniques, the value of the personal investment of time by a bureau's representative will generate long-term returns through repeat business and credibility in the marketplace.

The direct sales process involves several steps. First, there is the identification of prospects. Prospecting can take one of two directions. There is the location of prospects through such marketing techniques as direct mail and advertising. These techniques seek a response on the part of a planner and reflect to the bureau a degree of interest in its city. This may be called the "incoming" phase of prospecting. The other option available is that of literally calling, either in person or by telephone or through trade shows, potential prospects in order to determine their level of interest in the city. This could be called the "outgoing" phase of prospecting. Bureaus use a combination of these techniques to identify prospects. Because there are hundreds of thousands of associations and corporations which hold a variety of meetings, conventions and trade shows, the bureau's sales professionals assess potential clients on the basis of the planner's needs as well as the capabilities of the city which the bureau represents. In other words, bureaus which do not have large convention centers do not solicit convention and exhibits which cannot meet within their facilities. Careful analysis, therefore, of the group's requirements is essential to developing a viable pool of client prospects (see figure 5.1).

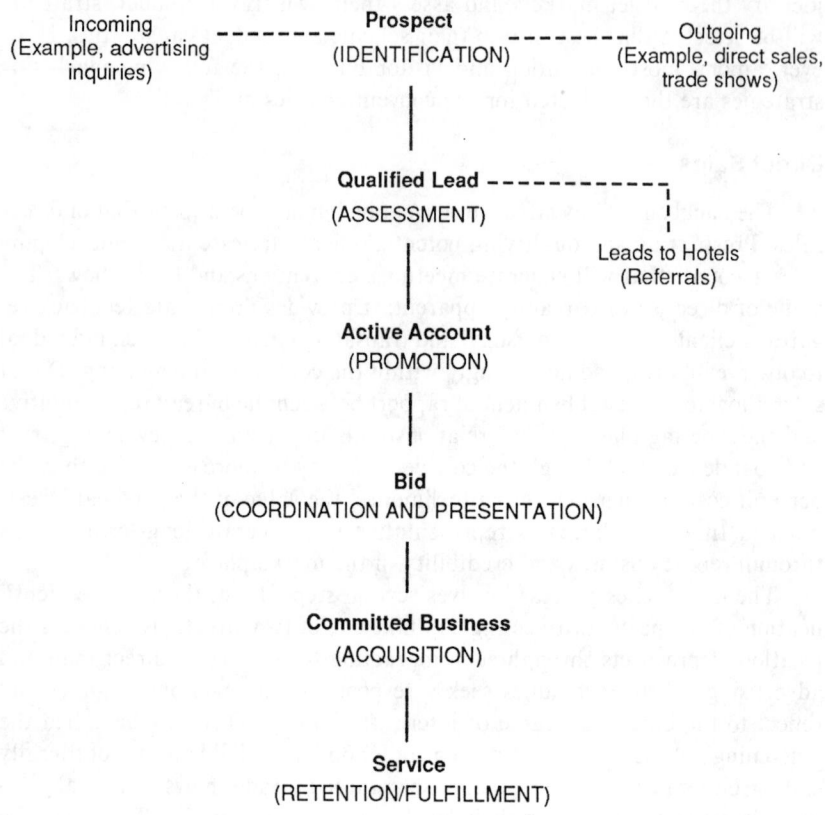

**BASIC STEPS
CONVENTION SALES**

Incoming
(Example, advertising
inquiries) – – – – – – – – **Prospect**
(IDENTIFICATION) – – – – – – – – Outgoing
(Example, direct sales,
trade shows)

Qualified Lead – – – – – – – – – – – –
(ASSESSMENT)

Leads to Hotels
(Referrals)

Active Account
(PROMOTION)

Bid
(COORDINATION AND PRESENTATION)

Committed Business
(ACQUISITION)

Service
(RETENTION/FULFILLMENT)

Source: © Richard B. Gartrell

Figure 5.1

There are at least six essential questions when prospecting; the responses to these questions can simplify the prospecting by quickly clarifying the interest level of prospective clients as well as their needs and requirements.

1. What is the schedule of future meeting sites?
2. What is the first uncommitted year for the meeting, convention or trade show?
3. Who will select the site?
4. When will the site selection be made?

PROCESS VARIABLES

Intrinsic Variables	Functional Variables	Negotiable Variables
• Decision Criteria • Decision Maker(s) • Local Support/Host • Personal Whim(s)	• Exhibit Space • Banquet Space • Breakout Rooms • Reception(s) • Plenary Session(s) • Sleeping Rooms • Open Dates of Convention Facilities	• Food Costs • Room Comp Policy • Reception (Sponsors) • Room Rates • Special Perks/Amenities • V.I.P. Treatment • Alternate Programming • Transportation/Shuttles • Availability of Dates • Proximity of Facilities • Weather

Source: © Richard B. Gartrell

Figure 5.2

5. What is the proper procedure for inviting consideration (for a city)?
6. What organizational member in (city) is the best local contact?

The responses to these questions will give a bureau representative sufficient information upon which to open a client account.

For the trade show market, the issue of date availability may be a more important criteria upon which to segment a market. If the objective for a convention center is to fill it with as much business as possible, particularly if it generates significant out-of-town visitors, then the development of a marketing strategy that will realize this objective is fundamental. Knowing which dates are open in the convention center and then identifying trade shows which might meet during such dates is a preferred strategy when targeting the larger trade shows.

There is considerably more information that must be obtained by a bureau among which is the following (see figure 5.2):

The *intrinsic variables* are issues that relate to the essence of the organization and can be influenced but not changed. Bureau sales personnel have to probe and understand who and what these criteria are and how they are influenced. The *functional variables* deal with meeting requirements; these are usually basic and necessary for the organization to achieve a successful meeting, convention or trade show. The *negotiable variables* are just that, items that can be mutually discussed between the meeting planner and the bureau or host facilities. Once these variables are determined, they are clearly stated on a sales lead document that is distributed to convention center and convention hotel facilities.

The resources that a sales representative can utilize in sifting through and identifying viable prospects are abundant. For example, the following are a few of the many directories that can be consulted for primary information on associations and their meeting requirements:

- *Encyclopedia of Associations* . . . lists more than 17,000 national trade associations and professional organizations;
- *Year Book of International Meetings* . . . lists 12,000 associations and is published by the Union des Associations Internationales based in Brussels, Belgium;
- The *Trade Show Bureau* . . . lists more than 8,000 shows conducted throughout the United States.

Also available are directories for national (example, ASAE's *Who's Who in Association Management*) and international (example, ICCA Membership Directory) associations as well as state associations (example, Texas Society of Association Executives) which provide basic information on professional and trade associations. The International Association of Convention & Visitor Bureaus (IACVB) has information on some 15,500 meetings stored in its INET computerized data bank which represents information that is shared among bureaus about meetings, conventions and trade shows, both domestic and international. Information about other international meetings might be obtained through state and federal tourism authorities, consulates, international airlines and hotels. There are commercial sources as well, for example, *Successful Meetings* databank of meetings.

The sales lead is the one major marketing tool convention bureaus use to promote bureau services to meeting planners. When properly used, the lead gains the most credibility with the hotel community and provides meeting planners with the most specific and concise information on any particular property. By utilizing the services of the bureau and allowing the bureau to solicit information and bids, the meeting planner is able to save an enormous amount of time.

Many bureaus design their sales lead forms to represent sizes of conventions or types of groups. Some will use color-bordered paper while others use colored paper. All sales leads contain fundamentally the same basic information. Once this information is compiled and entered onto a sales lead form, it is then distributed to the appropriate convention facilities. Ideally, the meeting planner will request in writing the names of properties or the type of properties to be included; if that is not the case, the bureau sales representative must converse with that planner to determine what he/she is looking for in order to qualify his/her needs on the sales lead form. In preparing the sales lead, the bureau is careful to include the following information (see figure 5.3):

- date—when the lead was mailed
- to—indicates the convention properties
- from—indicates the bureau sales person
- organization—name of the association, trade show, corporate meeting with whom the bureau is dealing
- contact—name of the meeting planner (include title)
- address/phone—the proper mailing address and telephone number; if the planner doesn't want telephone calls, simply indicate "no telephone calls please"
- meeting dates—specific dates as supplied by the planner (example, March 3–5, 1990)
- attendance—total number of people expected for the meeting, including spouses and visitors (example, 300 delegates/200 spouses/100 visitors)
- sleeping rooms—number of hotel guest rooms that will be needed for a particular evening (example, June 21–50 rooms; June 22–90 rooms). A hotel can better accommodate a group if it knows its room requirements.
- meeting room requirements—this requires very precise information as to general or plenary sessions, breakout rooms and their setting (example, 1 general session, theatre style)
- food functions—this too must be very complete and detailed, including the number of food functions and attendance for these functions
- exhibits—square footage, type of exhibits, move in and move out dates and hours, and length of trade show.

The lead form allows for the inclusion of other detailed information on rates, history and action requested. The more information provided on the sales lead, the better the responses from convention facilities. The sales lead confirms the conversation between the bureau sales person and the meeting planner. It further shows the convention facilities that the information provided by the bureau is in accordance with the wishes of the meeting planner.

Once a lead has been "qualified" and sent to the convention facilities and hotels in the community, it is imperative that follow-up begin. Based upon the decision date, the bureau needs to contact the planner to learn of the decision. Whether the city has been selected or lost to another location, a memorandum must be sent to the properties indicating the meeting planner's choice and any supportive reasons.

On the other hand, a lead may become a formal bureau client which is placed into the bureau's sales account files. Once an account file is opened for a client, it is systematically traced for review. These trace dates represent times

LEAD DEVELOPMENT

Greater Lexington Convention &
Visitors Bureau
430 W. Vine Street
Suite 363
Lexington, KY.   40507
(606)-233-1221

DATE: June 10, 1986

TO: All Properties

FROM: Jane A. Mullally

ORGANIZATION: Kentucky Medical Society - Annual Convention

CONTACT: Joe Customer   TITLE: Executive Director

ADDRESS: 123 Medical Way

               Nonesuch, Kentucky 40555

PHONE: No Phone Calls

MEETING DATES: January 5-8, 1988

ATTENDANCE: 750 delegates, 100 spouses

SLEEPING
ROOMS:

1/4 Sun	1/5 Mon	1/6 Tues	1/7 Wed	1/8 Thurs	1/9 Fri
		DATES			
100	400	500	500	200	-0-
		ROOMS			

MEETING ROOM
REQUIREMENTS: Mon-Wed (8:00 a.m.-noon) General Session, theater style,

                 700 people.

                 Mon-Wed (2:00 p.m.-5:00 p.m.) 5 breakout rooms, classroom

                 style, 500 people each.

FOOD FUNCTIONS: Mon evening reception, 800 people.

                 Tues evening banquet (dinner dance/800 people)

EXHIBITS: 100 - 10x10's (10,000 net sq. feet) - move-in 1/4; show

                 1/5-1/7; move-out 1/8.

PAST HISTORY/
FUTURE SITES: 1984-Louisville/Galt House $45 single/$55 double; 1985-
                 Bowling Green/Executive Inn $40 single/$50 double; 1986-
RATE HISTORY: Paducah/Holiday Inn $50 single/$60 double; 1987-Owensboro/
                 Ramada Inn $48 single/$56 double; 1988 open.

OTHER CITIES
UNDER CONSIDERATION: Louisville

DECISION DATE: July 28, 1986

ACTION REQUESTED: Please send your proposal directly to Mr. Customer and

                 copy the Convention Bureau.

LOCAL CONTACT: Mr. Joe Smith, 480 Limestone, Lexington, Kentucky 40567,

                 231-8696

Figure 5.3

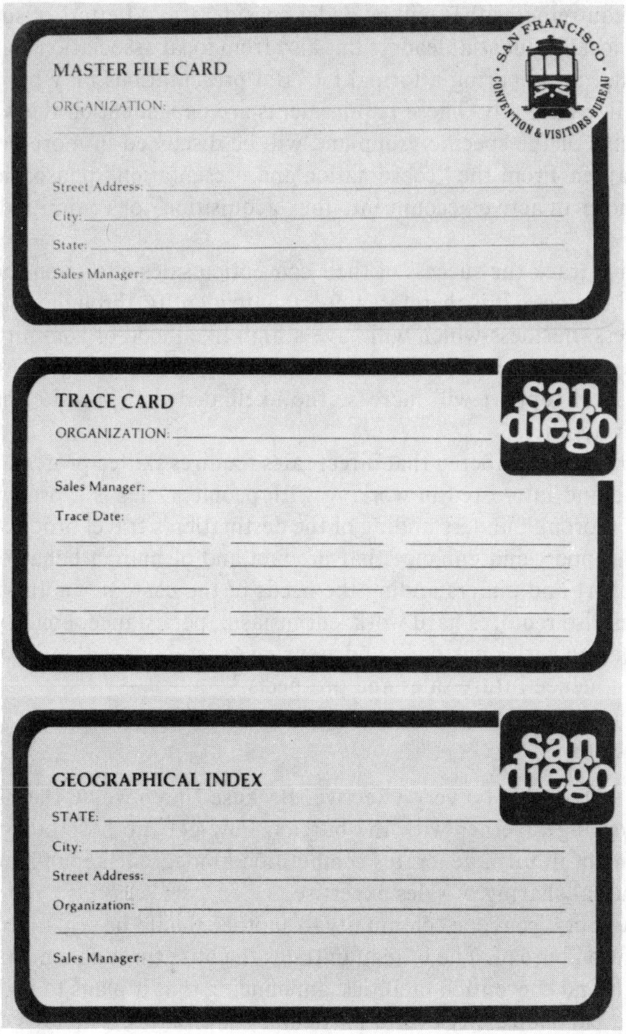

MASTER FILE CARD

SAN FRANCISCO CONVENTION & VISITORS BUREAU

ORGANIZATION: ____________________

Street Address: ____________________

City: ____________________

State: ____________________

Sales Manager: ____________________

TRACE CARD

san diego

ORGANIZATION: ____________________

Sales Manager: ____________________

Trace Date:

GEOGRAPHICAL INDEX

san diego

STATE: ____________________

City: ____________________

Street Address: ____________________

Organization: ____________________

Sales Manager: ____________________

Figure 5.4

which the bureau wishes to make additional contact with its clients to reassure them of their interest as well as to verify data about the associations' meeting needs. This process will occur throughout the time between prospecting and making a formal bid for that association's meeting, convention or trade show.

When the time is appropriate, a bureau will notify its local resources that a bid is being formalized for presentation to a specific organization. The solicitation of information by a bureau from its local resources is critical to the presentation of a total package that will entice that association to select that city. A full cooperative spirit is essential in being able to respond to the many complex requirements that will be under consideration. Letters of support not only from local influential leaders but also from local association contacts are fundamental in preparing a formal bid. Bid presentations may be in writing and/or delivered orally. These requirements are dependent on the wishes and requirements of the specific group and will be discussed in more detail later in this chapter. From the "coordination and presentation" phase, the bureau seeks to move an active account into the "acquisition" or committed business phase.

Bureaus track the success of their convention sales efforts on the basis of committed business. It is therefore important to identify, throughout this entire sales process, business which will have a high likelihood of committing itself to that city. The careful qualification of meeting requirements coupled with attaining local support will increase the likelihood that one site may be selected over another.

It must be remembered that direct sales requires skilled professionals who are excited and interested in working with people. Sales is a profession that requires a thorough understanding of the destination's travel product, the services that support and enhance that product and of human behavior.[1] Developing rapport and understanding the needs of the customer is fundamental; direct sales also requires hard work, enthusiasm, persistance, honesty and sincerity. Working with a customer and assuring satisfaction will build a clientele that will influence future sales and prospects.[2]

Sales Blitzes

Sales blitzes can be very effective. Because they involve the hotel community working together with the bureau, they get the hospitality industry excited which, in turn, generates competition among participants and allows for the mutual sharing of sales expertise.

A sales blitz from one community to another should be organized through the convention bureau. The bureau initiates the blitz through a memorandum to all hotels and convention facilities, announcing that it plans to make a sales blitz into a particular city over a particular set of dates. The type of calls to be made also should be shared in that first announcement (example, associations or corporations). The bureau will then determine who is interested in participating. Specific arrangements will be confirmed by the bureau as to transportation options, lodging and other specific arrangements (example, receptions). Costs should be individually handled by each hotel sales representative. Targeted leads for the blitz should be generated by the bureau. These leads can be distributed to blitz participants, allowing them sufficient time to schedule individual appointments. Participants should be allowed to make additional calls of their own. A minimum number of calls per day should be specified for each blitz participant. Information from the blitz should be gathered immediately by the bureau, transcribed and issued to all participants.

This allows for timely follow-up on each of the contacts. Such a sales effort allows for the gathering of a tremendous amount of information and the generation of sales leads for the hotel community. Such an effort, for example, was conducted by the Charlotte Convention and Visitors Bureau (North Carolina), targeting Atlanta. Representatives from the bureau and the hospitality and business community flew/drove into Atlanta, and over several days, made sales contacts.

Use of Local Organizations and Contacts

Many communities throughout the world are "major destinations" that are a draw in and of themselves and need no particular selling point other than their major tourist attractions. Such destinations might include London, Paris, New York City, San Francisco or Hawaii. But most cities need that something special to entice a meeting or convention to their communities. Probably the most important resource a city can use is a local member or a local chapter of a national or international association. Associations are made up of members, and members become the most important part of any association activity. Working with a local member of a local organization or a larger group could be the ideal approach to attract a meeting to a particular destination. Meeting planners listen to their members and their advice. Very seldom does an organization book a convention into a community without the local member's knowledge and support. Bureaus increase their effectiveness by taking the time to identify local resources who have relationships with larger national and international associations and organizations. The Raleigh Convention and visitors Bureau (North Carolina) has used this technique quite successfully as have many other bureaus.

Trade Shows

Trade show marketing is not a topic generic to all cities. In fact, there are two ways of exploring trade show marketing. First, there are those cities which have the facilities and wish to draw groups to their destination. Second, there are those cities which attend trade shows as a marketing technique. But first let us address those cities that have facilities and wish to attract business.

Cities with trade show facilities can readily identify the divergent needs associated with this segment of the market mix. In more cases than not, it is the most competitive because it yields the greatest return on the investment made by a bureau. As reflected in the 1985 Convention Income Survey sponsored by the International Association of Convention & Visitor Bureaus, the average trade show delegate spends $660.57 for on-site expenditures per show

Figure 5.5

versus $464.16 spent by convention delegates attending a non-trade show re-
lated meeting. Based on these statistics, the average trade show delegate spends
42.3% more money than a non-trade show delegate.[3] This economic impact
also was affirmed in a 1986 extension of that study which reflected a 9.7%
increase in delegate expenditures in U.S. cities (the data were adjusted for a
U.S. city comparison only in 1986).[4] The fact that trade show spending far
exceeds most other categories of group spending has stimulated an unparal-
leled growth in new convention center construction, expansion and renovation.
In fact, between 1970 and 1980 more than 100 convention centers were con-
structed adding over 30 million square feet of exhibition space into the market.
This trend has continued to accelerate, evidenced by the fact that over seven
million square feet of new or expanded exhibit space were added to the marketplace during 1985 alone.[5]

This increase in exhibit space presents a supply and demand challenge
which, if a bureau is to be successful, demands targeted marketing strategies
separate from those of an image building or destination promotion campaign.
While each city may take a different tack in marketing to the trade show
audience, there are some essential preparations which should be taken to yield
productive results.

Product knowledge is fundamental. Convention and visitor bureaus are, in their purest sense, marketing organizations. Bureaus are charged with enhancing the local economy through the expenditures made by convention and trade show delegates. In the context of trade show marketing, then, a bureau defines its product as the convention center or exhibit facilities available within that city. Basic product knowledge applies to the following:

A. Facility Capabilities:
1. Total exhibit hall square footage;
2. Individual capacities of meeting rooms and exhibit halls;
3. Capacities and dimensions of individual exhibit and meeting rooms; soundproofing of rooms;
4. Dimensions of service areas, for example, dock doors, freight elevators, main lobby and other public space;
5. Equipment inventory (chairs, tables, microphones, etc.);
6. Truck staging capabilities and marshalling area;
7. Availability of truck levelers on loading dock;
8. Show office dimensions and amenities;
9. Utilities including gas, water, electricity, compressed air;
10. And available food service.

B. Facility Costs:
1. Rental rate structure/package prices:
    a. Net and gross exhibit space cost;
    b. Package prices for multiple-day usage including both meeting rooms and exhibit space;
2. Costs associated with move-in/move-out days if not included in a package price;
3. Customer cost for any additional days beyond those included in a package price;
4. Limits on complimentary space provided for association use and/ or non-revenue areas (lounges, food service areas, registration areas).

C. Other Associated Costs and Considerations:
1. Meeting room set-up/tear down charges;
2. Cleaning (exhibit aisles, meeting rooms, registration areas, etc.);
3. Costs related to registration area and show office;
4. Utilities;
5. Freight storage;
6. Labor rates: current union charges for drayage, electricians, carpenters, teamsters, fork lift operators, cranes, and quality of the available labor force.

D. Exclusives:
  1. Union restrictions and limitations applying to exhibitor set up, operation and dismantling of display materials;
  2. Exclusives in terms of decorators, food service, concession stands, audio-visual, security, telephone service, and liquor service.
E. Insurance Requirements and Permits
F. Advance Deposits and Contracts

Though many of these criteria are basic and second nature to bureaus, only through a comprehensive understanding of the trade show product can a bureau identify its key benefits in comparison to its competition.

A second way of looking at trade shows is as part of a bureau's marketing mix. Trade shows are an extension of direct sales; they allow for one-on-one contact. Bureau representatives are able to visit with specific individuals who represent their target markets, assess meeting requirements and needs, maintain or develop awareness about their destination and the development of facilities and resources, and simply maintain a rapport and relationship with present and past clients. Leads can be generated as well as sales closed as a result of trade show participation. It is important for the bureau to recognize that it will not be able to reach everyone attending that particular trade show. However, the fact that staff is present and visible becomes an important factor in a destination attaining recognition and credibility among meeting planners. There is no question that trade show participation is costly; but it should be looked upon as an investment and a necessary part of any bureau's marketing mix.

Which trade shows should a bureau attend? That question is frequently asked and is not easily answered. Each bureau must assess which markets it intends to target. Once that is known, it is possible to ask whether a given trade show will have the kind of prospects a bureau wishes to target. If not, then there should be some concern as to the value of that trade show in light of the goals sought by that bureau. There is no shortage of trade shows; in fact, prioritizing is essential. The following is only a partial list of organizations which host trade shows:

- American Society of Association Executives (ASAE)
- Incentive Travel and Meeting Executives (ITME)
- Insurance Conference Planners (ICP)
- CONFEX (Conferences and Exhibitions) London
- Professional Convention Management Association (PCMA)
- National Association of Exhibition Managers (NAEM)

Appendix D lists and describes many major trade organizations. Bureaus have only limited resources and must be very prudent when identifying and selecting trade shows for their marketing mix. Among other concerns should be the geographic distribution of trade shows and their distribution over the calendar year. Both of these factors can enhance a bureau's marketing capabilities by distributing its exposure over both distance and time. Other variables also may include the quality of the show time provided for exhibit exposure, attendance by your competitors, the show purpose and style and the attendance record for that trade show in reference to your targeted audience. The continuity of your attendance is also an important variable in establishing credibility for a destination.

Simple attendance at a trade show does not guarantee success. In fact, a bureau must undertake careful planning in order to gain the maximum benefit from trade show participation. Some of those preparations include the following:

1. Designing a quality booth that will present the destination and its resources in the best possible light.
2. Identifying a target audience for a pre-trade show mailing and inviting them to visit your booth at the trade show.
3. Identifying selected individuals you wish to specifically visit at the trade show.
4. Setting sales goals for the trade show as they apply to prospects, potential leads and confirming of committed business.
5. Preparing and reviewing the kinds of information you wish to share with prospects when they visit your booth (for example, new facilities, new services, affirming their commitment, etc.).
6. Arranging a booth-manning schedule to insure that show times are adequately covered as well as to provide relief for booth personnel.
7. Decisions regarding the type and quantities of materials to be made available through your booth. Some trade shows have restrictions on these items, as well.
8. A decision as to the type of drawing(s) and/or give-aways planned for your booth at that trade show.
9. And planning the follow-up for each trade show contact.

When selling at a trade show, it is also important to respect the client; knowing the clients and their meeting histories is important to relating effectively with them at a trade show. Sales personnel need to be sensitive to a client's time and other obligations, and yet responsive to questions and concerns. Questions should be intelligent and open-ended to encourage dialogue. By knowing, listening and responding to that prospect, you are likely to increase the return on your investment as it applies to a given trade show.[6]

Advertising

Another primary marketing technique used by bureaus is advertising. Through the print media, for example, a bureau can create an atmosphere about a destination, project an image to a large audience, set itself apart from the competition and create a positive reason to visit that destination. But for many bureaus, advertising is not an option due to its potential cost and the limited resources of that bureau. However, for others, it is a must and the only way to project a constant and controlled reminder that the destination has value and is interested in business. One of the most successful campaigns launched during 1986 and 1987 and recognized for its creativity by the International Association of Convention & Visitor Bureaus was that of the Anaheim Convention and Visitors Bureau (California). By placing local personalities in the ads, Anaheim (see figure 5.6) projected an image of intense cooperation; the ads fed the imagination with creative settings and stimulating tag lines. Anaheim has one of the more creative approaches seen in recent years; yet ads can be any size or shape and run many frequency patterns to gain the attention of the audience. Trade publications abound, as well, and include the following:

- *Association Management*
- *Association and Society Manager*
- *Corporate Meetings and Incentive*
- *Insurance Conference Planner*
- *Medical Meetings*
- *Meeting Manager*
- *Meeting News*
- *Meetings and Conventions*
- *Successful Meetings*
- *Trade Show and Exhibit Managers*

In developing an advertising program for the convention and meetings markets, the following questions need to be explored:

- What are your target markets?
- What are the goals of your advertising?
- What publications best address your target markets?
- What kinds of costs may be involved for black/white or four-color ads? Sizes? Frequency of placement?
- Are tracking options such as a bingo response card available? Tip in card?
- What kind of timeline is there for development of your materials?

Figure 5.6. Two series of ads were developed each containing four different settings. Two ads from each of the series are shown here reflecting a creative means for including those individuals whose products support the marketing efforts of the bureau.

- What kind of placement schedule are you planning? Are there additional benefits for having your ads placed in specific issues?
- What kind of creative design are you planning? Does the ad have thematic consistency with the balance of your program? Is the ad meant to create an image or provide information?

The options for print advertising include not only trade publications but also newspapers and directories. A bureau must examine directories, for example, to ensure that the information listed regarding its destination is accurate and up-to-date. Many such listings are provided at no cost to the bureau as a service by the publication. Occasionally, a publication will offer the opportunity for an expanded listing or another type of incentive. Depending on the destination and the character of the publication, such decisions are universally the perogative of a specific bureau.

Advertising also involves non-print media. Radio and television have been used by larger bureaus that wish to penetrate a specific market in combination with the print media. Reno-Sparks and Las Vegas (Nevada) are, for example, destinations that have used the electronic media to enhance and promote their destinations. Though such promotions are usually visitor oriented, they will have an effect upon the perceived desirability of that location and may in turn influence meeting planners to consider that destination along with others.

Familiarization Tours/Site Inspections

Once a prospect is thoroughly qualified, one of the most effective means of convincing that planner that a specific destination should be selected for his/her next convention or trade show is to bring that association decision-maker to the city for a familiarization tour or site inspection. A distinction, however, should be made between the familiarization (fam) tour and the site inspection. A *fam tour* usually involves bringing several executives from different organizations to a city at the same time, with the support of a sponsoring airline and local hotels and attractions, for the purpose of providing a general overview of the destination's capabilities for handling conventions and trade shows. A *site inspection,* on the other hand, is conducted for one association executive or executives from the same association. Transportation is usually paid for by the association and is at the convenience of the executive or executives involved in the trip. The inspection is specifically tailored to that association's needs and meeting requirements for a specific year or set of dates.

The *fam tour* is the best way to sell a prospect with potential business for your destination but has never considered it as a future convention site. Qualifying the prospects before they are selected as fam tour participants is fundamental. A bureau does not want to host planners who may never hold their conventions in their area. Even more important, sponsors are relying on the bureau to qualify carefully those who are invited for a fam tour. Once participants have been selected for an announced fam tour, the following should be among things covered during their visit:

- Provide a general orientation to the city, particularly as it pertains to the location of the convention facilities, hotels, major retail sections, attractions and restaurants.
- Explain the transportation network available to and from the airport, between hotels and the convention facilities.
- Highlight any events, activities and attractions in your city, especially ones that may provide some special flavor or attention.
- Discuss special amenities and services that make your destination unique and special.
- Provide inspection tours of convention facilities, hotels and new developments.

A familiarization tour is for the benefit of all the participants. A bureau must be flexible in responding to their questions and concerns. In planning a fam tour, it is important to remember some of the following guidelines.

- Keep the fam tour small in number to provide individualized attention. The clients will be far more receptive to this format than being a part of a larger audience.
- Invite planners who have similar meeting needs; this will make it easier for the bureau to present information that is homogeneous rather than extremely different.
- Consider including spouses; this is likely to influence upper management executives and will enhance the overall impressions of the fam tour.
- Carefully select the time of the year and determine whether a weekend or weekday is best. Plan the fam tour around some key activity happening in your city.
- Be sure to maintain close liaison with fam tour guests prior to arrival, providing them with highlights of the fam tour, information on participants, what to bring and wear and any incidental costs they may incur.
- In setting the final itinerary, blend a mixture of business and pleasure; equally important is providing some free time for the guests to do things they wish.
- Include the bureau's membership; having their involvement is important in displaying a spirit of cooperation and enthusiasm.
- Develop information profiles on each of the tour participants for distribution to fam tour guests as well as local hosts and sponsors, including organizational history, meeting requirements and personal likes and dislikes.

- Have a general pre-fam tour briefing with all local sponsors and supporters, explaining details of the fam tour, guest background and professional expectations for the tour.
- A tour of the facilities should be interesting and creative; a sampling of what is offered is sufficient for a fam tour.
- Develop fam tour books which should contain detailed information on all convention facilities in the community for each of the participants. This resource can be taken back home and used for future reference.
- Print a program for all the fam tour participants and sponsors; include in that program detailed information about the fam tour, tour participants, sponsors and key bureau personnel.

A familiarization tour has to be done efficiently and professionally. The image and capabilities of a destination are being examined carefully by the tour participants and the tour serves as one effective way to display what a city can and cannot do. Clients are looking not only at the physical capabilities but also at the spirit of cooperation and rapport a bureau has with its members and the community.

A *site inspection* places more emphasis on business than pleasure. Such an inspection is planned around the time schedule of the executive who is coming to town. Based on his/her specific needs, interests and requirements, a comfortable schedule should allow sufficient time to tour each hotel and convention facility. Confirmation of this schedule is made with both the client and the host facilities. Much of the schedule is arranged after consultation with the client; the client should be allowed to identify what he/she wishes to visit.

Once the client arrives, it is important to adhere to the schedule. If the tour falls behind schedule, the bureau should call ahead. This demonstrates a professionalism on the part of the bureau and a sensitivity to the needs of others. Courtesy goes a long way in nurturing a spirit of cooperation. During the inspection tour, the role of the bureau is to observe, allowing the host facilities to do the talking. Between facility tours, supplemental information on such items as transportation or what other groups of similar size have done may be appropriate. Highlight the site inspection tour by including something special such as a lunch at a famous restaurant, an evening play, concert or sporting event or whatever might be of interest to the client.

Follow-up the site inspection tour with a letter to the client, addressing any issues or concerns that might have arisen. Follow up with letters to the sponsors as well, thanking them for their support and cooperation. Indicate to the sponsors what the bureau's next step will be in relation to the client. Again it must be emphasized that the site inspection is an opportunity for the meeting planner to get an intensive look at the meeting, convention and trade show capabilities of a destination.

Destination Publications and Brochures

A bureau's publications are its marketing and promotional tools, created to support specific programs and to respond to information requests generated by the consumer or clients. Destination planning manuals, visitor guides, maps and other related promotional brochures are part of the product and services provided by a bureau.

In designing publications, the first step is to determine the goal for each publication. Among questions that need to be explored are the following:

- What are the target markets (convention, trade show, incentive, etc.)?
- What tie-in will the publication have to a current advertising campaign, if any?
- What kind of creative image will the publication present?
- Will the publication showcase your destination, member services, and/ or educate clients and visitors about your destination?
- Will the publication be used as an incentive to solicit memberships as a part of a drive to increase revenues?

Once the goal of the publication has been determined, it is necessary to decide on the format of the publication. Among some of those items which may be included in a destination planning guide are:

- descriptions of meeting and convention facilities (convention center, convention hotels) including diagrams and floor plans (see figure 5.7);
- description of area attractions including a locator map;
- descriptive list of restaurants and other entertainment locations;
- maps of the area, downtown and university campuses if appropriate;
- transportation information including cost and time to and from the airport for taxi or shuttle services;
- list of convention services, such as badge companies, warehouses, moving companies and related services;
- promotional or educational articles if appropriate.

Such a resource planning manual becomes a key tool for planners as well as bureau personnel. Figure 5.8 is the Greater Lexington Convention and Visitors Bureau's (Kentucky) planning manual which is also tied, image wise, to their advertising campaign.

Development of this manual requires an adequate timeline for gathering information, layout, production and printing. Such timelines should include

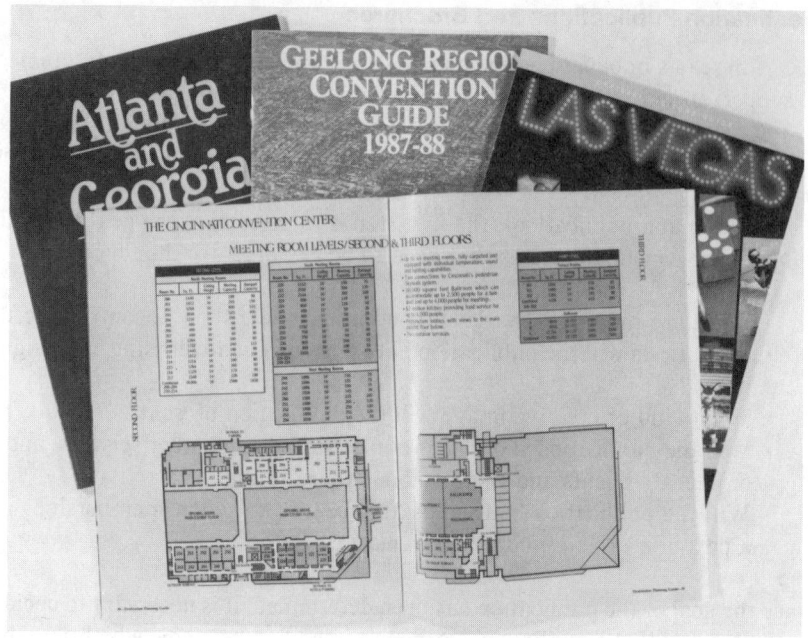

Figure 5.7

Figure 5.8

Figure 5.9

specific deadlines for the updating and inclusion of member services. All information must be carefully verified prior to its publication; the bureau may be wise to include a disclaimer statement that indicates it is not responsible for changes in services listed.

Costs for such a publication depend on many factors, which are the size of the publication, the complexity of the layout, the use of photographs and other graphics, the use of color, the quality of the paper stock used, and the quantity printed. Many bureaus assign staff to oversee the development of publications and brochures in order to ensure efficiency. The development or production of such materials may be contracted for through an advertising agency or through an outside publisher who specializes in convention and visitor publications. To reduce overhead costs, many bureaus have sold advertising, coordinated with the overall publication graphics, to offset the costs of the publications. Such advertising, when targeted to potential users based on the benefits of the content of the publication, lends credibility and may even enhance the appearance of the publication. Figure 5.9 is an example of a destination planning guide in which advertising has been included.

Brochures are another marketing tool for bureaus. They can be developed for use in direct mail programs, for use in response to visitor inquiries, and/ or for use in brochure racks at visitor information centers. Overseeing brochure inventory usually is assigned to a bureau staff member within the communications division. Brochures can be for specific projects or used in conjunction with special promotional campaigns. Frequently bureaus will have specific brochures for such items as:

- hotel accommodations/packages
- attractions
- restaurants/dining guide
- events and activities
- city map
- walking/driving tour(s)

A bureau usually has a generic image piece which sells planners and visitors alike on the amenities of the area.

Whether a large publication, a brochure or other promotional material, such publications support the overall marketing goals of a convention and visitor bureau. These publications are the products that project the destination's image into the competitive marketplace.

Direct Mail

Many bureaus use direct mail to generate an interest and awareness for their destinations. As part of a marketing mix, direct mail can extend a message on behalf of a destination into targeted market segments. The value of direct mail is that the audience can be carefully selected. For example, a bureau might purchase a specific mailing list of meeting planners from Meeting Planners International, or it might develop its own list of potential prospects based on an analysis of meeting capabilities from, for example, the INET system of the International Association of Convention & Visitor Bureaus. This selective list then becomes the bureau's resource for penetrating a selected market segment. Furthermore, a bureau will find that whatever it develops in the way of a direct mail campaign, the campaign carries a singular message and is not in competition with other ads. Some bureaus have developed rather extensive direct mail campaigns that include jigsaw puzzles, trivia cards, premiums or give-away items, audio tapes, plastic records or other items or gifts. All of these are designed to convey a specific message and to generate a particular response. Other direct mail programs can be far less expensive, involving image brochures and frequent mailings with a response card. Whatever the technique used by a bureau to highlight its destination, the goal is to gain the attention of a particular market segment. Direct mail provides a bureau with interested prospects who will require follow-up before a bureau is able to obtain committed business from them.

But a bureau has to be aware of the downside of direct mail as well. Too often, direct mail is classified as junk mail. Based on what one may receive in the daily mail box, the criticism may have merit. However, if markets have been carefully identified and selected and lists screened and cleaned, the likelihood of having a good response to a campaign increases. It is important to remember that direct mail is a means of addressing a large volume of prospects in order to identify through a response mechanism, those with an interest in your destination and product. The rate of return will average between 2%–4% and could be even greater if there is careful attention to the quality of the mailing lists. To be effective, the bureau must be prepared to handle the responses, quickly returning what was requested, sending a letter or placing a telephone call. The lack of immediate follow-up can dampen the impact and effectiveness of a direct mail campaign. Direct mail also infers a frequency; one mailing is not necessarily a direct mail program. The repetitiveness of a message into a market segment will greatly enhance prospects' awareness of a destination.[7]

Telemarketing

We often hear the phrase "reach out and touch someone." The telephone has become a primary tool for communications and for generating sales leads. Telemarketing can be described as one of three techniques: the one-on-one daily use of the telephone during a restricted time period to make calls to identify client prospects; the mass telephone campaign where a bank of telephones are manned by individuals calling specific markets for a specific purpose; and the computerized telephone message which automatically dials a number and makes a presentation. For bureaus, the third technique has not been a realistic option. However, the other two techniques have generated useful results.

Using the telephone for calls during a restricted period of the day offers a bureau sales manager the opportunity to prospect new clients. After carefully identifying a market segment, calls can be placed repeatedly to prospects to sort out their potential interest in a given destination. These calls allow for a personalized contact in which both parties can efficiently deal with the content of the call; needs can be identified and vocal reactions heard. The cost to the bureau is considerably less than having a sales representative on the road. In fact, considerably more can be accomplished daily than might otherwise be accomplished. The major drawback may be in getting past a secretary to speak to the decision maker. However, never underestimate a secretary who may be able to provide equally or more important or useful information. That person can establish whether the person called is really the decision maker for meetings, conventions and trade shows. Clarifying that issue could save the bureau many hours of work. Such individually targeted telephone calls should be used to prospect or update existing client accounts. The objective is to reach a targeted number of planners on a daily basis within an allotted time period.

A second telemarketing technique used successfully by bureaus is that of establishing a bank of telephones and making calls to a targeted audience during a specific time period. Such campaigns are usually coordinated through a specialty company. Often, these campaigns are used to build memberships. The Denver Convention and Visitors Bureau (Colorado), for example, used this technique over a week's period of time to identify short term business for the community. Corporate meeting planners were targeted, and calls were placed by selected individuals.

The value of telemarketing is the individualized contact with a prospect at a low cost compared to other marketing techniques. Callers may have a script, but more importantly, they must be enthusiastic and responsive to the needs and interests of those whom they call.[8]

Bid Presentations

After all the other marketing techniques have been employed and a bureau has a client who wishes to do business, it is then necessary for the bureau to pull together a bid presentation. The bid is the most critical marketing tool in obtaining committed business. Fundamentally, the bid should answer all the needs and requirements specified by an organization in a clear and concise manner. This bid may be presented to an individual, a small committee, a board of directors or a general assembly of hundreds or even thousands of people. The presentation may take place when decision makers visit your city or it may take place in another location. The presentation may be given to a client who is well known by the bureau or to a relatively new client. Each bid presentation will have its own unique character depending on the potential client and the character of the bureau itself. Regardless, the following are fundamental to the bid process.

Preparation

1. Request a "bid form" or information about the specific needs and requirements of the organization. This could be as short as one page or considerably more lengthy; it is the document that explains in detail what the organization needs in order to host its meeting. In Appendix G is a sample of the bid information needed by the International Association of Convention & Visitor Bureaus for its annual meeting.
2. Research the history of the organization for at least the past four years; analyze any discrepancies and clarify them with the organization's meeting planner. Such histories are available, for example, through the INET program of the IACVB.

3. Assess the strengths and weaknesses of your destination from the perspective of the meeting planner. If you cannot handle this group, inform the meeting planner immediately in writing. Always leave the options open for future meetings.
4. How is the bid to be made? Will the organization allow for an oral presentation or does it only accept written bids, or both?
5. Find out all the logistical details of the bid presentation such as:
   - location, date, and time
   - time limitations to the presentation
   - number of copies of bid required
   - size and setup of the room
   - whether you will have access to the room for preparation
   - number of people to whom the presentation will be made
   - names, titles, and addresses of people to whom presentation will be made
   - who the competition is, or who else will be making presentations
   - whether there are any restrictions or rules pertaining to the presentation (for example, only members can be present)
6. Meet with the leadership of the local constituency to discuss the strengths of the local chapter and whether there is anyone serving on the board or site committee for that organization. Clarify the role the local leadership will have in the bid presentation. Is there a local representative with a good public presentational style who would be advantageous to this bid? Then assess whether support from the surrounding areas can be obtained for this bid.
7. Classify the type of organization it is, for example, social, fraternal, political, professional, scientific, educational, etc., and then inventory the local resources as they relate to that kind of an organization. This may include major companies that may be engaged in a field of mutual interest, medical researchers, university departments, etc. This inventory of information then would be made part of the formal bid documents.
8. Analyze your market position; assess your competition and distinguish what makes your destination different or better than another. This positioning of a destination is important in identifying its uniqueness and giving it value as a meeting, convention or trade show location.
9. Contact previous host cities and ask for their help in dealing with the organization's planner; what was expected, were there any unexpected problems or surprises, and ways to deal with them interpersonally.
10. Work with the local representatives to pre-sell your destination through a letter writing campaign, including a variety of photographs or pictures.

Presentation

1. In compiling the presentation document, be sure it is complete, neat and easily readable. A summary page responding to the specific needs and requirements may be appreciated by the planner at the beginning of the document. Be sure the document is free of any misspellings or grammatical errors.
2. Personalize the bid document. Make the presentation appear to be tailor-made. Some bureaus even engrave the names of decision makers on the cover of the bid document, giving it an even more personalized touch.
3. Lead and include invitational letters in protocol order from the Governor, Senators, Mayor, local members, and the bureau. Each letter should not exceed one page.
4. If there is a "bid form" from the organization, be sure it is completely filled out with supplemental information provided as needed. Elaborate where appropriate, particularly in light of the research done prior to submitting the bid. Be sure to include color photographs and other descriptive brochures that sell the "sizzle" of your destination.
5. If an oral presentation is possible, choreograph the order and the scripts of each person who will participate in the presentation. Open with a local member of the group's constituency, followed by a mayor or other high ranking local government official. Then the bureau's sales executive should make a brief but detailed presentation that addresses the requirements of the meeting, convention or trade show. If an audio-visual presentation is available, make that presentation; then allow the local member to close the oral presentation. If time allows, ask for questions. Remain within the allowed time.

Needless to say, bid presentations are considerably more complex; but these general observations suggest the importance of the bidding process to a convention and visitor bureau.[9]

Convention Sales Files

Sales files are in actuality client accounts; these files are the system through which bureaus track all contact with a client. Files are opened on a daily or as-needed basis; in larger bureaus, the file clerks handle the processing and tracking of sales files. A file will usually contain a current profile of the organization, including the name of the meeting planner, current address and telephone number; a meeting history, indicating where that organization has met over the past five years or so; meeting requirements; a record of correspondence and other contact made by a bureau with that organization; and any other supplemental information that relates to that organization. These files are classified and maintained in accordance with the alpha-numeric sequences assigned by the International Association of Convention & Visitor Bureaus to international and national organizations. But since many organizations are not a part of that system, bureaus may have supplemental filing systems that account for their other files. For example, one system might be organized in the following manner:

10,000 series—IACVB alpha-numeric

9,000 series—other national/international

8,000 series—state and regional

7,000 series—corporate

6,000 series—travel/tourism accounts

5,000 series—university

4,000 series—government

3,000 series—local organizations

Each account will have a trace or tickler card that revolves that account back for review by a sales manager at least once each year. A geographic card will be made for each account, providing a sales manager with information as to which accounts are located in a given geographic area for sales trip planning purposes. The sales account also should have an alphabetical reference card so it can be located easily; accounts are usually filed by their numerical designation. A key-word card is also useful, particularly if the location of a word in the name of the organization is frequently turned around (for example, the Michigan Association of Accountants or the Association of Michigan Accountants). These systems are designed to organize the sales efforts, to increase the systematic retrieval and review of accounts, and to aid in the planning and execution of sales trips and programs.

The INET System

Over the past several years, the International Association of Convention & Visitor Bureaus has computerized its exchange of information. The founding principle for the IACVB always has been the exchange of information about organizations which meet the following criteria:

1. Meetings are held by a recognized organization.
2. Meetings are transient and solicitable.
3. Meetings are held regularly.
4. Meetings use 50 or more sleeping rooms.
5. Meetings are regional or larger in scope, or are state/provincial in scope but will meet outside their state or province.

Until recently, convention information was exchanged on a monthly basis on what was commonly called "blue sheets." A participating bureau would receive a package of convention reports to read. The INET system alleviated this cumbersome manual process with a modern electronic system that allows bureaus to obtain information at the touch of a button. More than 15,500 meetings are stored in the INET system. This information is gathered daily from the more than 300 member bureaus of the IACVB and fed into the system.

Each meeting held in a member bureau's area is reported in two ways. First, a bureau must report a meeting, convention or trade show when it is booked with a *Booking Notice* which is filed and entered into the system. If the bureau fails to report that meeting within 60 days after it has been held as reported on the Booking Notice, the bureau is notified that it is delinquent and no longer has access to INET information. In order to prevent that from happening, bureaus are asked to submit a *CCR* or *Confidential Convention Report* which supplies information about the meeting held. This report must be thoroughly complete, otherwise it is returned to the bureau for correction. Room nights, peak room nights, length of stay and total exhibition square footage are among the many variables reported on the CCR form.

After this information is entered into the system, it is possible for any bureau on INET to request information about an organization; this information comes out on a profile sheet with an overview of four years' history for that organization. This allows the bureau to make a quick assessment as to the consistency and growth of that organization's meeting needs. Updates of this information can be requested at any time.

In fact one of the unique characteristics of the INET system is the ease with which a bureau can obtain information. It is possible for bureaus to request information on meetings that are held in a particular city, during a particular time of the year or which have specific meeting parameters. Bureaus also have found the INET system useful for research purposes, particularly when a convention facility is being built in the community. The INET system has proven to be a tremendous value in assessing meeting information.

International Convention Sales

There are some differences between domestic and international marketing. On a closer examination, we find that the major differences tend to be related to geographic location, distances and variations related to languages and customs. We are a global village; the heterogeneous meetings, conventions and trade show markets are distributed around the world. Yet their requirements are no different than those of domestic groups. Assessing a destination's capabilities is in some ways even more important when dealing with international groups. In the international market, a city is, in principle, a venue

Figure 5.10

within a destination, for example, Los Angeles is a part of California and the United States. This relationship constitutes the basis of an international marketing philosophy; a city cannot be sold if the buyer does not want the country. When dealing with international groups, parochialism must give way to a much broader vision. Cooperative marketing with other cities, some of which may even be the competition, under a common umbrella may well prove to be the means to a successful end. Examples of the success of such international marketing cooperatives are those of Australia under the auspices of the Australia Tourism Commission and the Association of Australian Convention Bureaus, and the Southeast Asia countries through the Association of Asian Convention Bureaus. Both areas have experienced considerable growth in both the meetings and tourism markets as a result of their cooperative programs. Cooperatives also can reduce the individual costs for an international marketing program with more bureaus sharing the financial commitments. Cooperatives therefore can enhance a destination's profile in the minds of meeting planners as well as distribute the costs among the participants.

There are some special or specific requirements that relate to international marketing. For the most part, such concerns are largely a matter of common sense. Bureaus other than those in the United States have been dealing with international groups considerably longer and have a sensitivity to the individual concerns of the groups. However, there are a few issues that should be mentioned if a bureau is planning to engage in international marketing.

- *Linguistics* . . . while English may be understood by many international groups, certain international markets will require promotional materials in their language as well as the availability of interpreter services. A bureau may wish to consult with their consulates or the United State Travel and Tourism Administration office in a specific country to determine the best way to proceed. Being able to present materials in two or more languages may just be the deciding factor when preparing bid presentations or promotional materials. Translations should be done in a specific country or by someone who is a native to avoid any embarrassment through incorrect literal translation or language usage. Most convention centers outside the U.S. are built with the capability of providing simultaneous, multiple interpreter services for convention groups. For U.S. bureaus, being unable to provide this important service may be a drawback unless they have appropriate facilities and monitoring equipment. Having interpreter services for site inspections is also important; this may require a bureau to inventory its area to determine who is available to provide these important services. Appropriate signage also should be readily available in various languages to accommodate international guests (example: toilets); this signage should appear at hotels and shops throughout the community.
- *Currency* . . . if a bureau is interested in hosting international groups, it is essential that arrangements be established with local financial institutions to accommodate the need and demand for currency exchange. Travelers need to have ease of access to such personal services in order to make their visits comfortable. International hotel chains may be more readily able to accommodate such requirements than others.
- *Customs and Immigration* . . . A bureau needs to know and understand requirements that might impact an international meeting, convention or trade show. For U.S. bureaus, having such specifications stipulated in a bid proposal indicates to the meeting planner bureau understanding and sensitivity to such needs. Such requirements would include visa requirements for speakers and delegates, limitations or restrictions on the importation of printed or promotional materials and limitations or restrictions on exhibits.
- *Compatibility of Equipment* . . . Countries have different electrical power supplies; it is important that bureaus understand and know these differences and be able to accommodate them. The development of a reference file showing the compatibility between equipment and systems would greatly assist a meeting planner in determining audio-visual needs.

- *Trade Union Regulations* . . . Knowing local requirements and regulations is important; meeting planners do not wish to arrive in a country only to discover they cannot erect or mount their exhibits due to local regulations. Such requirements need to be communicated to the meeting planner early in the planning process.
- *Customs and Etiquette* . . . Every country has its own set of customs and rituals; though we may feel we understand others, it is important to be sure of the customs and rituals of a country and how they might impact on hosting a meeting, convention or trade show. An embassy or consulate can provide immediate information on specific customs, food or religious concerns. A social embarrassment is not desired by any bureau hosting an international group.

Working with international groups involves a longer lead time than when working with domestic groups. For a city that wishes to become involved with international groups, it may be wise to initially target smaller groups which have the potential to show tangible results. Once success has been seen and experienced, investment in soliciting international groups can then proceed. Some destinations will have a more attractive appeal for international groups than others; but it is the responsibility of the bureau to assess its destination and regional strengths to determine what kind of a positioning or marketing posture it wishes to take when soliciting international groups.[10]

Events Sponsorships

Too often bureaus operate in a vacuum. This is one of their biggest mistakes, since every bureau needs the support and understanding of the community if it is to be effective. The community needs to understand and appreciate the bureau's mission to bring as many people to the city as possible.

A good public relations program within the community is more important than a public relations campaign aimed elsewhere (public relations will be discussed in more detail in a later chapter). It is important to have the local community interested in bringing in visitors; and by understanding the bureau's mission and the services it can provide planners, there is a stronger likelihood that the community will be more responsive to visitors.

One approach to building this confidence in a bureau is to set up a monthly breakfast for people in the community who are influential in their own organizations. At that breakfast, the bureau provides an update of the resources and facilities available in the community and the services that the bureau provides a meeting planner. The objective of the breakfast is to make the association executives, political leaders and the business leaders comfortable with the fact that the bureau and the hospitality industry can accommodate the needs of their associations or groups. The breakfast also will enhance the image of the bureau and spread by word of mouth or through news features the value of the bureau to the economic vitality of the community.

Cooperative Programs

Working cooperatively within the community with key trade organizations will enhance a bureau's market presence and effectiveness. Among important organizations which deserve the support of a bureau is the Hotel Sales Marketing Association (HSMA), especially on the local level. As an arm of the hotel community, it is a vital part of the total convention marketing effort.

The bureau should lend its expertise to the local HSMA chapter to build an awareness of what is happening in the city and how that is likely to affect its members' selling capabilities. Building a better understanding of the "big picture" for hotel sales managers will help build unity in the community. Further, a bureau may wish to conduct seminars that explain bureau activities and services or host a special sales or marketing seminar that utilizes the talents of an industry professional. There is much that can be cooperatively done with members of the hospitality community. In previous sections, involvement with sales blitzes and trade shows has been explored. The hospitality community also should be included in the development of the bureau's annual marketing plan, not only reviewing recommendations but also offering sales and marketing suggestions. Another cooperative effort might include having restaurants set up table top booths at which they distribute their food in the form of hors d'ouevres; this exposes the restaurants to the targeted public being entertained and involves them with the programs of the bureau.

Cooperative programs go a long way in blending the bureau and the hospitality community into a unified marketing presence; they develop mutual respect and appreciation regarding the needs of each and the overall need for soliciting and booking meetings, conventions and trade shows.

Summary

This chapter has dealt extensively with the roles and responsibilities of a convention sales department. Based on an established marketing plan, bureaus undertake to influence meeting planners, association executives and exhibition managers through a variety of sales and marketing techniques. Being a people-oriented business, the primary focus of any sales effort is that of establishing rapport and a relationship with clients. Each technique also must be evaluated as to its effectiveness with a specific market, and many marketing strategies are designed fundamentally to position a destination in the minds of planners. Successful sales are premised on efficient and coordinated programming that involves an investment of both people and resources.

Discussion Questions

1. Why are convention sales important to a bureau and community?

2. What are the responsibilities of a convention sales department?

3. What are the steps involved in designing a marketing plan for convention sales? What are the issues that need to be explored in the development of such a plan?

4. Discuss the criteria for evaluating a marketing program; are these viable criteria or are there other alternatives?

5. What are the steps in direct sales? What questions can be asked to efficiently qualify a sales prospect? What do those questions mean?

6. What is the difference between intrinsic, functional and negotiable variables in the sales process?

7. Chapter five discusses two ways of looking at trade shows; discuss each perspective and the issues that are important to each approach.

8. What are the potential values in advertising?

9. Describe the difference between a familiarization tour and a site inspection. Outline at least four major steps involved in planning either a familiarization tour or a site inspection.

10. Why are publications important to a bureau and convention sales? What items should be contained in a destination planning manual? Provide actual examples.

11. Define and describe direct mail and telemarketing; what are their characteristics and how do they compare with one another as to potential cost and efficiency?

12. Why are bids important? Describe the process of developing a major convention bid, including a discussion of each element and why it is important to the overall presentation.

13. What makes international convention sales any different than domestic convention sales? Define and discuss concepts.

14. What is the purpose of sales files?

15. What is the significance of the INET SYSTEM to convention sales? What are the procedures and potential for the system?

Bibliographic Resources

1. Alessandra, Anthony, Phillip Wexler and Jerry Deen, *Non-Manipulative Selling* (Reston, Virginia: Reston Publishing Company/Prentice Hall, 1979).

2. Alessandra, Tony and Jim Cathcart, "Changing the Language of Selling," *Training and Development Journal,* November 1983, pp. 52–56.

3. International Association of Convention & Visitor Bureaus, *1985 Convention Income Survey,* July 1986.

4. International Association of Convention & Visitor Bureaus, *1986 Convention Income Survey,* July 1987.

5. Graveline, Dan, "Convention Centers," *Urban Land,* July 1984, p. 4; and David Listokin, "The Convention Trade: A Competitive Economic Prize," *Real Estate Issues,* Fall/Winter 1986, p. 44.

6. Trade Show Bureau, "You Make the Difference: A Guide to Professional Selling in Trade Shows" (January 1983); and Al Hanlon, *Trade Shows in the Marketing Mix* (Massachusetts: Wordsworth Publishers, 1982).

7. "Direct Mail," *MeetingPlace,* December 1983, pp. 6–10; Daniel Fitz-Gerald, "Managing a Mail Marketing Campaign," *Insurance Marketing,* September 1979, pp. 48 & 50; Sherril Sannella, "Follow-up Mailings—Make Them Work for You," *MeetingPlace,* October 1982, pp. 16–17; and Ed Camara, *Direct Mail Ideabook* (Camara Associates, New Bedford, Massachusetts, no date).

8. Roman, Murry, "Selling by Telephone: How to Create Campaigns That Ring Up Sales," *Marketing Communications,* March/April 1977, pp. 39–42; "Telemarketing: Part I," *Small Business Report,* August 1987, pp. 22–27; Troy Woodbury, "Telemarketing: Fast, Personal, Productive," *Courier,* December 1984, pp. 50–54.

9. Adapted from Wayne Chappell's seminar "Bid Preparation and Presentation" before the International Association of Convention & Visitor Bureaus, Tulsa, Oklahoma, 1985.

10. Katz, Kenneth, *Promoting International Tourism* (California: The Americas Group, 1986); Paula Ricciardi, "Tourist Boards: Your Foreign Connection," *Corporate Meetings and Incentives,* October 1985, pp. 77–82; J. Herbert Silverman, "World-Class Foreign Bureaus," *Corporate and Incentive Travel,* April 1987, pp. 16–26.

CONVENTION SERVICES: A SALES PARTNERSHIP

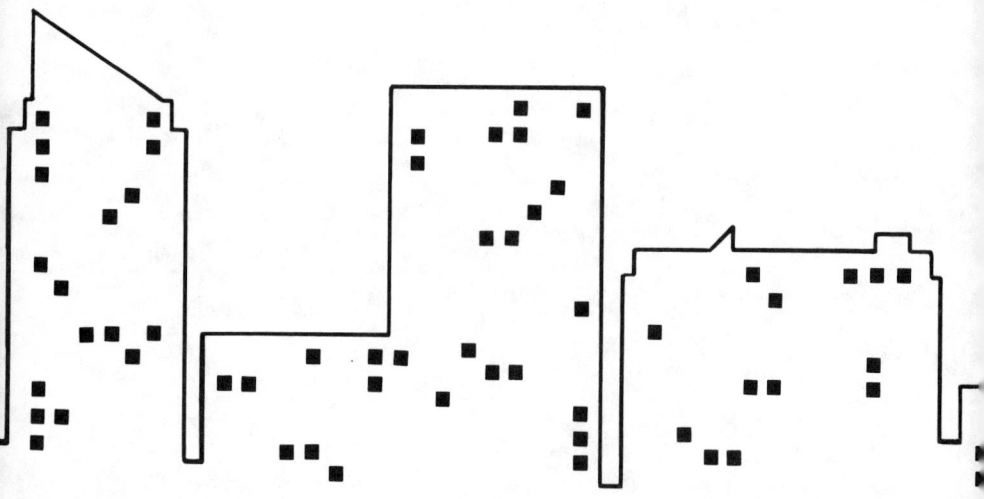

LEARNING OBJECTIVES

Upon reading this chapter, you will learn the
following:

- About "before" convention services offered
  by a bureau;
- About "during" convention services offered
  by a bureau;
- About "after" convention services offered by
  a bureau;
- About housing assistance provided through a
  convention bureau;
- About registration assistance provided
  through a convention bureau;
- About the concept of service as an attitude.

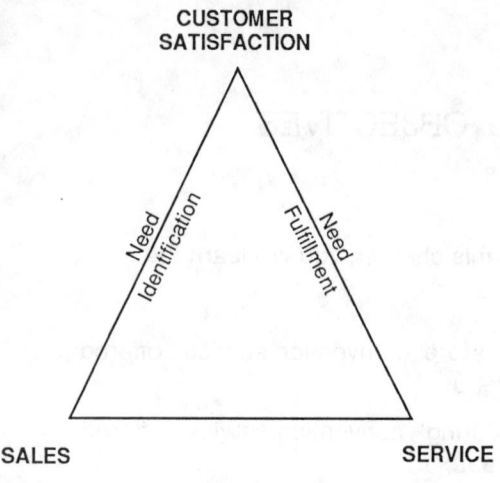

Source: © Richard B. Gartrell

Figure 6.1

Introduction

Customer satisfaction is premised on both identification and fulfillment of needs. This "eternal triangle" is the foundation of effective convention sales and marketing activities. Chapters Four and Five discussed the sales functions of a bureau as they apply to tourism and convention markets. Convention Services is a partner in those sales activities, ensuring that the client receives the support and assistance necessary to insure a successful program.

But service should not be confined to one area within a convention bureau. Service is an attitude that should permeate the entire bureau staff. *Time* magazine carried an article in which it questioned the consistent lack of service being provided by a society that is service and information oriented.[1] The foul-ups, miscommunications and arrogance of those serving others are a sad testimony; they generate distrust, frustration and disillusionment. And ultimately, these behaviors suggest to the customer that they should seek other sources for the services or products they wish.

For those in the travel and tourism industry, service is an essential part of any client relationship. The sale may satisfy customer needs but the fulfillment of those needs comes with the services rendered. The performance of convention and visitor bureau personnel and the physical environment in which a bureau operates communicate the attitudes and dependability clients can anticipate. Bureaus must provide discernible levels of service in order to meet client expectations. In order to do this, competent and competently trained staff is essential. Contrary to the perceptions held by many, the travel and tourism industry is not an easy place to work. It requires highly motivated, people-oriented personnel who are skilled and talented and willing to dedicate long hours to ensure that clients receive the very best assistance available. Clients and their needs differ dramatically, and bureau staff must be flexible and adaptive, as well. High standards and expectations of performance are critical to building quality service and customer satisfaction.[2] Sensitive inter-personal skills enhance a relationship and assure clients that the bureau understands their needs and concerns.[3] The challenges are many and the opportunities unlimited. Businesses which have accepted the challenge and are dedicated to improving their service have found an enthusiastic response from clients. Though this chapter will focus on the operations of one aspect of a bureau, convention services, it does not limit service simply to those few who have a direct responsibility for that area of programming support. For the convention bureau, service is part of its total operations, from the attitude of the receptionist to that of the chief executive. Simply labeling one part of the operation "services" does not relinquish that responsibility from the balance of the staff. Meeting planners, tour planners and visitors are all clients who deserve the most professional assistance available.[4]

Convention Services: Structure and Responsibilities

Convention and visitor bureaus have long had staff assigned to ensure that the meeting planner receives appropriate support in producing a successful meeting, convention or trade show. Often a division of the convention sales department, convention services personnel act as professional consultants to meeting planners. They are well informed professionals who provide the meeting planner with a liaison to the local community and its many resources.

Depending on the size and budget of a bureau and its location, convention services may be a one-person operation or a larger department of its own. Destinations which tend to attract large groups requiring multiple hotels, large numbers of registration personnel and other related services usually will have a full department to accommodate their extensive needs. It is important that whatever the organizational structure, the convention sales and service areas recognize their interdependence. The convention services department must assure convention sales that it will deliver those services that have been promised by convention sales personnel in negotiations with a meeting planner.

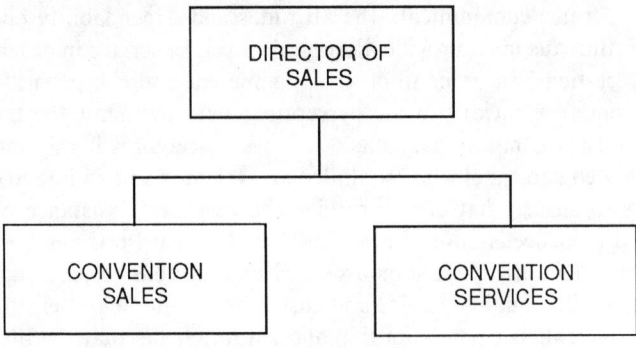

Figure 6.2

The responsibilities of convention services can be described chronologically: before, during and after a convention is held. Regardless of the phase, convention services personnel serve as a vital communication link between the meeting planner, hotel and convention facilities and bureau members and providers of goods and services. The successful convention services department maintains effective communications between all of these diverse audiences.

"Before" Responsibilities

These responsibilities may vary among bureaus depending on size and budget. Generally speaking, however, most bureaus can provide meeting planners with the following assistance prior to the holding of a meeting, convention or trade show.

1. Site Inspection. Often seen as a sales strategy, the site inspection enables the planner to view first hand the convention and meeting facilities of a community. This service also includes meetings with managers of hotels and convention facilities as well as providers of local services, such as transportation. A site inspection is a good opportunity for the bureau's services personnel to meet with the prospective client; assurances of competent assistance from the bureau is another aspect of sales.
2. Pre-Convention Publicity. Associations and trade organizations are always seeking ways to improve convention or trade show attendance. Such groups can work with a convention and visitor bureau to design a program that will develop awareness as well as build attendance. Such efforts might include some of the following options:
   • a current list or directory of the major media in a bureau's area, including names and addresses of both print and broadcast media,

to enable the association to produce and disseminate pre-convention press releases and to invite media representatives to its program for local coverage.

- a comprehensive press kit of feature news releases, editorials and photographs for use in association newsletters, magazines and other related publications.
- slides and photographs on the city's convention facilities, restaurants and attractions.
- loan of the bureau's promotional slide, video or 16mm presentation on that destination to generate interest and attendance.
- camera-ready materials that the association can use in developing its registration packets, including such items as housing forms and maps (downtown areas and/or convention center and hotels/transportation network).
- a generic image brochure that can be sent to delegates to increase attendance.

3. Pre-Convention Tours. Assistance can be given in arranging pre-convention tours of the city and adjacent areas.
4. Post-Convention Tours. A bureau can provide assistance with the planning of tours for delegates following the completion of a convention. Though a bureau does not conduct such tours, being a liaison between certified tour operators and the meeting planner is one of the many servicing functions of a convention and visitor bureau.
5. Handicap Resources. To ensure the availability of all programs to delegates, associations may request of the bureau information about local resources for the handicapped.
6. Spouse Programs. Many associations also plan programs for spouses and children; bureaus can provide local resources for such programs.
7. Speaker Resources. Names of potential local speakers can be provided for programming consideration.
8. Central Housing. Assistance including hotel reservations and confirmations for groups can be provided when multiple hotels are being used.

Bureaus have been very creative with their "before" assistance to associations, including the creation of posters for mailing to convention delegates to encourage attendance, providing "how to" publicity booklets to help the association in its public relations efforts and the inclusion of articles or forms to assist the meeting planner, such as the National Association of Exposition Manager's INFORM-A-GRAM #82 which lists the kinds of services associations can obtain from a convention and visitor bureau.[5]

"During" Convention Assistance

Once a convention or trade show moves into a city, a bureau will provide services to support its program. Among "during" services are the following options:

1. Registration Assistance. Bureaus have a cadre of trained personnel who can provide large associations with registration assistance for arriving delegates. Assistance may include not only people but also typewriters and name badges.
2. Opening Ceremony. The bureau can arrange for a welcoming speaker for an opening ceremony; this might be the mayor or other noted business, education or political figure with an interest or relationship with the organization sponsoring the convention or trade show. Such requests usually have to be made far in advance to accommodate busy calendars.
3. Hospitality or Information Desk. Bureaus often will be asked to provide a hospitality or information desk for convention delegates. This is an opportunity to respond to delegates' questions about things to see and do. Frequently this also may include a display of restaurant menus for delegates to view when considering dining options for their evenings.
4. Shuttle Transportation. Though these services are usually paid for by an association, shuttle services are arranged months in advance of a convention or trade show through a bureau. Shuttle systems require knowledge of the number of hotels being used by delegates, the schedule of events for the convention or trade show, and the number of delegates that must be moved from location to location. Shuttle services usually involve a coordinator and volunteers who assist with dispatching the coaches from the various pick-up and drop locations.
5. Emergency Services. If the convention or trade show is large, it usually has planned for and secured professional emergency services (such as paramedics) to be present on site. There will be many groups that will want to know how to handle emergency situations if they arise, rather than incurring costs for on-site paramedics. Knowing the emergency procedures and resources of a community is among the services a bureau provides.
6. Supplies and Services. The ability to assist a meeting planner in securing supplies or services at the last minute, for whatever reason, is another service a bureau offers.
7. Sponsorships. During a convention or trade show, a bureau may be asked to assist with the sponsorship of a reception, meal or event. These requests are usually negotiated in the site selection process.

8. Destination Display. A bureau may request, or be invited to present, a display during the convention or trade show preceding the one which will take place in its city as a means of developing awareness and building attendance for the forthcoming convention. Such displays usually are placed in the general registration area and include the distribution of promotional materials for the forthcoming convention location.

9. Welcome Banners. Many associations will request that welcoming banners be displayed for delegates at the airport, convention center and host hotels. Bureaus can assist in arranging for these. Some cities are able to provide welcome banners in their downtown areas as well; these are usually reserved for very large and influential groups such as political conventions.

Some bureaus have developed training programs among host hotels to inform employees about a large incoming convention or trade show. These programs of pride have included welcome buttons that are worn by employees, as well as tokens which are provided to the delegates to give to employees who demonstrate outstanding service attitudes. Awards to the most outstanding employee are usually part of the latter program. Bureaus also have been called upon to assist with last-minute difficulties. Such situations may involve working with local law enforcement agencies to resolve a particular issue, or working with labor negotiators to settle a labor dispute. Bureaus even have dealt with parking problems for downtown convention delegates by developing, in cooperation with their city government, a parking pass which allows registered delegates to park without penalty at city meters during a specified time period. Such "during" assistance provided by a bureau assists the meeting planner in producing a successful event.

"After" Convention Assistance

Even after a convention or trade show departs, the assistance a bureau offers a planner is not quite complete until some of the following are performed.

1. Thank You Letters. The bureau will want to issue thank you letters to the meeting planner, his/her board of directors and officers and any other members involved in the planning and hosting of the convention or trade show in its city. This letter should be from the bureau's chief executive and may include a special thank you letter from the mayor or other dignitaries. Thank you letters also should be issued to special speakers and guests of the convention. A list can be obtained from the planner.

2. Program Critiques. In cooperation with the planner, the bureau must perform a critique of the convention or trade show. This information is a vital part of the report that must be filed through the INET system. Such critiques include the number of actual hotel rooms picked up, peak night information, food functions and overall meeting performance. Even if the group is not a transient and solicitable piece of business, this information is still useful historical information for future planning and should be a part of that organization's account file with the bureau.

3. Post-Convention Difficulties. If difficulties or misunderstandings arise, the bureau is able to assist both the planner and the appropriate facility. Contracts should be written for all agreements with regards to hotel room rates; complimentary hotel rooms; exhibition space, including move in and break down times; and any other negotiable items. The bureau acts as a liaison and cannot assume responsibilities for misunderstandings and related difficulties. But there is more potential for a successful convention and trade show to return than if there are dissatisfaction and frustrations.

The professional handling of all arrangements prior to and during the actual convention or trade show is fundamental. Appropriate contact by a bureau following the completion of a convention or trade show also is important. It reflects professionalism as well as sincere interest on the part of the bureau as to how, and whether, the needs and expectations of the planner and the delegates were met. Such service creates a positive feeling about the city and opens the door for the association or organization to return at a future date.[6] Convention services are a precious resource. The professional assistance and advice a bureau can provide from the early planning stages through adjournment are an invaluable asset to any planner. Those involved with convention services probably have the most to do with ensuring that both the bureau and the association accomplish their common goal: a successful meeting, convention or trade show.

Housing Assistance

Whether it is called "housing assistance" or a "housing bureau", the objective remains the same: to provide a large convention or trade show with central registration for delegates when multiple hotels are involved.

Following a site inspection and selection of a city for a meeting, convention or trade show, the planner identifies hotel properties which will house attending delegates. When only one hotel is required for a meeting or small convention, the hotel handles all delegate reservations directly through its front desk or reservation department. However, when two or more hotels are required, the convention and visitor bureau becomes the coordinating agency for the planner and a central source to which delegates turn for reservations.

The bureau steps in because individual hotels cannot be asked to process reservation requests for another property, nor are associations in a role to handle the reservations: they do not wish to assume the responsibilities nor do they understand the individual hotel procedures for confirmations. Some larger associations initially handle their delegate requests but rely on individual hotels to supply the confirmation directly to the delegate. When the bureau becomes involved in coordinating housing for a particular convention or trade show, area hotels know that the bureau will place delegates in accordance with their individual requests and that reports on delegate housing will be accurate and current. The procedures, therefore, for housing assistance are relatively simple.

Once the hotels have been identified and the planner has negotiated acceptable room rates and any other contractual needs relating to room assignments, the planner provides the bureau with a list of the properties selected. The bureau's housing assistance or housing bureau designs a housing application listing the hotels, their rates, a map locating them in relation to the convention center, and any other information needed to process a reservation. Such items should include areas in which to indicate: hotel preference; name, address, and telephone of delegate; number of persons per room; and credit card number for confirmation and/or late arrival guarantee. This form is forwarded to the planner for duplication and distribution; it may be a separate mailing or included in the registration form sent to all association members. The form lists the bureau's return address and deadline date. The deadline date is usually a cutoff date that guarantees room availability and/or convention room rates. The housing bureau also may verify with the hotel and the planner any specific information regarding individual hotel room blocks, i.e., type of rooms, special instructions regarding the room block, locations for officers, board of directors and staff.

Once the delegates receive their registration information and make a selection regarding hotel preferences, their hotel reservation form is mailed directly to the convention and visitor bureau. In some cases, bureaus also will accept telephone reservations and upon receipt of such, have in-house forms that request the same information that would have been processed on the mail application. Some bureaus restrict telephone reservations to three weeks prior to the opening of the convention. Delegates usually are asked to indicate more than one hotel preference in the event their first choice is filled. Reservations are handled by the bureau on a first-come-first-serve basis and date stamped upon receipt. If all a delegate's preferences are filled, then the bureau assumes the responsibility of placing him/her in a facility that meets the needs as far as room rate and proximity to the convention center are concerned. The association assigns all VIP reservations individually and handles complimentary room assignments as well. If VIP reservations affect a room block, the bureau is appropriately notified and takes this into its room block counts.

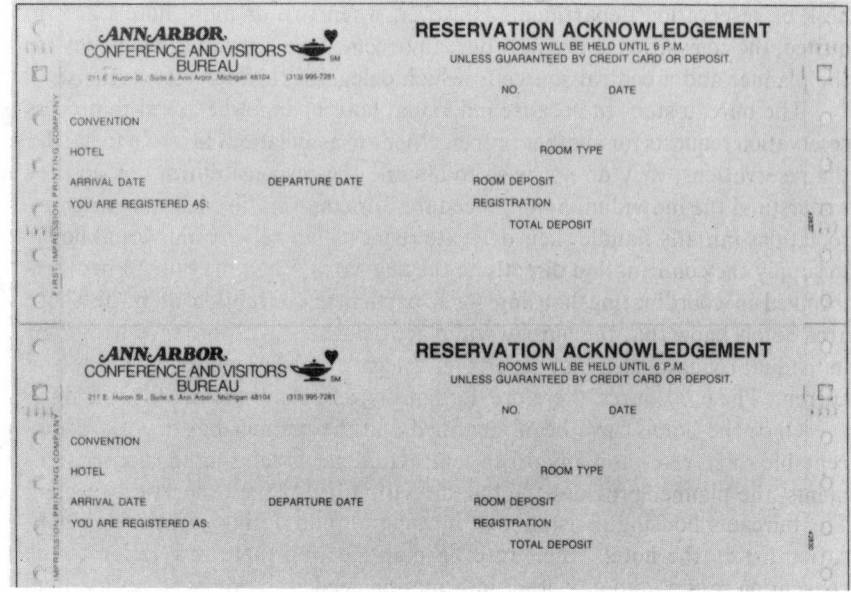

Figure 6.3

There is an established cut-off date for the receipt of reservations. This date is mutually agreed upon by the hotels, the association and the housing bureau. Usually it is three weeks to a month prior to the primary arrival date. At this cut-off date, the hotels have the option of releasing any unused rooms in the reserved block for general sale. Hotels also have the option of accepting further convention delegate reservations. The housing bureau will continue to accept delegate requests and will attempt to place them at properties still wishing to accept convention reservations.

Some bureaus accept deposit checks along with the reservation request; such checks are usually made payable to the bureau and endorsed over to the appropriate hotel upon assignment to a room block. In such cases, a cancellation notice of at least 48 hours should be required for receipt of a full refund of the deposit; this usually applies to both credit card or cash deposits. Prior to the cut-off date, such requests for cancellation, as well as reservation changes, must be sent in writing to the convention housing bureau. After the cut-off date, such changes and cancellation may be accepted by telephone by the convention housing bureau.

With the advent of computerized housing assistance, bureaus can now quickly acknowledge (see Figure 6.3) delegates' reservation requests and placements. Bureaus do not, for the most part, confirm reservations; that is presently the responsibility of individual hotels, though other arrangements are being explored between hotels and bureaus. As a result of the computerization of these operations, however, bureaus have become more competitive, offering the meeting planner options he/she may not have considered in prior years. Computerization allows for timely statistical reports to the planner and the hotels; these reports, if done prior to computerization, were manually compiled and typed and then sent to the planner or the hotels. Now planners can receive an alphabetical listing of delegates and their hotel locations or an alphabetical listing of delegates by hotels. It also is possible to provide the hotels with up-to-date lists of delegate reservations and any changes in those reservations. During the months prior to the convention, the bureau can rapidly provide the planner with general statistical information, such as the number of reservations processed and their locations. Other characteristics of computerized housing programs include such features: classification of delegates into sub-categories for meeting purposes, break down of delegates as to state of origin, listing of delegates' date of arrival and/or date of departure. The efficiencies of these programs have greatly enhanced the capabilities of the bureau in providing meeting planners with timely and useful information as well as advising hotels regarding usage of their room blocks. Except for reservations that may have been made outside these channels, the statistical information on room use and room nights greatly enhances the reporting capabilities of the bureau, particularly as it applies to the INET system.

Regardless of whether a bureau operates its housing bureau manually or through a computer, a good working relationship with the hotels, in particular their reservation departments, is essential. Weekly, if not daily, communications with those reservation personnel is necessary to insure a smooth running procedure. Frequently, though, communications do break down. When this happens, you have the embarrassing and unnecessary overbooking of a property. An easy way for this to happen is if the hotel reservation department accepts delegate reservations by telephone and places them in the reserved room block controlled through the convention and visitor bureau. Unless the hotel notifies the bureau, overbooking results and can be a major embarrassment for the hotel, the bureau and the planner. Hotels need to understand and respect the housing bureau procedures and guidelines. Close communications between hotels and bureaus can reduce the likelihood that overbooking will occur and satisfy the hotels, which need to know how the sale of their room block is proceeding. In turn, delegates do not wish to be pushed from office to office seeking a room reservation; they also wish timely confirmation of a room for their convention. If bureaus and hotels mutually strive for the efficient processing of reservation requests, acknowledgements and confirmations, then the meeting planner can feel confident that the housing of convention delegates will be a success.

Registration Assistance

For larger conventions and trade shows, registration assistance provided by a convention and visitor bureau is expected. Such arrangements are negotiated as part of the total, mutually arranged services between the meeting planner and the convention bureau. The degree of services will vary from city to city. The individuals staffing registration areas present an important image, and bureaus find it beneficial to carefully train these people. For some bureaus, they are volunteers who enjoy working and serving others. In other bureaus, they are permanent, part-time employees "on call" and financially compensated for their efforts. Still other bureaus contract with outside individuals, agencies or bureau members to fulfill these registration obligations. Whatever the format, the impressions conveyed by registration personnel are an important part of the bureau's total marketing endeavors.

Registration positions may be generally classified into the following categories:

1. Registrar. This individual types name badges for late-registering delegates. Badges for convention delegates are usually prepared well in advance of the convention or trade show and placed into registration kits for the delegates to receive at the registration counter.
2. Clerk. This is a non-typist who assists with the general distribution of materials at the registration counter.
3. Exhibit Registration Clerks. These individuals assist exhibitors with badges and exhibit booth locations.
4. Cashiers. These individuals are specifically assigned to ticket sales and/or the handling of a cash box or cash register. These people should be bonded since they are also responsible for receipts and equipment for charge cards. Forms should be provided to allow the cashier to tally all receipts and money and balance on a daily basis. If large amounts of money are collected, arrangements should be made for balancing the books frequently throughout the day with receipts and money turned over to the convention meeting planner or an association executive.
5. CRT Operator. This person inputs information from attendees into the CRT system which may produce a computerized badge or other related information. Larger conventions may utilize computerized registration forms which are forwarded to a company contracted by the association. Prior to the opening of the convention, CRT terminals are moved on site at the convention, and training is provided to those who will staff these terminals.

6. Room monitors. Though many associations use their own volunteers, some conventions will contract for room monitors to be posted outside a meeting room to check credentials and badges. These are often employed at major exhibition halls and food functions. Room monitors also may be asked to distribute questionnaires, count attendees and collect and tally questionnaires.

7. Message Clerk. The message clerk will receive incoming messages and post them on a prominent and easily accessible message board. If emergency messages are to be hand carried onto an exhibit floor or into a meeting room, that message clerk needs to be properly credentialled to permit access to those locations.

8. Information Clerk. An information clerk may be contracted to provide delegates with information on local points of interests, attractions, scenic areas, restaurants and other details of interest. Information clerks also have informational booklets available for the delegates.

9. Hostesses. Usually assigned to work in a hospitality room, hostesses often pass out information, maintain the general appearance of the room or assist a delegate as needed. They also may be assigned to a spouse's hospitality room or a lounge area in the exhibit hall. For some associations, these activities are supported by sponsoring organizations.

10. Secretary/Show Office Receptionist. This person is assigned to work in an area other than registration. This individual should possess good office skills and be able to respond to last minute problems. Some associations will bring an administrative assistant to handle these responsibilities.

11. Supervisor. In some cities, a supervisor is assigned when there are at least six registration personnel working. The supervisor works directly under the meeting planner and sees that all personnel are at their appropriate work stations. It is the supervisor's responsibility to schedule, with the approval of the meeting planner, breaks, lunch and dinner periods. The supervisor is responsible for gathering timesheets at the end of each person's scheduled time of work, verifying information provided and returning all worksheets to the convention bureau.

Duties of registration personnel may vary somewhat; however, all personnel need to be carefully screened, selected and trained by the convention and visitor bureau prior to being assigned to a convention (see Appendix H). They should understand that part of their job is to make the delegates feel welcome.

Each assigned registration person also should be involved in a briefing conducted by the meeting planner or his/her designee prior to the opening of the convention. This ensures a clear understanding of the procedures to be observed during registration and throughout the convention. The briefing may be as short as thirty minutes or as long as four hours, depending on what is to be accomplished. Such items as the color code of badges, cashier procedures, registration procedures, handouts and other policies or procedures need to be explained and understood. These understandings are essential for the smooth and efficient handling of delegates, whether at registration, the entrance to an exhibition or elsewhere in the convention.

Registration personnel should be arranged and negotiated at least two months prior to the convention. When requesting personnel, it is important that the planner have a description of needs and responsibilities. Further, the bureau should assign the same people to certain duties throughout the entire convention; this ensures continuity of personnel and reduces the disruptive nature of having to train people daily.[7] When negotiating for registration assistance, the planner will want to know:

- current rates for each position
- minimum hours per call
- overtime policies and rates
- method of payment
  —advance payment (some request 80%)
  —cash at the end of the assignment
  —invoicing after the conference
- when payments are due (net 10 days, etc.)
- extra expenses
  —charges for mileage
  —transportation fees
  —parking charges
  —meal charges
- cancellation policy for personnel

These contractual items will vary from city to city and must be clarified and mutually agreed upon between the bureau and the meeting planner.

Other Servicing Assistance

Convention and visitor bureaus receive requests for other types of assistance as well. Among those requests are:

- assisting with a mailing to an association's membership to stimulate convention attendance;
- providing a special "service lead" to bureau members informing them of the forthcoming convention or trade show and indicating any special needs, suggesting that local suppliers contact the planner directly;

- supplying promotional letterhead for use with pre-convention mailings by the association to its membership;
- providing specialty items for pre-convention promotions as well as during the convention, including buttons, lapel pins, balloons, posters, golf tees, note pads, pens, program shells (brochure covers) and more.

These special requests must be handled individually by each bureau and negotiated to mutual satisfaction between what the bureau is capable of doing and what the planner is desirous of having.

Costs of Services

It would be inappropriate to attempt to list the cost of services suggested in this chapter; for many bureaus, these services are provided without cost to the planner. For services such as housing and registration assistance, costs are negotiated between the bureau and the planner. Such costs should be given to the planner prior to the selection of a convention site so they do not come as a surprise from the bureau. Most bureaus are extremely reasonable about what they can provide a planner; this, of course, is in relation to the convention bureau's size and budget. Because there seems to be an ever-increasing request for bureau services, many bureaus are reevaluating their policies concerning the cost of many complimentary services.

Summary

Service is a verb. It is an active concept. It is an attitude that permeates our thinking and our behavior.[8] Meetings, conventions and trade shows come and go, but they are composed of people who attend for a variety of reasons and who return to their places of work enthused and excited as a result of their attendance and interaction with colleagues. They leave a city with feelings and impressions. And it is the responsibility of the convention and visitor bureau to support the efforts of the association or sponsoring organization to ensure that its attendees' time in the city was a good experience. Smiling faces, words of welcome and encouragement, a willingness to go one step further are all a part of the total package that makes up the travel product. The bureau can sell the city and its attractions and convention resources, but the city and its own attitude toward others lets delegates know how welcome they are. Services are both the tangibles that can be arranged and negotiated and the intangibles that fulfill expectations. Fond memories of a city's friendly service is the real product all convention bureaus want delegates to take home.[9]

Discussion Questions

---

1. What is service? Why should we be so concerned with service in our society today? What steps might be taken to strengthen our service attitude in the travel and tourism industry?

2. List and explain the services a bureau provides meeting planners before, during and after a convention. Why should a bureau be concerned with these matters? Shouldn't planners be responsible and able to resolve these issues without the need of a convention bureau? Discuss the liaison role of a convention bureau.

3. What are the responsibilities of a housing bureau? Why is it important for a bureau and a hotel to maintain effective communications? What are the benefits of a housing bureau for convention delegates?

4. What do registration personnel do for a convention? Why are they important to a major convention or trade show? What has to be carefully planned for when using registration personnel?

Bibliographic Resources

---

1. Koepp, Stephen, "Pul-eeze! Will Somebody Help Me?" *Time,* February 2, 1987, pp. 48–55; and Jeremy Weir Alderson, "Is Service As Bad As Time Says?" *Meetings and Conventions,* July 1987, pp. 50–57.

2. King, Carol A., "Service-Oriented Quality Control," *The Cornell H.R.A. Quarterly,* November 1984, pp. 92–98.

3. Dessler, Gary S., "Interpersonal Techniques Boost Your 'Hospitality Batting Average' ," Florida International University *Hospitality Review,* Fall 1983, pp. 21–28.

4. Wyckoff, D. Daryl, "New Tools for Achieving Service Quality," *The Cornell H.R.A. Quarterly,* November 1984, pp. 78–91.

5. National Association of Exhibition Managers, INFORM-A-GRAM #82, "Site Inspection: Convention Bureau Services," 6 pages, no date.

6. Gartrell, Richard B., "Convention Bureaus: One-Stop Convention Shopping," *Association Management,* November 1984, pp. 101 and 103.

7. National Association of Exhibition Managers, INFORM-A-GRAM #92, "Registration: A Team Approach," 2 pages, April 1986.

8. Gartrell, Richard B., "Service Is A Verb," *Courier,* October 1984, pp. 146, 148, 150.

9. Watkins, Dal L., "When Service Is The Product," Professional Notes for the International Association of Convention & Visitor Bureaus Newsletter, 2 pages, 1986/1987.

MEMBERSHIP MARKETING

7

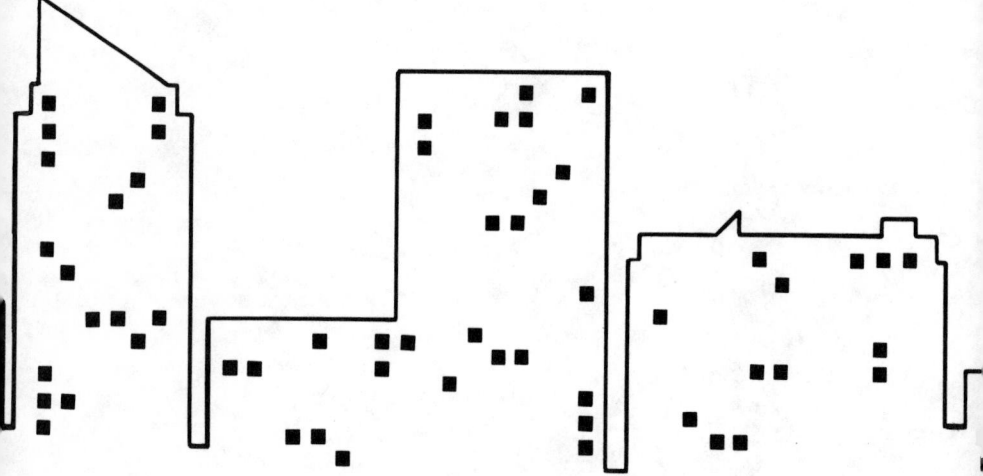

LEARNING OBJECTIVES

Upon reading this chapter, you will learn the following:

- The importance of membership development and retention;

- How to plan a membership marketing program for a bureau;

- The value of well developed promotional tools;

- The motivations that govern membership investments;

- The diversity of categories for membership investments;

- The importance of membership services;

- And the talents and skills needed to sell memberships.

Introduction

Members of a convention and visitor bureau are partners in the marketing of a destination. They are a fundamental part of the image that is projected. Without their investment in the sales and marketing programs of the bureau, the effectiveness of the bureau is limited. Members therefore provide a distinctive character for the destination by offering their products and services to those groups interested in visiting that community, whether it be a convention, trade show, group tour or a vacationing family.

Membership marketing is a critical aspect of a convention and visitor bureau's total programming; through such efforts, the bureau is able to share its story with community businesses, thereby enlisting their interest and involvement. While many bureaus receive public funds for their marketing endeavors, membership revenues represent another effective way to develop and expand the flexibility of a bureau's resources. Bureaus have found that membership marketing also brings to light a broad range of skills, talents and contacts upon which it can draw for brainstorming ideas and executing programs. Through the bureau, various community interests can be coordinated to promote that destination.

Within bureaus, there are usually assigned staff with primary responsibility for developing and implementing a membership marketing program. This chapter will consider staff responsibilities and the constituent parts of such a membership marketing program.

Membership Planning

Not unlike any other aspect of destination marketing, developing a membership marketing program requires thoughtful deliberations. Knowing who to approach and how to approach them is the beginning of a successful program.

In a recent association journal, several questions were suggested that need to be asked when beginning to plan a membership campaign.[1] These questions have been adapted for a bureau's membership program.

1. Where are we now as a bureau? What is it about our bureau that has brought members in over the past year? What are the members' sentiments about bureau programming and membership benefits?
2. Where do we want the bureau to go from this point? What kind of growth do we foresee? What kind of growth in members do we need? How can we increase member retention from year to year? What are our goals?

3. Do we see a gap between where the bureau is today and where we would like to see it over the next few years? What kinds of programs need to be implemented to reach those goals? What are the effective timelines?

4. What are the ways in which we plan to reach the goals established for the bureau? What strategies are in place?

Planning is not a difficult undertaking but, so often, planning is not part of the membership marketing process. Based on these questions, a bureau has to consider its "situation" as it begins to develop the various components of a membership program. Success is not attained by telling a staff member to simply go out and obtain memberships.

Thought must be given to the "hows" and "whys" of such efforts, and the situation analysis begins to focus on the needs of a bureau and the goals that might be established for a membership program. The situation analysis also should consider those factors which may influence prospects one way or another; for example, what is the reputation of the bureau? Are people in the community vaguely aware of what a bureau is, what it does and why it does it? Does the community have an interest in convention and tourism marketing? Have there been circumstances within the community that might hinder a membership program or distract from its focus? Who is the competition? Is the bureau's membership program being launched at the same time as another major association's program? What resources within the community are being equally vied for by the bureau and other organizations? Does the community have the resources to sustain a number of membership programs by various organizations? The answers to these questions need not be long or complex, but the responses will give a bureau a much better idea as to what it might expect when planning a membership marketing program. The information gleaned from such a situation analysis will help a bureau determine its potential dues structure or require that it look for alternative ways to obtain memberships (example, through a bartering system, where service in lieu of payment is provided for a bureau membership). The situation analysis also will help the bureau understand various motivations that may be required to enlist membership investments.

From the situation analysis phase, membership marketing emerges into the development of strategies and collateral materials that will support that marketing effort. Effective membership marketing strategies focus efforts in a uniform direction, identifying high potential prospects for bureau membership as well as a plan that will involve them in various bureau activities. For example, it may be found that a direct mail solicitation would not be as effective as planned personal calls. However, a series of follow-up mailings might be more appropriate to reinforce what was shared during the personal membership solicitation call. Such follow-up mailings might include a welcome letter from the bureau executive, informational materials on the bureau's programs, and announcements about key membership meetings and social events. Potentially successful strategies for membership marketing include:

• **Personal Calls** . . . utilizing this strategy requires that a target audience be carefully identified for potential interest in bureau programs and staff be thoroughly trained in how to approach the prospect and present the bureau. Personal calls are a maximum way of insuring personal communication; further, they allow for dialogue, clarification of questions and responses to mutual feedback. Though time consuming, the investment in personal calls to develop memberships allows a bureau to reach out and have personal contact with its prospective members. The bureau is then no longer simply an organization but a person through whom a message is carried. Here are some additional steps for planning personal sales calls for membership development:

1. Plan ahead; know why you are making the call and what it is you wish to accomplish. Is it simply to inform the prospect about the bureau or is it to solicit a financial investment? When making the appointment, be sure the prospect understands your intentions as well and not caught unaware of who you are and what you represent. This also will ensure clarity in mutual communications and reflect courtesy and professionalism on your part.

2. Know your prospect; research the interests and the nature of the company he/she represents. Be prepared to discuss any relevant information you may have gathered, particularly as it relates to the mission and programs of the convention and visitor bureau.

3. Be sensitive to the needs of the prospect; the task of the bureau is to nurture the member, to provide information and to assist where necessary. Be excited about what the bureau is doing to help the community and why the firm's investment is important.

4. Develop rapport. Make the prospect feel comfortable and relaxed enough to communicate with you. Encourage the prospect to share concerns and insights; let the prospect do a majority of the talking. Practice the concept of active listening, using open-ended questions that will draw out the prospect.

5. Be efficient and punctual. Recognizing that you are meeting with an executive, arrange sufficient time to conduct the call in a relaxed yet efficient and professional manner, not overstaying the invitation.

6. Be assertive in directing the membership interview; do not allow yourself to be placed on the defensive. Be prepared with positive responses to what otherwise might be negative questions or issues. Be assertive in promoting the value of the bureau's programs and how the firm's investment will enhance the capabilities of those programs on behalf of the community.

7. Be positive in your communications; never argue, since that may prevent the attainment of your objectives. The sales person may obtain a membership investment but lose the goodwill of that member if there are arguments. Look beyond what is said for hidden meanings or concerns. Recognize that in some cases you may not be successful in selling someone on the character and value of the bureau and accept that reality. Be positive, walk away and trust that with time, as a result of planting the seed, that executive may wish to become involved with the bureau. His/Her goodwill is important, and learning more about the value of what a bureau is to its city may be a significant measure of accomplishment. When leaving the appointment, be aware of what is said; much can be learned after the first "good-bye".

• **Direct Mail** . . . is frequently used in support of personal calls and other marketing strategies. The volume of printed materials arriving daily on anyone's desk is almost overwhelming; direct mail may stimulate interest, or it may affirm a personal call or telemarketing program. Direct mail that is consistently sent and scheduled to arrive on a specific day of each month can draw attention to the importance of the bureau and its programming. But alone, direct mail is often less than successful in generating bureau memberships, primarily because it lacks the personalization that can be attained through personal calls and telemarketing techniques. Blending direct mail with other program techniques is a preferred membership marketing strategy.

• **Telemarketing** . . . is close to a personal call in that it personalizes the communication; such calls allow for immediate feedback from the prospect. The bureau representative and the prospect can discuss mutual questions of interest; programs can be outlined and closure attained, similar to what can be obtained through a personal call. Telemarketing also is cost-effective in that time is used efficiently. It has one essential drawback—there is no personal face-to-face contact with the prospect. A lot can be gleaned from verbal interactions; however, a face-to-face meeting can be arranged at another time.

Special promotions that integrate a series of specific strategies also can be developed. Establishing a membership committee is a fundamental part of a successful membership program. Such a committee can help with the identification and solicitation of new members as well as assess current members' interest, involvement and potential concerns. A membership committee also can effectively respond to membership attrition by contacting members who indicate they may not wish to renew their investments with the bureau. In essence, the membership committee is important and can serve a variety of roles in assuring a quality and enthusiastic membership in support of bureau programs.

The membership committee can initiate promotional contests among the bureau membership to determine how many existing members can help identify and recruit additional members. Such contests not only generate an esprit de corps but also expand networking among members that the bureau needs for effective destination marketing. Such contests further expand the capabilities of bureau staff by making the full membership responsible for membership development, enabling the bureau's staff to serve more in the capacity of support personnel.

The importance of a membership committee cannot be underestimated; such a committee carries the mission and programs of the bureau into the community and greatly influences the perceived image of the bureau. The membership committee can be an exciting and dynamic component that enlarges the bureau's reputation and respect within the community.

Another technique that has been used by associations with some degree of success[2] might be equated to a pyramid. The officers contact other board members who, in turn, contact six to eight members. In this way, the association is able to contact each member at least twice a year. More importantly, board members have an ongoing sense of what the membership feels and can meaningfully discuss their interests and concerns. The membership is not insulated from the leadership, and the leadership is able to be more responsive based on the immediate interests and concerns of its members.

Needless to say, the kinds of membership marketing techniques that might be developed are limited only by the creativeness of those responsible for membership development. Programs can be formulated and techniques used, but the bottom line is people. The bureau makes an effort to identify and solicit members who are willing to invest in programs designed to develop the economic vitality of that community. Those members share the message and mission of the bureau with others and serve to personalize what might otherwise be a distant and impersonal program.

Membership Promotional Tools

Impressions are important; and there is no more important an area for impressions than membership solicitation. The bureau is eager to generate interest in its programs, and the first impressions should reflect both the professionalism and the dynamism that exist within the bureau. In many cases, the prospect will have heard little or nothing about the bureau or think it is the same as another organization (e.g. chamber of commerce). Information materials prepared for member prospects should not only project a quality impression but also educate the prospect about the character and mission of the bureau. In developing membership materials, it is essential that those involved with membership solicitation be included in the design and writing of

Figure 7.1

those materials. They are the ones who must "sell" the bureau, respond to inquiries and work to retain members. They are the ones who are attempting to align the interests of the bureau with the interests and concerns of the member prospect. Some of the following guidelines may be found useful when developing various membership promotional materials.

1. Promotional materials should make the prospect want to read them. Promotional materials should look inviting and interesting; they should evoke curiosity and reflect pizzazz. Copy may be limited, and the inclusion of photographs, illustrations and graphics is essential. Figure 7.1 reflects two bureaus' materials used to gain the attention of prospective bureau members.
2. The membership promotional materials should be more than the sum of their parts. They should communicate many unwritten messages in addition to the printed words. The promotional materials should tell the membership prospect that there is more to the bureau than meets the eye. Such is communicated in part in the Boston solicitation brochure (Figure 7.2).

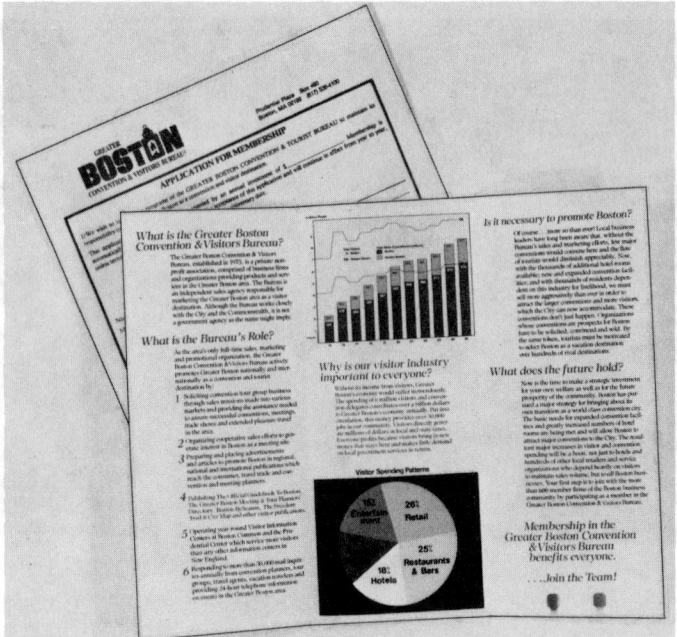

Figure 7.2

3. Promotional materials should reflect the personality of the bureau. For example, if the bureau considers itself a "sophisticated organization", then its materials should reflect that image. An example (Figure 7.3) of such an image is distinctive in the membership materials presented on behalf of the San Francisco Convention and Visitors Bureau (California). The silver and white folio, coupled with the informational pages, suggests and reflects a quality image. If the bureau is known for its tourism efforts, its materials should reflect that orientation. If the bureau is known for its high tech or educational orientation, then a western theme would be inconsistent. The promotional materials must be a qualitative representation of the bureau's character.

4. Promotional materials should have a clean and uncluttered design. For the most part, the bureau is making a presentation to a company's chief executive officer; there is not enough time to wade through material to grasp an understanding of what it is or what it says. Therefore, it is essential that membership materials be concise, precise, clean and easily readable. Let the membership salesperson, on behalf of the bureau, supplement and complete the presentation package with materials appropriate to the prospect.

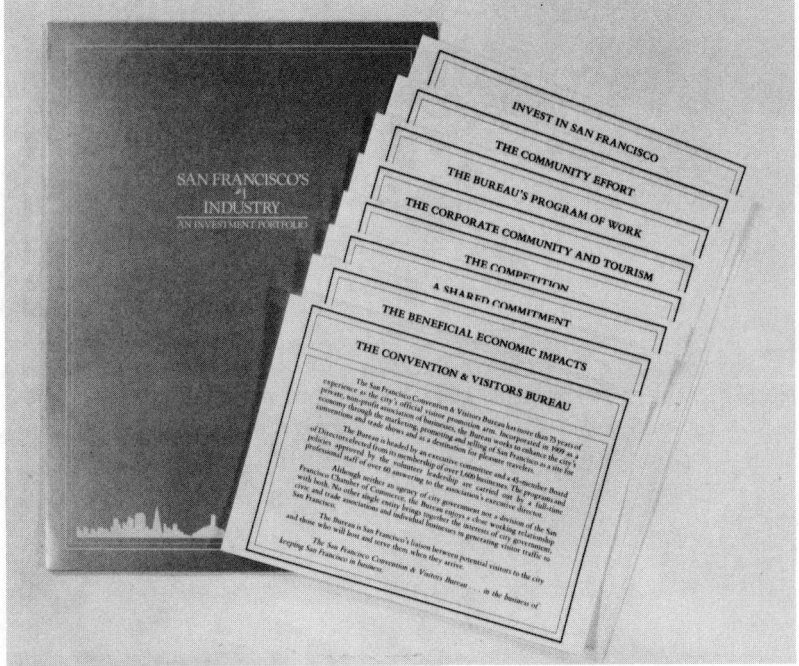

Figure 7.3

5. Tangible membership benefits should be clearly stated. Prospects want to know immediately what they receive as a result of their investments in the bureau; there need not be a philosophical discussion as to the value of membership per se, but rather a clear and easily comprehended listing of benefits. In discussion, the membership salesperson can tailor the benefits to the interests of the prospect.

   When designing these materials, several observations must be made. First, using trained graphic artists is highly recommended so that the materials have a quality layout, appearance and contemporary look. Second, the materials should not attempt to list everything a bureau does or all the publications it produces. Remember that the purpose of membership promotional materials is to gain the attention and interest of prospects, thus it is necessary only to tease them with the potential of what a bureau means to the community and, in turn, what their investments mean in reaching community objectives. Third, consider the use of testimonials as a way to enhance the promotional materials. Testimonials have their role in sharing with others how one feels about an investment with the bureau. Identifying key and influential individuals for these testimonials can enhance a membership campaign significantly. Fourth, providing prospects with a full membership list or a sampling of the membership

Figure 7.4

also may influence them; knowing they are joining a popular team of investors in the bureau's future is a significant motivator. Fifth, it may be appropriate to include a membership application in the promotional piece; such an application may reflect exclusivity in that not just anyone can join the bureau, but one must apply and be accepted for membership by the board. Figure 7.5 is a sample of the application form used by the Boston Convention and Visitors Bureau (Massachusetts).

A sales letter also may accompany the promotional materials or be sent ahead of a personal call. This letter should generally introduce the bureau. It also may indicate that a membership salesperson may be calling to arrange an appointment or visit via the telephone regarding an investment in the bureau and its importance to the community's economic future. Whatever may be said in the letter, it should capture the prospect's interest and attention,

GREATER

CONVENTION & VISITORS BUREAU²

Prudential Plaza   Box 490
Boston, MA 02199   (617) 536-4100

APPLICATION FOR MEMBERSHIP

I/We wish to support the programs of the GREATER BOSTON CONVENTION & TOURIST BUREAU to maintain its responsibility to promote Greater Boston as a convention and visitor destination.

This application for membership is accompanied by an annual investment of $_____. Membership is automatically renewed on the anniversary date of the acceptance of this application and will continue in effect from year to year, unless terminated by written notice to the Bureau, prior to anniversary date.

PLEASE PRINT OR TYPE

Phone: _____

Name of Organization_____

Member of Record_____Position/Title_____

Address/Street_____Zip_____

Mailing Address_____ Zip_____

Category (Listing in Membership Directory)_____

Description of Business_____

Number of Employees_____Number of Branches/Locations_____

Reason for Support (Joining)_____

Recommended By (Name)_____Company_____

Duplicate Mailing (if any)_____

Name_____Position/Title_____

Address (if different)_____

Signature/Member of Record_____Date_____

Make Checks Payable To:

Greater Boston Convention & Tourist Bureau
Prudential Plaza
P.O. Box 490
Boston, MA 02199
ATTN: Accounting Dept.

FOR OFFICIAL USE ONLY
Authorized Approval_____
Payment Received_____
Anniversary Renewal Date_____

Your continued investment in the work of the Bureau is necessary for the future of Greater Boston and can only enhance stability of your business.

Your membership investment is a tax deductible business expense.

White — Bureau Copy   Canary — Member Copy

Figure 7.5

otherwise it will be discarded. The letter should be concise and precise so that it can be easily and quickly read. Remember that chief executives value their time and wish to handle matters, including mail, as efficiently as possible.

All membership promotional materials must be written and designed to motivate the prospect to want to invest in the bureau's programs. Understanding motivations for "joining" an organization is an important aspect of membership marketing.

Membership Motivations

"Why should I join?" Though a simple statement, the implications are far reaching. Being able to articulate what it is a bureau has to offer prospective members and aligning that with their interests is what membership marketing is all about. However, there is no unified, definitive and universally accepted theory of motivation to guide a bureau in developing its marketing programs. It is essentially up to the bureau to define, as a result of membership communications, those reasons which motivate prospects to invest in the bureau's programs. Several such reasons have been ascertained.

First and foremost, when a prospect invests in a convention and visitor bureau, the bottom-line motivation is a business benefit. That prospect perceives a real value of bureau membership to his/her own business. This motivation can be divided into four broad categories.

1. A prospect wishes to do business with visitors, whether groups or individuals. Such businesses exemplify what is commonly called the "tourism industry," composed of hotels, motels, restaurants, attractions, tour companies, rental car agencies, cruise lines, airlines, bus companies, convention facilities and such related convention services as those provided by decorators, speakers bureaus and meeting planners. Membership bureaus publish a "services directory" that lists their members under their type of business. These directories are distributed to planners (see figure 7.6).

2. Prospects may wish to invest in a bureau in order to do business with other bureau members. These businesses provide a broad range of goods and services to those in the "tourism industry" and represent a wide variety of community businesses. Such businesses include hotel and restaurant purveyors, accounting firms, plant decorators and contractors. These businesses do well when the tourism industry is doing well and feel the impact of economically soft times. This networking is not limited to those businesses which support the tourism industry; such networking is critical to the stability of any business and working with other bureau members opens numerous opportunities.

GATHERINGS, a collection of highly entertaining menus, makes every occasion special. The Junior League of Milwaukee's new cookbook showcases the quality Wisconsin cooks are known for. Over 400 tested recipies are gathered together and presented in 10 chapters of menus that have pleased hundreds of critical palates. A hardbound, 200-page coffetable edition, it is illustrated with 31 poster-quality color pages. Published May 1987.

HOMETOWN INC.
1518 E. North Ave.
Milwaukee, WI 53202
(414) 276-9311
(800) 242-9328
Contact: James Barry

Packaged wet and dry ice, for all special events. Also deliver diesel fuel, gasoline and lubricants.

WE'LL DO IT-TWO
9402 N. 107th St.
Milwaukee, WI 53224
(414) 354-2228
Contact: Lori L. Brigham
Debra J. Arnold

We'll Do It-Two offers numerous unique services to businesses, private individuals and professionals. All types of shopping, cleaning, party planning and general delivery are just a few of the available services geared toward anyone with little time to spare.

**ILLUSTRATED
BUSINESS GUIDES**

**CARTOGRAPHICS
INTERNATIONAL INC.**
2733 W. Wisconsin Ave.
Milwaukee, WI 53208
(414) 344-5110
Contact: Mike McMahon,
Tom Winkel

Cartographic International Inc. produces and markets beautiful four-color maps which provide an unusual 3-dimensional view of Milwaukee. This very functional map also provides an index to the who's who of the Business community. Provides visitors and residents alike an easy to use guide. For information how your business can participate please contact us at (414) 344-5110.

**INDUSTRIAL THEATRE
PRODUCERS/CONVEN-
TION PRESENTATIONS**

M & W PRODUCTIONS, INC
P.O. Box 93910
Milwaukee, WI 53203
(414) 272-7701
Contact: Michael Wilson
or Tom Marks

Complete industrial theatre shows, and convention production services. Quality entertainment, motivational programs, and presentations. Our staff can conceptualize, design, cast, direct, choreograph, and staff an event custom written for your company or organization. As a Milwaukee based company we afford you substantial savings by locally producing your original and unique presentation.

LANGUAGE SERVICES

**IVERSON LANGUAGE
ASSOCIATES, INC.**
P.O. Box 09337
Milwaukee, WI 53209
(414) 476-3119
Contact: Steven P. Iverson

Iverson Language Associates, Inc. offers language services in 20 languages, including American Sign Language. We also offer translation services and interpretation, all at competitive rates. Other services include travel, telex, immersion programs and cultural presentations. We also arrange special programs such as tours for non-English speaking groups.

**MAILING &
PACKAGING SERVICES**

CAPEADAN SERVICES
3617 N. 55th St.
Milwaukee, WI 53216-2811
(414) 444-0892
Contact: Dave Hogrefe

With over 20 years of experience, Capeadan's Mailing and Packaging Division can help you complete your most challenging programs: mailing list rental; mail processing; automatic inserting; folding; metering; polyethylene, shrink,

bookfold, sleevewrap packaging' cheshire, PS, piggyback, heat seal labeling; zip sorting;mail tracking and 5-9 digit zip-code conversions. Call us today to find out how Capeadan can assist with your next convention or seminar.

FEDERAL EXPRESS
133 W. Wisconsin Ave.
Milwaukee, WI 53203

Nationwide Overnight Service. For package pick-up and information call 1-800-238-5355.

MEDICAL SERVICES

**MILWAUKEE REGIONAL
MEDICAL CENTER**
1000 N. 92nd St.
Milwaukee, WI 53226
(414) 778-4570

An academic health center offering medical care, education and research. The MRMC acts as the service organization for its seven regional members.

**MEETING/CONVENTION
PLANNERS**

**ALL AROUND MILWAUKEE
TOURS & EVENTS!**
see page 36

**BARKIN, HERMAN,
SOLOCHEK & PAULSON**
see page 7

CORCOM, LTD.
207 E. Buffalo St.
Suite 401
Milwaukee, WI 53202
(414) 347-1818
Contact: Sandi Wietzel

Corcom, Ltd are specialists in structuring events and fine tuning the details that make successful meetings. From planning to publicity, support literature, invitation packages, special activities and general logistics—we'll make your meetings work. Call us at (414) 347-1818 for free estimates when you're planning corporate sales meetings, customer special event activities, educational conferences, VIP meetings, trade shows and conventions.

21

Figure 7.6

3. Prospects also may wish to do business directly with the bureau. Needless to say, the bureau is like any other business enterprise and must rely on the community's business resources. Such resources include printers, graphic artists, office supply companies, specialty companies, travel agents and entertainment companies among others. Investing in the bureau strengthens not only the bureau but also the business.

4. There are also those businesses which may not feel a direct effect from their investments in the bureau but wish to invest and strengthen the overall tourism industry. These businesses always benefit from a strong economy and may even benefit indirectly from the tourism industry through the use and reuse of funds received from the infusion of new revenues into a community. Such organizations usually include banks, major manufacturers and utilities; these companies usually acknowledge that revenue generated through tourism helps make their communities appealing places in which to live.

There may be other reasons for wanting to invest in bureau programs; such reasons may be allied to other motivational theories such as Maslow's "Need Theory," specifically social needs, Likert's "Human Relations Theory" which encourages participation and involvement in team efforts, or some other aspect of motivation, such as wanting to be involved in a new experience, wanting to be included in a team to enjoy the congeniality of group participation or wanting to obtain some degree of recognition either individually or corporately.[3] Whatever the motivation, bureaus benefit greatly from membership investments be they financial support or contributions of time and talents.

Membership Investments

Why do we continually use the term "investment" rather than "dues"? There is more to being a bureau member than simply writing out an annual check; a bureau seeks the full involvement of its members in support and advocacy of its mission and programs and therefore sees memberships as "investments" and not just "dues."

Explaining the "dues" structures for membership in a convention and visitor bureau is complicated. Each bureau has its own formula as to what the investment will cost. In 1986, a survey of bureaus was conducted in an effort to determine the character of those various formulas.[4] A couple of principles are reflective of these diverse results.

1. Each membership category usually will have a different investment formula. Retail businesses, for example, may have a different level of expectation than airlines. The former may be based on gross sales receipts or number of employees, while the latter may be based on the number of seats into an area or the number of employees. Several bureaus categorically utilize the same formula across all membership categories; however, this is not usually the case. The following are some examples of investment structures.

Corporate

Example #1

A. Large Corporation $3,000
B. Medium-Size Corporation $2,000
C. Small Corporation $1,000

Example #2

A. Corporation Gross Sales Over $5 million $5,000
B. Corporation Gross Sales between $3–5 million $4,000
C. Corporation Gross Sales between $1–3 million $3,000

Retail

Example #1

1–2 Employees $100
3–5 Employees $150
6–10 Employees $200
Over 11 Employees .... $250 + $5
per employee

Example #2

Gross Sales under $1 million $625
Gross Sales $1–3 million $1,250
Gross Sales $3–5 million $2,500
Gross Sales over $5 million $3,750

2. Within categories there is usually a differentiation made between various types of members, for example, distinctions between convention hotels, resorts and motels. Distinctions also are made between restaurants with and without lounges. In retail areas, the distinction is usually between small, medium and large companies predicated on the number of employees. Distinctions are made between publications that sell ads and those that do not. Below are examples of investment schedules for various categories which differentiate within a single category.

Hotels and Motels

Convention Headquarter Hotels .... $14 per room
Hotel with Meeting Space .... $13 per room
Downtown Hotel .... $12 per room
Motel with Meeting Space .... $10 per room
Motel .... $9 per room
Resort .... $10 per room
Other Accommodations (e.g. RV Park,
Campground, Mobile Home, etc.) $250

Visitor Attractions

Small Amusement Park $200
Small Nonprofit Attraction $200
Large Attraction $400
Major Sport Attraction .... Individually
Set with CVB

3. Investment schedules will differ considerably between bureaus, reflecting the individuality of each destination. Understanding other areas' investment formulas can help in formulating limits of resources for one's own area. For example, knowing that one major metropolitan area charges $22 per hotel room for a downtown hotel, but that several other destination cities of similar size charge between $12 and $14 per room for hotel memberships may be of distinct value in assessing the quality of one's own membership investment schedule.

In developing an investment schedule, a bureau must carefully assess community resources. Following such an assessment, it is possible to divide memberships into investment categories. These categories might include the following:

Advertising Agencies/Graphic Arts

Attractions/Amusement Parks

Banks/Financial Institutions

Business/Professional Services

Corporations

Convention Services

Hotels and Motels

Non-Print Media

Print Media

Purveyors

Real Estate

Restaurants

Retail/Shopping Malls

Transportation

Utilities

Such lists and assignment of investment dollars per category are usually reviewed and updated on an annual basis.

Some bureaus prefer a simplified membership structure; others have very complex structures. The end result remains the same, that of securing memberships from businesses that wish to invest in the bureau's programs and the future of their community. Once a member has invested in the bureau, membership services and member servicing become paramount concerns.

Membership Services

Membership services are programs and activities available only to those who have invested in the bureau; non-members do not have access to such services or are charged a steep premium for them. For example, if a bureau develops a newsletter that receives broad distribution throughout the business community and also is sent to planners and association executives, the bureau may make advertising available to members only; non-members are restricted from advertising in the publication unless they join the bureau. Bureau members also may receive certain publications from the bureau without charge; a non-member might have to purchase them for a considerable price. How specific bureau member services are handled are again policies of the individual bureau.

What are some of those services? Following is a list of some of the most common services offered by convention and visitor bureaus.

Networking

New Member Receptions
Business-After-Hour Mixers
Trade Shows
Recognition Programs
Legislative Status Reports
Legislative Issue Surveys
Annual/Semi-Annual Social Functions
Breakfast Meetings
Educational Seminars

Exposure

Free Listing in Bureau Publications
  • Convention Planning Guide
  • Tourism Planning Guide
  • Convention Services Directory
  • Visitors Guide
  • Specialty Guides (e.g. Lodging, map)
Newsletter
Annual Report
Cooperative Advertising Opportunities

Incentives

Group Insurance Plans
Discounts from other Bureau Members
Discount Bank Card Interest Rate

Other Services

Convention Leads
Group Referrals
Mailing Lists
Convention Calendars
Access to Slide/Film Libraries
TV Taping
Computerized Housing System
Convention Marketing Committee
Tourism Marketing Committee
Convention Services Committee
Distribution of their materials at the Visitor Information Center

Involvement is the critical term when dealing with bureau members. It is one thing to simply provide literature, but it is quite another to involve them in meaningful ways on behalf of the bureau. Of course, not every member will want to participate actively. There are those who invest in the bureau to sustain its programs as part of the quality of the community; there are others who join and may appear at only one or two meetings during a year. Then again, there are those who wish to be involved in everything. The bureau must balance all levels of participation, including as many members as possible in the life of the bureau and, at the same time, moving forward with its destination marketing responsibilities. This tightrope walk is important in the retention of members.

Membership Assimilation and Retention

Communication is the key to survival; maintaining a liaison with members is crucial to a bureau's ability to grow, respond to marketing challenges, flex under financial or economic pressures and demonstrate a vitality for the future. Simply securing a member is not enough; that member must be assimilated into the life of the bureau. When this is accomplished successfully, the likelihood of retaining the member increases. Many bureaus utilize the assimilation timeline (figure 7.7) in their membership marketing programs. Obviously, the most effective retention program is that of communicating with members to keep them informed of programs and activities. This communication can be via short letters in which important statistical information is shared (e.g. convention bookings increased this past quarter 12% over the previous year); the announcement of a major convention booking (e.g. the securing of the 20,000 delegate American Medical Association Annual Convention); happenings within the bureau itself such as staff adjustments, awards or special recognitions, or a myriad of other possibilities. As long as the information is meaningful there is never a fear of communicating too often. Executives are busy, but by repeatedly sending good material to members on a regular schedule, continued awareness of the bureau is ensured. It will also increase the likelihood of active membership involvement and, of course, provide for the advocacy of the bureau among other members of the community.

When it comes to retaining members, a renewal timeline (figure 7.7) is also frequently used by bureaus. This timeline suggests meaningful ways of communicating with the members to let them know about the positive things that have transpired over the previous year and to thank them for their investment and confidence in the programming of the bureau. This timeline puts into perspective the value of the member to the bureau. It gives that member sufficient reason to renew and retain its investment in the bureau. The mechanics of notices is a function of the bureau's accounting and membership personnel, but posturing the bureau in the eyes of the member is the responsibility of the bureau's president, supported by the public affairs or communications staff. When communication channels are effectively utilized throughout the year, the likelihood of retaining members is considerably greater.

Nothing is more exciting in membership marketing than bringing a new member on the bureau team and knowing that the business and the bureau will benefit mutually from the relationship. Developing loyal supporters is equally rewarding, particularly if they were originally skeptical about the purposes and programs of the bureau. The bureau benefits tremendously from being able to draw on the reservoir of resources and talents found in the members who invest in the bureau. The successful bureau sees membership marketing as an essential public relations opportunity. That is why those who are selected to work with membership development are a critical part of the bureau team and its ability to achieve marketing goals.

Membership Personnel

Developing and maintaining membership requires a full time staff with appropriate clerical support. Identifying prospects, making presentations, responding to questions and asking for the commitment require a sense of dedication and purpose along with the sales skills that bring successful efforts. But equally important is the reality that those in membership are working with people, serving as the personal liaison for the bureau in the community, nurturing relationships and thriving on the stimulation that comes through human relations.

NEW MEMBER ASSIMILATION TIMELINE

	DATE MEMBERSHIP RECORDED	PLUS ONE WEEK	PLUS 30 DAYS	PLUS 90 DAYS
COMMUNICATION	THANK YOU LETTER	WELCOME LETTERS	WELCOME LETTER	POST CARD (optional)
CONTENT	"Pleased to learn from (Rep) that you have joined; want to join him/her in welcoming you. . ."	"Welcome to our partnership. . ."	"Here is printout of your account record. Is everything correct? Please make any changes, additions, etc. and return to my attention. . ."	"We haven't seen you at an orientation or reception. These are two benefits of membership you will want to take advantage of . . ."
SENDER	Membership Development Manager	President or member of Executive Committee/Executive Dir	Membership Services Manager	Membership Representative
ENCLOSURES/ COMMENTS	PACKET: Program of work, Cablegram, Convention Calendar & Update, Member Logo, CSG, Decal (when appropriate).	Embossed invitation to orientation or reception. Where appropriate use Executive Committee member's stationery.	Computer printout.	Use discretion in sending.

MEMBER RENEWAL TIMELINE

	BILLING DATE MAY 15 NOVEMBER 15	REMINDER DATE JUNE 15 DECEMBER 15	DUE DATE JULY 1 JANUARY 1	30 DAYS DELINQUENT AUGUST 1 FEBRUARY 1
COMMUNICATION	LETTER	STATEMENT WITH "REMINDER' STAMP	MAILGRAM	NOTE CARD
CONTENT	"We've enjoyed our last year . . . it's time to renew our partnership . . ."		"Just to remind you that dues are owed now. . . your membership has lapsed today. . ."	"I notice you have'nt paid. . . tried to reach you by phone. . . give me a call. . ."
SENDER	President	Accounting Department	Public Affairs Director	Membership Representative
ENCLOSURES/ COMMENTS	Invoice.	None.	Membership Brochure	Optional.

Source: San Francisco Convention and Visitors Bureau

Figure 7.7

(Continued)

	PLUS 6 MONTHS	PLUS 8 MONTHS	AS APPROPRIATE	AS APPROPRIATE
COMMUNICATION	INFORMATION SHEET	EXECUTIVE DIRECTOR'S LETTER	INVITATIONS	PHONE CALLS
CONTENT	"Have you used your membership?"	"Thought you"d like to know latest developments . . ."	"Join us for: New Member Reception New Member Orientation Business Exchanges Other Events"	"Just to keep in touch . . ."
SENDER	Membership Representative	Executive Director	Communications Manager or Membership Representative	Membership Representative
ENCLOSURES/ COMMENTS	Hand deliver during personal call when possible.	To every member-- don't ask for anything. Sent in February or August as update. Text will vary	RSVP where appropriate.	None.

(Continued)

	60 DAYS DELINQUENT SEPTEMBER 1 MARCH 1	90 DAYS DELINQUENT OCTOBER 1 APRIL 1	GOOD-BYE ON GOING	DATE RENEWAL CHECK RECEIVED
COMMUNICATION	LETTER	LETTER	LETTER	LETTER
CONTENT	"Our programs are still being implemented to serve you."	"It has been 90 days - in accordance with our by-laws we must cancel your membership."	"Sorry you found it necessary to discontinue your membership. . ."	"Thank you for renewing. . ."
SENDER	Membership Development Manager	Executive Director & Board Members	Public Affairs Dir.	Membership Representative
ENCLOSURES/ COMMENTS	None.	None.	None.	Personalize each letter.

Membership staff must be thoroughly familiar with the operations of a convention and visitor bureau. They need to be aware of and fluent in responding to inquiries regarding the bureau's strengths and weaknesses. They have to be familiar with programs in order to respond to questions that might be posed, such as why the bureau hasn't chosen to pursue the international market or why the bureau can't correct the available air service. They must have excellent interpersonal communication skills and a personal as well as a professional presence. They have to reflect confidence. Though it might be assumed that any person with sales skills should do well in membership, it must be remembered that closure in membership development means asking for the prospect's financial investment in the bureau, and frankly, not everyone is comfortable asking for money.

Often staff who are selected for membership development tend to have the least experience in the industry; it is imperative then that they be thoroughly trained, knowledgeable not only about convention and visitor bureaus but also about the dynamics and issues facing the tourism industry as a whole. They have to be well indoctrinated, but that is only part of their necessary training. They also must acquire a thorough knowledge and understanding of their business community—the types of businesses, their leadership and how they interrelate with one another. For this reason, transfer from one bureau to another is not as easy for membership staff as it is for sales and executive personnel. But this kind of knowledge makes them a valuable bureau resource which can influence greatly the community's perceptions of the bureau. Regardless of where they are or what they are doing, creative and motivated membership salespersons will make an opportunity out of every social and business contact, whether a breakfast meeting, a concert or a casual evening on the town. Knowing who to call is the most efficient and effective means for developing a qualitative and supportive bureau membership.

Membership salespersons also must be credible; they reflect the bureau and its level of professionalism. It is important that they be respected and have a reputation for integrity. Experience as a product salesperson does not necessarily mean a salesperson will be effective or believable in membership sales.

Selling means not only asking and obtaining a commitment, it also means doing what might be best for the prospect. The membership salesperson must be a sensitive listener, seeking to understand what it is the prospect seeks and whether it can be obtained through an investment in the bureau. Though it doesn't occur often, declining a membership investment may be necessary at times. Reasons that may precipitate such an action might include the following: the business is new and not well established and needs a longer track record (e.g. tour company emerging in a competitive environment); a company which refuses to invest in the bureau according to the bureau's investment portfolio; or a company that has performed unethically. The reputation of the bureau is important, and the quality of its membership will impact that perception.

Among traits that a bureau might seek in a membership sales person are the following: organization skills (for maintaining and tracking of prospects and clients); stamina (to maintain the required day-to-day year-round performance of soliciting membership investments); courtesy and common sense (respecting others and thinking through what and how calls need to be handled); and a strong ego (accepting the challenges of the position but being able to handle rejections that come when investment opportunities are declined).

Compensation for membership personnel varies among bureaus. Many bureaus place such personnel on salary, and consider them a vital part of their "team." The advantage is that they are guaranteed a basis for living while memberships might be cyclical; the disadvantage is that without an incentive they may not work as hard in securing membership investments. Of course, a salaried position could be modified to include an incentive program that is based on a commission or formula for attaining members. Another common method of compensation is by direct commission, the advantage being that the person earns in direct proportion to the amount of work expended in securing membership investments. The disadvantage of straight commission is that a membership person may not wish to do other related tasks unless they are directly related to sales.

Whatever the method of compensation, membership sales personnel are critical to the financial stability of the bureau as well as to its standing in the community. Their professionalism is directly correlated to the stature of the bureau and its leadership.

Summary

Membership marketing creates a broad awareness of bureau programs and its mission throughout the community; successful recruitment of members also provides the bureau with strong advocates and a stable financial setting. The bureau serves its community as a marketing organization that seeks to enhance the economic vitality of a community. In return for those efforts, membership investments demonstrate the confidence a community has in bureau programs. Classifications for membership and investment schedules may vary considerably among bureaus, but regardless of the type of membership program, bureaus benefit through the talents and resources that members bring with their investments. Memberships are more than dues; memberships are investments—investments in the present and investments for the future.

Discussion Questions

1. Are we playing a game of semantics when using the terms "dues" and "investments"? Does one reflect a better image than the other?

2. Why should a business invest in a bureau's programs? Develop a series of reasons for making an investment for the following: hotels, restaurants, travel agencies, airlines, cruise lines, attractions, retail businesses, corporations.

3. How can a bureau that receives funds through room tax revenues justify to prospective members their need to invest in a bureau?

4. How can a membership committee help a bureau develop its membership program?

5. Develop a list of questions that identify various motivations for investing in a bureau. Identify each question as to the type of motivational premise it suggests.

6. What are some reasons why a membership should be retained in a bureau?

7. Develop an interviewing schedule of questions, and identify the kinds of talents or skills they are to elicit (e.g. stamina, ego, courtesy, etc.) for a membership salesperson.

Bibliographic Resources

1. Patrick, Georgia Lakaytis, "Member Marketing Plans," *Executive Update,* September 1987, pp. 39–45.

2. "Membership Promotion: What's New? What's Old?" *Elected Leader,* 1987, pp. 23–27.

3. "Membership Development and Maintenance," pp. 121–137, and "Motivating Members and Employees," pp. 139–157, in *Principles of Association Management* (Washington, D.C.: American Society of Association Executives, 1975).

4. "Membership Directors Shirt Sleeve Conference, Bureau Comparison Survey, 1986," unpublished manuscript.

COMMUNICATIONS MARKETING

8

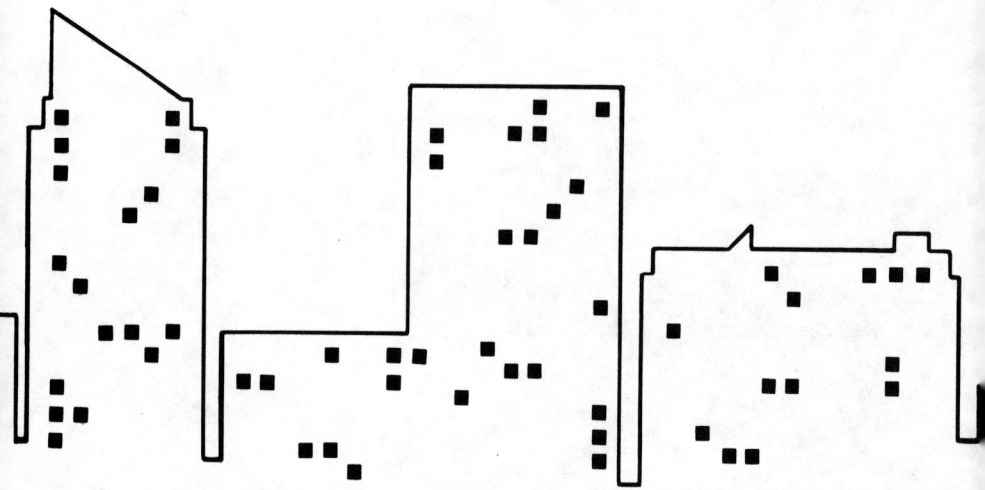

LEARNING OBJECTIVES

Upon reading this chapter, you will learn the following:

- About the complexities of communications marketing and its importance to a convention and visitor bureau;

- About the symptoms of ineffective community relations, the axioms and techniques for implementing effective community relations programs;

- About the need for an effective public relations program for a convention and visitor bureau;

- About the need for establishing program objectives, conducting a public relations audit, and the techniques that can be used in a public relations program;

- About the resources available for the development of a public relations effort;

- And about the need for and techniques that might be used to assess the effectiveness of a public relations program.

Introduction

Too often, we tend to dismiss the importance of communications. Because we all can speak and hear, we assume that when we transmit a message to another, it is accurately received and the recipient listened without distraction. That is a naive assumption. Communications is much like a kaleidoscope, with changing images and patterns, beautiful yet very complex. For convention and visitor bureaus, communication becomes an even more complicated process. As an organization, the bureau is competing for attention similar to many other organizations; without a clear sense of purpose and a well-developed communications program, the bureau cannot distinguish its message from the many others that flood the communication channels.

Bureaus are always attempting to establish and confirm their credibility as destination marketing organizations; attaining this credibility in the eyes of many diverse audiences makes the mission of the bureau easier to attain. But often, bureaus do not have a well-established image within the community and thus the community's expectations for a bureau are less than what a bureau is able to deliver. Bureaus also have difficulty with levels of expectations; without an understanding of what a bureau is and can do, the community may not be aware of what a bureau can accomplish. This can, in part, be overcome by involving people in various phases of planning and development, including boards, committees and special programs. Through involvement, a bureau can enhance its credibility, creating greater expectations about what it can and will accomplish as a marketing organization.

As suggested, information alone will not increase the stature of a bureau within its community; it takes the involvement of people. Like any communication behavior, the bureau must overcome competing messages to position its importance in the economic life of the community; develop understanding as to its mission and need for program and financial support through mutually acceptable agreements; and be seen as an acceptable catalyst for action that will, through its marketing endeavors, generate new sources of revenue by bringing into that community meetings, group tours and visitors from outside the area.

The dynamics of effective communications marketing requires skilled leadership that understands the challenges of the marketplace, senses trends and opportunities and is able to effectively communicate those observations to various constituents. This process requires a visionary leader with strong human communication skills. It also requires an understanding of the communication process itself, that it is complex, subject to change and multidimensional, including cultural, sociological and psychological variables.

Communications marketing is an effective way of dividing and examining those communication behaviors in which a bureau must engage if it is to develop an identity and image. This chapter will examine, as a part of communications marketing, both community relations and public relations. Community relations are isolated because of their tremendous importance and affect upon the effectiveness of a bureau. Without the undivided attention and support of its destination community, a bureau cannot be a successful marketing organization.

Community Relations

As we explore some dimensions of community relations, it will be placed into a framework represented by the acrostic, "S.A.T." The S.A.T. represents understanding the (a) *s*ymptoms of terminal community relations, (b) *a*xioms for developing better community relations, and (c) *t*echniques for implementing effective community relations.

Symptoms

Like the medical profession, one cannot prescribe a remedy without a diagnosis of the symptoms that determine the nature and extent of the illness. The same kind of principle can apply to community relations. To better understand what might be symptomatic of poor or terminal community relations, the following symptoms are offered for consideration.[1]

1. Does the community have a misunderstanding about the purpose, mission and operations of the convention and visitor bureau? Communities vary considerably in size and it may be necessary to place this question into a perspective that segments the community. For example, do those who are involved with visitors understand the mission and operation of a convention and visitor bureau? It is important that there be an understanding as to the bureau's primary program objective, to solicit group business and to generate new revenues for the community. The bureau requires support and an identity to accomplish its goal, and there must be an awareness of this throughout the community to enable the bureau to network, gain support and obtain coverage of its marketing activities. Although the bureau exists within a community, its marketing activities are focused outside the community, attempting to bring visitors into the community. The bureau provides its community that critical presence in competitive marketplaces.

2. Does the bureau have difficulty networking with community agencies for special projects? Respect is required to negotiate mutually beneficial arrangements for programs, special events and other marketing activities. If a bureau cannot obtain that kind of support, a major problem in community relations exists.

3. Does the bureau find it difficult to obtain support for convention bids from local chapters and members of associations? Many times, a bid is enhanced by having support from local chapters and members; without this kind of cooperation, the bureau is less than totally effective in its bidding procedures. Therefore, it is important that the bureau maintain a reputation that encourages local association chapters and members to want to support its convention bids.

4. Is the funding of the convention and visitor bureau diverted to non-convention and non-tourism projects? When this is done, it may be reflective of political processes which do not value the bureau as a destination marketing organization. Politicians always will attempt to satisfy divergent audiences which pull at them, and frequently this can be accomplished through allocation of funds such as the hotel occupancy or room tax, especially if governing legislation is permissive. The bureau has to be proactive, constantly bringing before such entities the importance of its programming along with clear accountablility. If a bureau is dependent solely on such public funds and diversions occur, needless to say, that bureau is unable to establish a quality program not subject to enormous pressures and change. A bureau can avert some of these pressures by having a qualitative and quantitative contract with governing political bodies that establish some stability in the level of funding, thus assuring the bureau that it can move forward without the fear of funds being lost. It should be noted that such groups as the National Association of Exposition Managers (NAEM) and the International Exhibitors Association (IEA) have taken a vocal stand for the use of room tax revenues to support convention bureau activities and not be diverted to other programs by political bodies; in fact, their memberships will remove from consideration, or not select, a specific destination for a convention if at least 50% of such funds are not used to support the marketing efforts of a convention and visitor bureau.

5. Does the bureau face the loss of other public funds? Though founded in 1896, convention and visitor bureaus do not always receive the respect they merit; as marketing organizations, they tend to be visible and vulnerable. Bureaus rely on a variety of funding sources, including public funds from grants. Grants are sometimes subject to competition and in other situations based on an allocation formula.

The former always means that the final allocation may be a portion of that sought based on the total sum available and/or the number and size of requests submitted. Public sector funding enhances the capabilities of a bureau and, in part, reflects the confidence those public bodies have in the mission and operations of a bureau. If the bureau is doing its job, documenting and sharing that information, then there should be sufficient public support for those endeavors to ensure their stability in markets that continue to grow in competition. It also must be noted that there has been a growth in bureau funding to ensure that it can adequately address these changing market trends. This growth is usually reflective of continued, if not increased, public support.

6. Has the private membership of the bureau stagnated or decreased? The strength of private memberships or investments reflects, in part, the confidence and commitment of the community to the bureau's programs. A vibrant bureau will have no difficulty in soliciting, gaining and retaining members; but if the bureau is ineffective, for whatever reasons, obtaining and retaining membership investments may be severely hampered. If programs are being fulfilled, there needs to be an effective communications of those ideas and successes. Such stories affirm members and their investment and assure the bureau of continued investments.

7. Are the hotels/motels dissatisfied with the bureau's program of work? Bureaus must consider those immediately involved in the industry who compose the travel product for a destination. A program of work cannot be developed in isolation of those with a vested interest in its design and performance. It is difficult to satisfy everyone all the time, but it is necessary to allow all to provide input and observations as a program of work is being undertaken. Because hotels/motels feel the impact the quickest, they have to be included in the development of an annual program of work; and though they can be vocal, it must also be remembered that the bureau provides stability for the destination, while there is frequently significant turnover in hotel personnel. The bureau is not in competition with the hotels; quite the contrary, bureaus rely on a cooperative relationship in order to be effective in executing their annual program of work.

8. Does the bureau find it difficult to obtain media coverage or interest? This relationship will vary considerably too; larger bureaus which have communication personnel may be able to establish rapport with media representatives more effectively than smaller bureaus which do not have such dedicated personnel. But there are many other factors, as well, which can impact media relations; a bureau that is part of a parent organization such as a chamber of commerce or a governmental unit may have difficulty in establishing a separate identity and

therefore may not receive the media attention it wishes, particularly as it relates to specific marketing activities. On the other hand, such a relationship may generate more effective media relations. It is difficult to categorically state that any one situation may contribute to more or less effective relationships with the media. But generally speaking, if a bureau, regardless of its structure or size or staffing, continues to be frustrated in its media relations, it is apparent that there is not a good image as to its purpose, mission and operations. Media support is necessary in sharing the importance of its programs with the community.

9. Does the bureau have the support and involvement of major corporations? This becomes a particularly important issue for large bureaus which have private membership investments; but even without such investments, a bureau needs to have the support of its business community, as well as any other defined groups such as the arts or university community, in order to accomplish its task of coordinating those resources which support convention and tourism programs. Of course, the support may come in the fashion of financial investments or in-kind donations to the bureau's efforts. Such resources are important in insuring the achievement of marketing goals. Such investments also will be easier to obtain when there is an energetic program that projects positive and affirming results. Each bureau has to determine in what manner these results are to be quantified and how frequently they are to be shared with members as well as the community in general.

10. Is the bureau confronted with legislation that fails to take into consideration its impact on the convention and tourism industry? Often, political solutions may be sought that have implications on the convention and tourism industry but which are not immediately seen; how visible a bureau is may mitigate such legislative efforts and provide a qualitative look at the economic importance of conventions and related group business.

11. Does the bureau appear on listings of community agencies or sources of information on the community? For many, this may not be a problem, but if a bureau is frequently overlooked for such listings, it may reflect again a lack of an image that establishes its value and credibility to that community. Constantly monitoring such listings and reminding compilers that the bureau should be included is the least that can and should be undertaken to rectify such oversights.

There may be other identifiable symptoms suggesting difficult community relations. Regardless of the size, stature, structure or successes of a bureau, effectively networking and communicating the bureau's message is an expectation that must be accepted and vigorously pursued.

Axioms

Now that the "symptoms" have been generally identified, the axioms begin to specify those kinds of programming efforts that must be considered and undertaken by bureaus if they are to be effective in developing positive community relations. Of course, the actual setting in which a bureau operates will, in part, influence which or how well any of these axioms can be implemented, but they serve as a useful starting point.

1. First, the convention and visitor bureau needs to include in its annual marketing plan specific objectives and strategies for community relations. By establishing goals and outlining program strategies, a bureau can assign its resources, both financial and personnel, to insure that those objectives are attained on schedule. This also gives community relations a priority among all the other marketing endeavors and clearly establishes an agenda for the bureau within its own community.

2. The bureau should consider carefully the composition of its board of directors and allow that board to be the basis of community outreach. This may mean that some board seats are specifically designated for certain community groups, such as representatives for the arts, university, attractions, regional business communities, political entities or others to insure a broad representation. Such a dedication of board seats may be formalized in the bureau's by-laws or made a board policy. By taking such an action, the board becomes a distinctively distributed body which can serve a vital role and link in developing positive community relations.

3. The bureau may wish to establish a community relations committee. In fact, this is almost an imperative. Such a visitor industry council can provide the bureau with tremendous support, provide insights and recommendations for programs and serve as a voice for the bureau's programs throughout the community. Bureau volunteer leadership can be a valued asset in establishing credibility for the bureau and seeing that its story is told often.

4. The bureau should use board members and membership volunteers as much as possible for community relation purposes. Too frequently, the paid staff are perceived as having a special interest; but when volunteers are mobilized, the bureau can be far more effective in having its story told to the community. Volunteers also lend important credibility to the bureau's programs through their own stature within the community. What better way to affect perceptions than to have respected community leaders telling the story. When engaged in such community relations activities, such volunteers need to have visibility.

Depending on the circumstances, this recognition might include reference to their involvement with the bureau in a speech introduction, use of their names on bureau letterhead, serving as a spokesperson for the bureau when making pertinent presentations; they might be provided with business cards that indicate bureau board membership, recognizable lapel pins, uniforms or casual wear that can be worn when engaged in social functions. The bureau's volunteers are its most effective tool for developing positive community relations.

5. Most bureaus produce a newsletter. Their schedule may fluctuate—some are monthly, others bi-monthly. The newsletter can carry important information about bureau programs and their development. It can introduce new bureau members, announce recently held or booked conventions, highlight special events or activities, and provide other pertinent information. The newsletter serves as an important communications link between the bureau and the community; it also may be used as a marketing tool, mailed to targeted planners to share with them the things that are happening within that community in the hope that an awareness of such activity will reflect favorably on the destination's potential as a future meeting or tour site. Newsletters share information, keep individuals informed of programs and program accomplishments, stimulate interest and aid in the development of an allegiance to the bureau's mission and purposes.

6. Bureaus should develop a consistent message to their communities through the use of terms that represent the significance of what a bureau is able to accomplish. Key words that are easily recognizable are important in developing credibility for the bureau; these words might include: "economic development," "economic vitality," "economic impact," "employment opportunities," "tax benefits" and words of similar significance. Bureaus are marketing organizations, but their activities have an economic impact. That message must be clearly and consistently related to the bureau's board, membership and community. Investments in a bureau support the economic vitality of a community; marketing is necessary in order to establish a market presence that will allow the completion of a sale. The hosting of a convention or tour affects the host hotel and convention center, but it also impacts the community at large through delegate expenditures and subsequent tax revenues. Capturing the significance of these transactions is important, but it is also necessary to share that information with the surrounding community, particularly the community leadership.

Telling the bureau's story may seem mundane or repetitious, but the message must be stated again and again. Sometimes a particular event will occur that highlights just how economically significant the industry is. For example, a corporation may move its training resources into a community, requiring hundreds of its employees to spend a week at a time over a year or two year period, staying at hotels, eating at restaurants and utilizing retail outlets. The bureau can capitalize on such an investment by sharing with the media the significance of such an activity in room-nights, economic impact and image development. A major association's annual convention and trade show may be secured involving 20,000 delegates for a four day period; this offers the bureau the opportunity to again preach the economic significance of having such groups in the community. Whatever the situation, if it is newsworthy, the bureau needs to capitalize on it to ensure that the impact message is accurately related to the community, and in turn, the community sees the need for a vital and energetic bureau. In order to accomplish this, there are certain techniques which a bureau might employ for effective community relations.

Techniques

When the bureau begins to develop its plan of work and the strategies to be employed to reach the association or tour markets, it has to first divide those general, broad markets into viable segments for specific appeals. One message cannot be employed effectively to all markets segments; what might appeal to medical groups may not appeal to major trade shows or tour planners. The same principle applies to community relations. Effective techniques can be employed by a bureau to enhance its image within the community, but the community must first be divided into segments with which the bureau can work. Among these segments might be included: educational community, arts and cultural organizations, public sector or governmental organizations, major corporations and the private business sector, hotels and the hospitality industry and any other easily identifiable segment. Techniques employed for one market segment may be found useful in others, thus overlapping. But to segment allows some market-specific efforts to be undertaken that lend credibility to the bureau and enhance its overall community image (see figure 8.1).

1. *The Educational Community.* This is not restricted to communities with colleges and universities; it involves all communities because of their high school and technical college systems. Techniques that a bureau might employ to enhance its image and relationships with educational institutions include the following.

a. Volunteer to serve as a guest lecturer; this might involve economic classes, career education classes or travel and tourism classes. Students become more informed not only about what a bureau is and does, but also the importance of the travel and tourism industry as a whole.

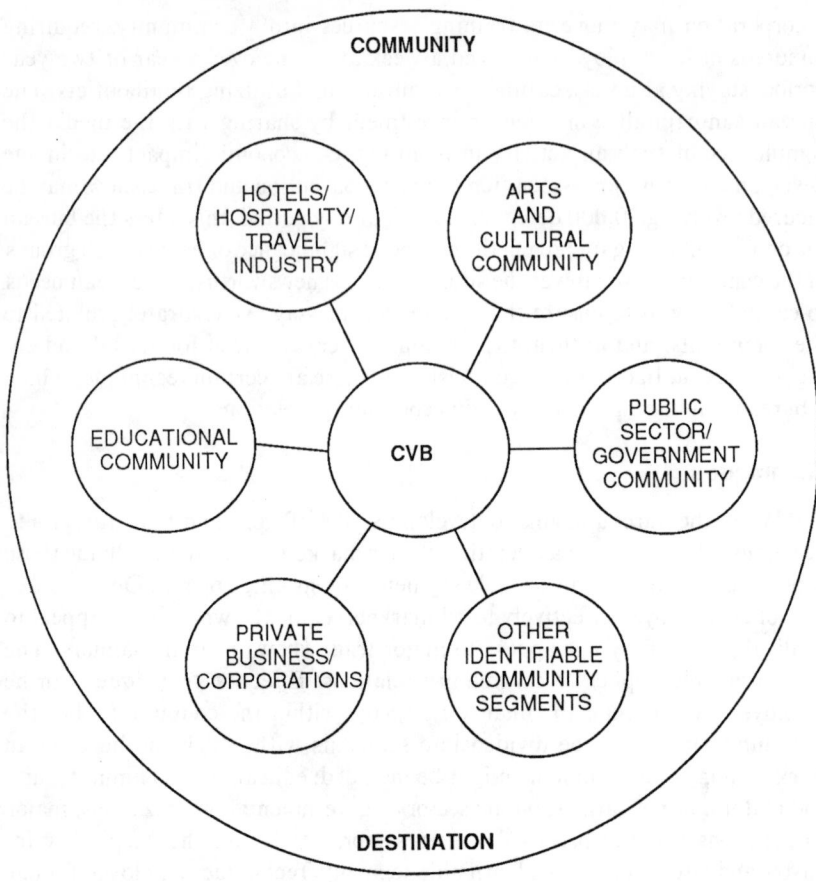

Figure 8.1

b. The bureau might support scholarships for local students enrolled in a culinary arts, hotel management, travel and tourism or similar program. This nurtures rapport between the bureau and those educational institutions and lends credibility to educational endeavors.

c. Bureaus also can benefit by investigating potential internships with various departments such as marketing, journalism, advertising, computer sciences, hotel management, business administration, travel and tourism or similar programs. Students frequently are required to complete a required number of hours as part of their undergraduate program and are seeking internships to provide such an opportunity. The internships should not be seen as an opportunity to have a "gopher" on staff but as a means of mutually reaching established goals. For the student, it is exposure to the industry that might not otherwise be obtained; for the bureau, it means having a qualified candidate participate actively in the bureau's programs. Such internships might specifically involve research projects, qualifying sales accounts, staffing visitor information centers, writing press releases and preparing media kits, designing and writing publications or providing computer assistance. The options are many and valuable to both parties. Secondary institutions frequently have cooperative clerical training programs which can, to some degree, be of tremendous value to a bureau seeking support staff.

d. The bureau may find working with an educational institution of value in distributing informational materials to visiting parents, faculty, sports teams, summer camp participants or at freshmen orientations.

e. The bureau also may wish to work closely with alumni groups; through such groups, the bureau might identify individuals who would be influential in bringing group meetings or tours to the community.

f. Creatively, a bureau can design discovery tour programs for local historical points of interests, sites or homes, attractions, cultural events, and art institutions for inclusion in school curriculums. Such endeavors have to be coordinated with faculty as well as curriculum specialists for the appropriate school systems. One example is to use a map with locations and distances as part of a planned math exercise; it teaches not only geography, but also math skills.

g. The bureau may be wise to include key leaders from the educational community on its board; such professionals will offer useful insights as well as serve as advocates of bureau programs. They also can coordinate the relationships between the bureau and educational institutions.

2. *Arts and Cultural Organizations.* In its marketing endeavors, the bureau serves as the umbrella destination marketing organization for a community, particularly as it applies to groups and visitors. It is important that a bureau work closely with the arts and cultural organizations in providing an atmosphere and quality of life that contributes to a community's appeal. Specific steps might include the following:

a. Sponsoring a marketing seminar for the arts to demonstrate ways the arts community can market effectively to tourists. Such a program was undertaken by the San Francisco Convention and Visitors Bureau (California) and opened creative communication channels between those in the arts community and those dealing with visitors.

b. Serving as an umbrella organization for producing an ongoing calendar of arts events; this might be a separate piece or included in a periodic calendar of events. Such an effort also might include a recorded message that lists current arts events.

   c. Developing tour packages that focus on offerings from the arts and cultural communities; such events might be theatre performances, musical performances, special festivals or walking tours of the visual arts. The Ann Arbor Convention and Visitors Bureau (Michigan) has developed several tours focusing on the arts which have enhanced the image and quality of that community. One such tour package had a French flavor, embracing dinner at a French restaurant and tickets for a performance by mime artist Marcel Marceau.

   d. Hosting familiarization tours for both meeting and tour planners; including arts attractions among sites visited enhances the offering of the arts community and opens the door for creative planning (example, hosting a reception at the local art museum).

   e. Holding board meetings throughout the year at local arts attractions exposes everyone to their value.

   f. Placing a key representative of the arts community on the board, thus providing the opportunity for mutually supportive roles.

   g. Depending on the nature of the bureau's advertising program, developing a cooperative advertising program with the arts community directed at meeting and tour planners. Such a program was developed in Canada and involved the Toronto Convention and Visitors Bureau. If advertising is not a major agenda item for the bureau, it may be involved in other promotional efforts such as auctions, give-aways or door prizes; using an art object as a gift can serve a bureau well. The Lincoln Convention and Visitors Bureau (Nebraska) used a sculpture as a trade show give-away.

   h. Depending on the existing levels of community activity, a bureau may wish to propose the development of an arts festival or special event to be coordinated through an arts agency or in cooperation with the bureau. Such events require considerable time in establishing a viable agenda as well as obtaining appropriate financial support; bureau staffing is usually not sufficient to handle the coordination of such events. It is recommended that a broader, community supported structure be given responsibility for administration and operations; the bureau can provide invaluable marketing expertise and would not have suggested such a development unless there was perceived to be a need and resources for it.

   3. *The Public Sector and Government Organizations.* It has been stated previously that bureau executives are marketers who manage in a political environment. Political leadership needs to be informed and worked so it becomes supportive of bureau programs. Among some techniques that might be employed to reach and work with public sector and governmental organizations are the following.

a. Political leaders should receive the bureau's newsletter regularly to keep them informed of key events and activities and to enhance their perception of the value of the bureau to the community.

b. The bureau regularly should invite the political leadership to all bureau functions and events, especially social events, familiarization tours, sales blitzes and receptions. Their involvement in such events benefits the perception of the bureau by those involved (especially planners), as well as providing the bureau with an opportunity to demonstrate the effectiveness of its marketing endeavors.

c. Not only should the community's political leaders receive the newsletter, they should also receive a copy of the annual report, convention calendar and publications as they are revised and reprinted. This again draws attention to the bureau. They may even be provided a quantity of the bureau's publications for use and distribution through their offices.

d. When bidding for conventions and trade shows, use solicitation letters or letters of invitation from various political leaders; having the Mayor, City Council members, or even the Governor supporting a bid can be impressive and important to the image the bureau wishes to project. Further, it integrates their interests with those of the bureau. The list of those who might be included on such a resource list will depend on the local area; include local, regional, state and federal elected representatives when considering invitation letters.

e. Many times, incoming convention groups will seek welcoming remarks from the Mayor or someone of equal stature for their opening ceremony or convocation. Develop rapport with the elected political leadership and learn who is willing to address such groups; it may even be necessary for the bureau to prepare those remarks, but that is not important. The important issue is having an elected official serve as a spokesperson for the bureau and the community in welcoming a convention to town. This provides the bureau with an opportunity to advise that spokesperson as to the economic importance of such a group and its value to the community. In the end, all benefit.

f. Provide elected officials with easily understood statistical information regarding the importance of meetings and tourism; such a booklet was prepared by the Sydney Convention and Visitors Bureau (Australia) and graphically demonstrates the economic impact of groups. Figure 8.2 is a sample of several pages from that booklet. There is no question that elected officials are literally pulled in diverse directions by their constituents; and it is important that those community, regional, state and federal elected officials understand not only the mission of the bureau but its impact on the economic vitality of their

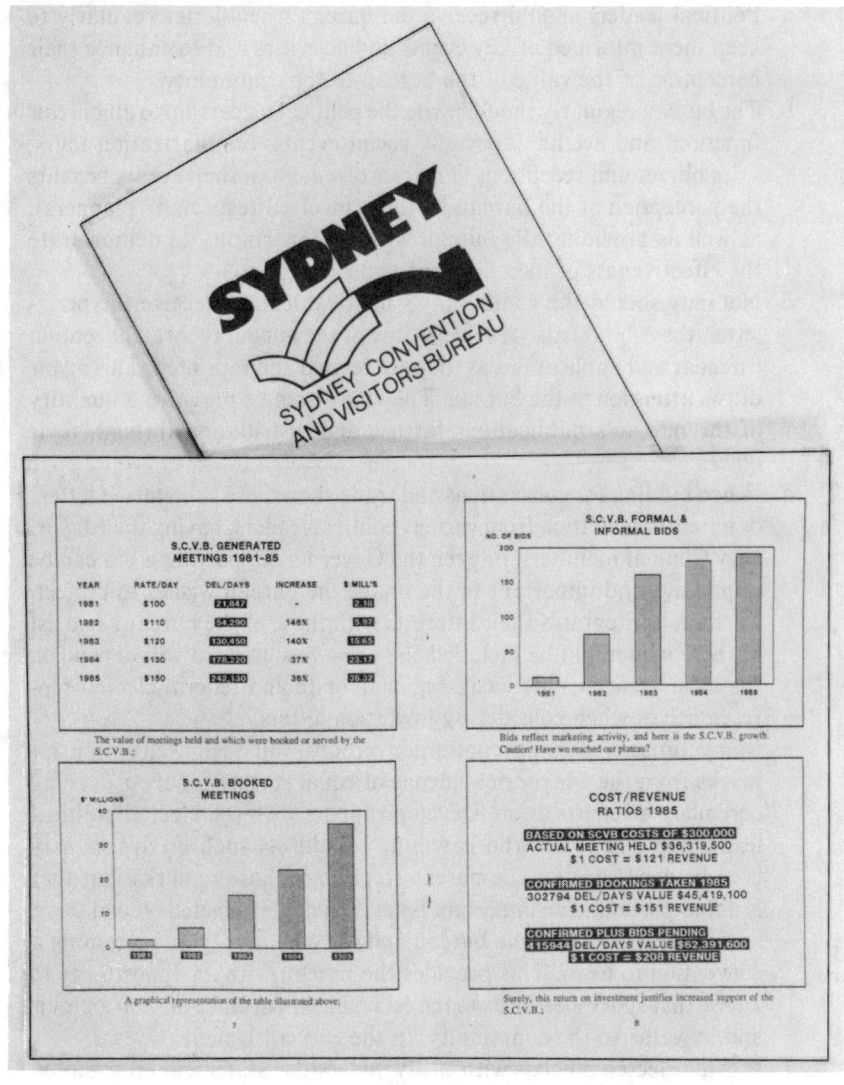

Figure 8.2

community. There is no better way to address this than by sharing with them in a clear and concise manner, similar to the Sydney example, just what the economics of the business means to their community.

g. Recognizing elected officials can be an advantage to the bureau, particularly if they have taken an assertive role in supporting the bureau and the travel industry and/or in encouraging economic growth for their area. "Ambassador" awards can be given to them and also to non-elected industry and volunteer leaders at the bureau's annual dinner function.

h. One way to insure a liaison with elected officials is to develop a Government Relations Committee composed of volunteers from the membership as well as from bureau board members. This committee can serve as a forum for discussions on specific legislative matters. In addition, the committee provides a means for elected officials to transmit concerns for consideration and if necessary, potential recommendations for action by the board.

i. When dealing with other public agencies, the bureau should encourage inclusion of designated bureau personnel and board members on key committees that might influence the events and activities of the community. Such committees might include festival or special events (example, art festival, bicentennial committee, annual bike race or marathon); economic development (example, convention center development, urban development, downtown development authority, waterfront improvement); or those that deal with issues of civic pride (example, ethnic/neighborhood celebrations, park celebrations, historic site commemorative). The bureau should be sensitive to the character of each committee and to the capabilities of its staff in accomplishing its fundamental mission and programs; in many cases, the bureau can provide wise marketing counsel to these committees and organizations, thereby enhancing its stature within the community through a spirit of cooperation and assistance.

j. The media represent a key liaison needed to insure that the bureau's message is communicated to the community; having a media representative on the bureau's board is highly recommended as is establishing a media relations committee which can assist the bureau in meeting with and maintaining a positive profile among local, regional and state media representatives.

k. Knowing and remembering key anniversaries and birthdays for elected and key non-elected officials is another way the bureau can maintain a positive profile within the community. Caring enough to remember their interests is a powerful affirmation of the bureau's desire to maintain quality relationships among its diverse constituents.

l. Though bureau members may receive a listing of the membership, it is important to remember to send a copy of this document to elected and key non-elected officials to show the broad base of community support. This may be accomplished with a simple letter of courtesy indicating a desire on the part of the bureau to keep them informed of who bureau investors are and what those investments mean for the total program.

Of course, there may be additional creative techniques that can be employed to keep public sector organizations and elected officials informed of what the bureau is all about. The simple truth is that the message must be repeatedly stated to insure that it gets through the competition and is noticed and appreciated by those to whom it is targeted.

4. *The Private Sector and Major Corporations.* The convention and visitor bureau must maintain its liaison with the private sector if it is to be successful in accomplishing its stated mission and program objectives. The private sector can provide considerable flexibility to the bureau not only with and through its volunteers but also with and through its financial investments. Therefore, it is fundamental that a solid community relations program be developed, focusing on the value and benefits of private sector business involvement with the bureau.

> a. Depending on the bureau's organizational structure, it is important that the bureau be an active member of the area chamber of commerce and be represented either by board members or key volunteers on various chamber committees, such as marketing or legislative. The bureau also should plan to address the chamber annually to share its mission and programs. Many chambers have "soap box breakfasts" at which the bureau can make such a presentation. If the bureau is a division of the chamber, the principle still applies. Even more important is bureau representation on the chamber's general board of directors as well as representation on the executive committee. This insures full communication about the bureau's programs among the leadership of the chamber.
>
> b. Similar to that which was recommended for elected and key non-elected officials, a bureau can develop a program to recognize members of the private sector for their support of travel and hospitality programs within the community. Such awards may be granted at the bureau's annual dinner. Companies that contribute large sums over a considerable time span or which sponsor or underwrite key bureau programs need to be recognized publicly and saluted. There may be other volunteers who give of their time and talents in support of bureau programs, and they, too, should be annually saluted. The Fairbanks Convention and Visitors Bureau (Alaska) developed such an awards program to bring about greater public awareness of its activities as well as to thank those who supported the bureau and the industry.
>
> c. It is important that the bureau ensure that its message is told before as many groups as possible throughout the year; community, civic and church groups are always seeking speakers for their programs. Having a dynamic visual presentation can excite the audience and greatly enhance the image of the bureau within the community.

d. The bureau should insure that press releases, as well as the newsletter, are sent to the editors of key business and corporate publications within the community. Frequently a story is picked up from a newsletter and leads to additional interviews. It is important that all channels of communication be inventoried and that the bureau's economic impact and marketing activities are communicated to all audiences.

e. When working with large corporations, the bureau also must respond to their needs and interests. In some cases, they may not wish to have any major publicity about a key sponsorship. On the other hand, most corporations seek a stronger profile within their communities and if they are involved in sponsoring a key bureau program, they no doubt will want to be recognized and publicly saluted. Such sponsorships might involve funding an audio-visual presentation; sponsoring a board room (such an activity was accomplished at the Atlanta Convention and Visitors Bureau) and having the company name placed on that room; sponsoring an information center and having the company name placed on that center (such was accomplished by the Denver Convention and Visitors Bureau); or participating in and underwriting a new festival or special event for the community.

f. When working with public sector agencies, using key chief executive officers on behalf of the bureau may be more effective than using bureau staff. Having the support and influence of the private sector has its advantage; using bureau staff might be seen as self-serving while the use of more influential corporate chief executives may insure a more assertive and effective means for handling key issues and result in more positive reactions. Using such supportive talent is also an asset to the bureau and relieves the staff of tremendous pressures.

g. When soliciting membership investments from major corporations, it is essential that any special reception be of the quality and caliber their targeted chief executives would expect; having key corporate business members present would provide tremendous credibility among invited chief executives. Being sensitive to the corporations' particular needs and stroking them accordingly is another way to demonstrate professionalism.

5. *Hotels/Hospitality—Travel Industry.* Bureaus are a part of this dynamic industry, and it may be taken for granted that members of this industry automatically know and understand what the bureau does and how it accomplishes its programs. That is a grossly inaccurate assumption. Hotels tend to have a high turnover of personnel, thus what might be understood by staff today may not be the case tomorrow. That is but one example. Because 98%

of the travel industry tends to be composed of small businesses, there are many within the industry who do not perceive themselves as part of "an industry" and thus they tend to ignore or lack interest in what the bureau undertakes on behalf of its community. Several steps might be undertaken to mitigate this.

a. Over a year, it might be advantageous for the bureau executive or the top leadership of the bureau to meet with the general managers of the hotels or other travel related businesses, sharing with them information about the bureau and/or seeking their input regarding their role in meeting bureau goals. If individual meetings are not feasible, another more advantageous format must be sought to encourage communication and involvement. It may be felt that once this is done the job is completed, but the bureau must monitor the turnover among such positions and meet with new personnel upon their arrival in the community.

b. Members of the community's travel industry should receive the newsletter. It may be to the advantage of the bureau, if something special was noted either as an enclosure to that newsletter or within the newsletter itself, to entice particular interest and involvement in specific bureau programs. Some bureaus will feel that this is an inconvenience and that bureau members should be treated equally; there is no question that that principle is correct. But if a bureau finds a lack of interest or involvement from those who benefit the most from its programs, then assertive means are needed to draw attention to the value of bureau programs and what they are missing when not involved.

c. Sometimes a bureau establishes advisory committees on which members of the travel industry are seated; it is within that forum that ideas and input are sought and/or their involvement is encouraged. This may, in some cases, prove to be a very effective means for reaching out and involving bureau members.

d. Just because they are part of the industry does not mean bureau supporters should get less recognition for their time, talents and efforts; in fact, when planning an annual dinner and identifying potential awards, those within the industry should be among those reviewed, recognized and saluted for their contributions.

e. The bureau's newsletter may wish to focus on key developments happening within the industry. If there are no new developments, an article focusing on a hotel, convention facility, key trade show, meeting planner, group tour or the like could be an appropriate way of integrating individual industry interests with those of the bureau. Such articles indicate to meeting and tour planners the strength of the area, drawing their attention to what is happening and/or is available.

f. The bureau also may wish to hold special training for hospitality personnel; with turnover so great, one way of enhancing their effectiveness is to provide a program that orients them to the community and presents insights into a service attitude. The Boise Convention and Visitors Bureau (Idaho) developed such a "Host" program for its hospitality industry and community.

It is obvious how important community relations are to a bureau; though the bureau's main efforts are outside the area drawing group business into the area, it is important that the local community not be ignored. It is its support and investment that allow the bureau to accomplish its annually stated goals and programs. It is the quality of the tourism product and convention facilities that entice the meeting and tour planner; the quality of the destination itself attracts attention and interest. When there is a dynamic bureau which demonstrates positive and effective relationships among its many diverse constituents, it is likely to have an influence on a meeting or tour planner. The strength of a bureau lies in its relationships with its community; without a good relationship, the bureau lacks a key attribute for effective marketing. Needless to say, there may be plenty of other ideas regarding ways to work with and encourage support from various community segments; each bureau must be creative and responsive to its own particular setting to remain viable. It is hoped that the foregoing suggestions will stimulate additional ideas of equal or greater benefit.

Public Relations

Public relations can generally be described as all those things that a bureau does that can be interpreted as projecting the most positive, honest and accurate image possible to the general public about the organization.[2] The bureau always is eager to develop programs that will gain the broadest acceptance.[3] Similar to community relations, there is a need to develop credibility and goodwill with one's constituents; public relations has become an essential, if not critical bureau function.[4] What composes public relations functions may vary considerably among bureaus but might be summarized as every means of communication, every impression made and every message delivered, including:

- The voice quality and attitude of the person answering the bureau's telephones;
- The graphics and appearance of bureau stationery;
- The graphics and quality of the newsletter produced monthly or periodically by the bureau, including consistency of graphics, layout and perceived value of the included stories and information;

- Thematic and graphic consistency among various publications produced by and through the bureau and whether they project a unified image for the bureau;
- The quality of media presentations reflecting the professionalism of the bureau;
- The quickness of responses to letters or telephone inquiries for information. This also applies to the responsiveness of bureau staff to telephone calls from planners, community representatives, peers and other constituents;
- The responsiveness of the bureau to member requests for advertising graphics, slides or other promotional materials;
- Professionalism in staging and executing seminars, conventions, trade shows or other programs that bring attention to the bureau as a sponsor;
- The quality of the exhibition booth and representation of the bureau at trade shows;
- The timeliness of press releases with current and worthy news items about bureau programs and developments;
- The quality of the bureau's annual report and its distribution to targeted constituents;
- The credibility of bureau staff when making a public presentation, presenting testimony before legislative bodies or representing the bureau on committees or other public forums;
- The quality, use and distribution of photographs taken and sponsored by the bureau.
- The rapport the Bureau has with print and nonprint media.

That is just a beginning; public relations involves considerably more, but by focusing on some of the essential dynamics, it demonstrates just how critical the public relations activities of a bureau are in developing and maintaining a viable image within its community, among its peers and within the marketplaces it targets. What then are the elements of a public relations program and how does a bureau examine what should or should not be included? The balance of this chapter will explore these considerations.

   1. *Program Objectives.* What should a bureau consider first when developing its public relations program? Not only does a bureau need to consider whether it can accomplish a public relations program, but how and with what resources. Similar to a marketing plan, it must first begin with what the objective or objectives for its public relations program should be. What is to be accomplished? Some of the "goals" or "objectives" might include the following phrases:[5]

- To keep the general public informed about . . .
- To heighten awareness of the bureau . . .

- To disseminate information about its services . . .
- To share information on the impact of . . .
- To gain a commitment to the bureau through . . .

These are only beginnings and reflect some of the possibilities that might be included in a public relations program.

2. *Program Audit.* It may seem like the inevitable chicken and egg controversy, but once a bureau has identified its program objectives, it is necessary to conduct what is commonly called an "audit". An audit is a means of looking at, examining, reviewing or monitoring existing programs. For example, figure 8.3 is a modification of a public relations audit presented at a seminar sponsored by the International Association of Convention & Visitor Bureaus. The audit requires a thoughtful analysis of practices, or lack of practices, by a bureau. The findings then become the foundation upon which public relations program goals and objectives can be designed or refined. The "audiences" with which a bureau must interact are then identified and how the bureau wishes to relate to each is carefully molded into a coherent program based on what has been revealed through the public relations audit.

Being objective with responses to the audit will benefit the bureau over the long term; that is the value of undertaking such a program analysis, for it identifies both strengths and areas that need program and staff attention.

Though there have been some suggestions as to potential phrases for goals, and though there has been a suggested form for a public relations audit, the audit does overlook one of the most important points of contact by a bureau, that being with the general public through the telephone operator/switchboard and/or receptionist. What impressions are received by those publics who call or come in contact with that front office person? Do they feel good about their encounter with that staff person? Do they have a good feeling about their encounter with the bureau? Is that person courteous and responsive to the person calling or walking into the office? Does the bureau appear professional in its dealing with people?

The intent of an audit is to examine all phases of the bureau's public relations activities; such activities far exceed how the bureau relates to the media or how frequently it issues press releases. It may be necessary for a bureau to go well beyond that in order to do a thoroughly reliable and credible assessment of its public relations activities.[6]

The audit is a form of research that provides useful insights for the bureau. Another aspect of such an audit is that of assessing the attitudes and images people hold of the destination. It must be remembered that the bureau, though desirous of favorable impressions and feelings about itself, is in the business of selling a destination, and knowing what and how people feel about that destination will impact not only the marketing program but also on the public

A PUBLIC RELATIONS ASSESSMENT FOR CONVENTION AND VISITOR BUREAUS

TARGET AUDIENCES	1 Why should this audience be interested in the Bureau?	2 What is the Bureau's goal for targeting this audience?	3 What message does the Bureau want to communicate?	4 By what means is the Bureau communicating its message?	5 What action does the Bureau wish the target audience to take?	6 Are there wa in which th Bureau can ex its message
CLIENTS • Meeting Planners • Assn Executives • Exhibition Mgrs • Group Tour Planners • Incentive Planners • Travel Agents • Repeat Convention Clients • Convention Delegates • Tourists/Visitors						
MEDIA • Media • Trade Press • Consumer Press • Magazines • Directories						
PRODUCT/SERVICES • Convention Center(s) • Hotels/Motels • Attractions • Local Services and Vendors						
LOCAL ORGANIZATIONS • Business Community • Educational Institutionals • Civic/Community Groups • Governmental Units						
BUREAU STRUCTURE • Board of Directors • Committees • Membership • Employees						
FINANCIAL SOURCES • Grants • Governmental Units • Foundations • Member Sponsorships • Other Sources						
OUTSIDE RELATIONS • Other Convention Bureaus • Other Regional/State Marketing Organizations • Trade Associations • Other Audiences						

Figure 8.3

relations efforts. The intent of any public relations effort is that of generating positive publicity; for the bureau, this has a two part meaning that covers not only the bureau itself but also the destination it represents. Knowing what images are held allows the bureau to address them in a positive manner.

Understanding not only what is being done and why, but also how people feel about a destination is part of the research that must be undertaken by a bureau if it is to develop a viable and credible public relations program. Once that is accomplished, a program can be outlined that will benefit the bureau and the destination it represents.

3. *Program Techniques.* The complexity of any public relations program will depend on the kinds of resources a bureau is willing to dedicate toward those efforts. The suggested public relations audit also will imply ways of reaching critical audiences the bureau wishes to influence. Public relations techniques may vary from audience to audience, and the intensity of their usage from bureau to bureau. The skill with which such techniques are used also will vary depending on the talents and competencies of those assigned such responsibilities. The public relations efforts of a bureau is not the area to which beginners are assigned; developing favorable images requires sophisticated personnel who enjoy working with diverse groups of people on behalf of the bureau. The techniques that are available are also varied and flexible and, when placed into a coherent program, can be useful in communicating the bureau's message.

As suggested by the title of this chapter, bureau communications are another aspect of marketing. Publicity is sharing with diverse audiences the program developments of the bureau. These efforts must be integrated into the total marketing plan developed annually for the bureau. The time and allocation of resources warrants careful planning and execution in order to enhance the images of the bureau and the destination it represents.

What are some of the events and activities through which a bureau can generate publicity:

- an announcement about a major convention or trade show selecting the city for a future date, including the economic significance of such an event;
- an announcement about major hotel or meeting facility expansions;
- an announcement of a major membership campaign or a new promotional campaign for the destination, which might include a press conference with visual aids and distribution of media kits;
- an announcement about the bureau's annual meeting, including economic impact statistics for the previous year and/or information about the major speaker or program;
- an announcement about a major familiarization tour or oversea trade mission, who is involved and what it will mean to the destination;
- announcements about new staff appointments, the publication of new brochures or research studies from the bureau or the availability of new services for meeting and tour planners.

Needless to say, there may be hundreds of other potential ideas that warrant being shared with various audiences. By sharing such information, the bureau establishes its importance and significance within its community as well as its credibility among its diverse constituents. Items prepared for promotional purposes must be timely (not released a month after the event), relevant (related to the audiences for which they are intended) and of interest (having some human interest or reason for wanting my attention). What then are those forms of travel publicity that a bureau can effectively use to tell its story?

Working with the Media

An important part of any bureau's publicity program is that of establishing mutual respect with media representatives, both print and electronic. For the most part, the media are under considerable pressure to meet deadlines; they may or may not have worthwhile materials to work with. This is where a bureau can be of assistance; the bureau can support and nurture the media by leading them to important stories or by giving them ideas upon which to base an article, feature or telecast. The bureau should never send the media a story that is not newsworthy. When this happens, it affects the respect and credibility of the bureau as a viable source for quality information. It must be remembered that if the bureau wishes to increase the awareness of the general public regarding bureau programs on behalf of the destination, it must first raise the awareness of the media. This takes an investment of time and a relationship in which there is mutual trust, respect and appreciation for one another's needs.[7]

When working with the media, there are certain guidelines to follow:

- Don't assume that the media understand or appreciate bureau programs; take the necessary time to explain them and to nurture productive relationships.
- Be assertive and take the initiative in sharing with the media information about bureau programs and concerns; provide them with accurate information about bureau performance or major developments. Demonstrate that the bureau is a reliable source of information about convention and tourism marketing activities.
- Invite the media to be present at major bureau functions and committee meetings; this is particularly useful for events such as the annual dinner, familiarization tours, kick-off ceremonies for a promotional campaign or similar activities. Allowing the media to participate in various committee meetings also may be beneficial, particularly if the issues at stake are significant, for example, the legislative concerns over tax deductibility of business meals.
- Provide the media with sufficient lead time when requesting story coverage and/or photographic coverage so their personnel can be scheduled efficiently; this well may increase your chances of media coverage.
- Prepare printed materials for the media in a professional manner, insuring that the information is complete, accurate and presented in an acceptable format. The easier the bureau makes it for the media, the

greater the likelihood that materials will be used. Editors do not have a lot of time to crawl through a mass of information looking for key points.

- Reciprocate when asked; if effective and mutually acceptable relationships are to be developed with the media, it is important that a bureau not only provide information but also follow through when the media request something. Trust is then developed.
- Do not assume that what the bureau wishes to release to print media will be effective with the electronic media. Target your materials to the type of media being selected. For electronic media, for example, include graphics and visuals that might be used along with the story.

Following are elaborations on specific publicity techniques which might be used by a convention and visitor bureau.

Press Releases

The press release is one of the most effective means of communicating messages on a regular basis. There is no guarantee that every release will be used, but through repetition, it may reflect to the media a level of activity that warrants greater attention. Press releases should adhere to the "K.I.S.S." principle, "Keep It Short and Sweet". The most important information should be carried at the top of the story, followed by specific details and elaborations. The first two lines should carry the critical "Who, What, When, Where, How and Why" information. Both sentences and paragraphs should be short; the release should be typed, double-spaced, on one side of white 8½ × 11 paper. If it exceeds one page, there should the phrase "more" at the bottom of the first page and "30" or "###" used at the end of the story. The bureau should include the release date as well as the person at the bureau to contact for further information. If photographs are included, they should be quality black and white prints, with identification and captions taped to the back of each. If the event is known in advance, photographic coverage by the media can be requested. When distributing releases, include not only community media sources but also travel trade media sources.

Press Kits

Several observations have been made about press kits and their contents. One set of observations indicates that such kits should only contain stories and photographs.[8] Another perspective seems to indicate that a press kit should contain not only stories and photographs but also background information, brochures, maps, business cards and other pertinent information. Sometimes press kits are referred to as Press Information Kits or Media Kits. The key point to remember is to remain flexible with the development of press or media kits; if the bureau is providing specific information about its performance over the past year, the stories and photographs in a press kit also should be specifically related. A more complex or detailed media kit may be forwarded to media representatives as an informational piece or in preparation for a familiarization tour of the area. In that particular situation, the kit serves as useful background material for the media and helps place such a visit in perspective.

Feature Articles

Because of their size, some bureaus are able to develop feature articles on their destinations through their own staffs; others may contract with a freelance writer to develop such in-depth materials. A feature is usually lengthier than a press release. For the bureau, a feature might provide information about some major event happening in its community, giving descriptive and detailed information. For example, articles might focus on specific arts, cultural events or festivals, seasonal events such as cider mills, the evolution of an historical attraction or an in-depth analysis of the community's convention facilities. Usually such articles will be featured in magazines or as a special article in a newspaper. Timelines for publications have to be considered when developing such materials. Feature articles can be seasonal or they might be tied into a special campaign being developed by the bureau.

Press Conferences

A press conference must be thoroughly warranted if it is to be a successful event. For example, announcing the performance statistics for the bureau for the past year may not warrant a press conference; yet, if the bureau is sponsoring an overseas trade mission or a familiarization tour of the area, bringing the participants before the press for interviews might be a worthwhile activity. Press conferences require thoughtful planning and execution; they should include brief but formal statements by the bureau followed by a question-and-answer session. Media deadlines must be taken into consideration when scheduling a press conference; invitations should include all area media representatives from radio, television, newspapers and magazines. Press kits should be available at the press conference for each of the attendees.

Travel Writers

The bureau should have as part of its public relations program the development of close liaisons with travel writers. A first step might be to host travel writers on a familiarization tour of the destination allowing them to see the various product offerings on a first-hand basis. It is worth the investment of the bureau's time and resources to become a member of travel writer associations. One of the most prestigeous is the Society of American Travel Writers (SATW). The Society's objective is to provide readers with objective information based on first-hand knowledge of a destination. There are also many unaffiliated writers seeking ideas for stories; these people can be of equal value to a bureau in promoting some aspect of its destination.

Public Speaking

One of the greatest fears among executives is having to make a public speech; yet for the bureau, public presentations are one of the most effective ways to get its story told throughout the community. A bureau should identify potential speaking opportunities; such opportunities abound through a community's many civic and professional clubs and organizations. Once a list of these is developed, the bureau should contact each indicating an interest in making presentations before its members. A basic presentation that can be used by bureau staff or board members should be developed. A slide show can provide colorful graphics to keep the audience interested in its message. Further, this type of presentation assures that the same message is being projected into the community regardless of who the spokesperson may be. It is important for the bureau to determine the types of questions that are likely to be asked and to prepare responses to be made. Fielding questions can be an art; it is usually during such dialogues that the audience becomes even more intrigued with the bureau's programs and their benefit to the community. Rehearsal assures a professional presentation.[9]

4. *Program Resources.* The public relations field abounds with resources to assist a bureau in the development of its own program; this chapter is not intended to serve as an inclusive statement on public relations but only to provide some ideas, direction and resources upon which bureaus can draw. The following is not an exhaustive list but some recommended resources for further study.

a. **Public Relations**

Benn, Alec, *The 23 Most Common Mistakes in Public Relations* (New York: American Management Assn, AMACOM, 1982).

Cutlip, Scott M. and Allen H. Center, *Effective Public Relations,* 3rd ed. (Englewood Cliffs, N.J.: Prentice-Hall, 1964).

Louis, H. Gordon, *How to Handle Your Own Public Relations* (Chicago: Nelson Hall, 1976).

Martinez, B. and R. Weiner, *Guide to Public Relations for Non-Profit Organizations and Public Agencies* (Los Angeles: The Grantmanship Center, 1979).

b. **Media**

Close, Jeffrey S., "The Media Tour: A Marketing Tool That Works," *Association Management,* March 1982, pp. 73–77.

Cochran, Linda Ray, "Beyond The Typewriter: How To Develop A News Release," *Association Management,* March 1983, pp. 97–101.

McGuire, Jack, "Let's Clear The Air About Public Service Announcements," *Association Management,* December 1983, pp. 143–147.

Pesmen, Sandra, *Writing for the Media: Public Relations and the Press* (Chicago, Ill.: Crain Books, no date).

c. **Public Speaking**

Alessandra, Anthony and Jim Cathcart, "Selling Your Ideas to Different People," *Association Management,* September 1983, pp. 109–115.

Feudo, John A., "Coping With Podium Panic," *Association Management,* March 1987, pp. 83–84.

Friend, William, "Now That Your Speech Is Over, How Do You Answer the Questions," *Association Management,* April 1981, pp. 90–95.

Hanna, Michael S. and Gerald L. Wilson, *Communicating in Business and Professional Settings* (New York: Random House, 1988).

Vardaman, George T., *Making Successful Presentations* (New York: American Management Assn, AMACOM, 1981).

Other resources come in the form of directories which provide valuable lists and descriptive information about media and other public relation resources. These include the following:

- *Roster of the Society of American Travel Writers*
- *Travel Market Guide* (publications that publish SATW member works)
- *Travel Photo Source Guide* (photographic specialities of the photographic members of SATW)
- *Fact Book of the Touristic Press* (Published by Lufthansa, roster of travel writer associations around the world)
- *The Folio 400* (magazines in the U.S.)
- *Working Press of the Nation* (4 volumes)
- Gebbie's *All-In-One Directory* (short version guide to publications, electronic media and specialty press)

Regional media contacts also can be compiled by a bureau for use with local and regional programming. The above resources along with other regional groups can be consulted for information.

5. *Assessing Public Relations Efforts.* Measuring the impact of public relations activities is a difficult task. Since publicity is uncontrolled and placement not guaranteed, there is frequently a reluctance on the part of bureau management to include it in established marketing goals. However, the dedication of bureau resources is too valuable not to consider it a viable marketing activity and not to subject it to assessment procedures. Such procedures can benefit a bureau by demonstrating channels of communication which tend to be more effective than others in utilizing bureau publicity.

There are two fundamental ways to assess publicity. The first is through what is commonly called a quantitative measurement. Here, publicity is evaluated on the basis of its process, reflected by some of the following indicators:

Number of Releases

Number of Placements

Circulation of Print Media

Total Reach/Exposure of Electronic Media

Audience Demographics

Geographic Distribution

Column Inches (print media)

Air Time (electronic media)

Equivalent Advertising Costs (column inches)

Equivalent Advertising Costs (air time)

In the case of print media, clippings of media placements can be obtained through a clipping service; each clipping is identified by publication, date and circulation. Clippings are accumulated, catalogued and filed by subject matter or some other criteria; a monetary value for each clip, equivalent to advertising space, may be assigned in order to assess the real value of those placements. Of course, not every bureau has the budget to afford a clipping service and thus will have to rely on its own monitoring techniques.

Electronic media may be willing to provide the bureau with the estimated value of a news placement or the costs that would have been incurred by a bureau for a public service announcement.

There is now growing interest in assessing publicity efforts by qualitative measures of effectiveness. Qualitative measures require greater sophistication, expertise and financial investment on the part of the bureau. Such efforts might include "pre/post market testing" to determine what the awareness or acceptance of the travel product might have been before and after a specific publicity effort in a specific market through specified media. Another qualitative measure is "controlled market comparison". This technique compares sales efforts in test markets where publicity was a part of the marketing mix with markets where there was no publicity. A third method is "conversion studies".[11] The quantity of responses received as a result of a publicity program will reflect which media generated the best results. However, the results of a conversion study will reflect who came and spent time and money as a result of the inquiry. This may or may not correlate with the quantity of responses received through a specific media. The value of such a study is that it allows for a qualitative assessment of the success of a publicity program and its impact on the community.[12]

Summary

The communications marketing efforts of a bureau must be pivotal if a bureau is to have effective community relations and an aggressive publicity program. Such marketing efforts have to be integrated into the bureau's total marketing scheme, assigned priorities, allocated bureau resources and audited for effectiveness. The bureau may wish to conduct assertive sales efforts to bring new sources of revenues into the community, but it also must conduct an effective communications program if it is to sustain credibility as an umbrella destination marketing organization for its community.

Discussion Questions

---

1. Why is communications described as a kaleidoscope?

2. How does "involvement" relate to the credibility of a bureau?

3. What is the "S.A.T." of community relations? Describe and discuss each aspect of the "S.A.T."

4. Eleven symptoms are identified as contributing to ineffective community relations; identify and discuss at least four which you feel are the most important and justify your position.

5. Six axioms for effective community relations are presented; identify and discuss each of those axioms and why it is important for a convention and visitor bureau.

6. Various community segments are identified; select three and discuss the strategies that would enhance the credibility and perceived value of a bureau by those community segments.

7. Why should a bureau set objectives for its public relations program?

8. What is a public relations audit? Describe and discuss.

9. Describe, discuss and evaluate the various forms of publicity available to a bureau as part of a public relations program; why is publicity an unreliable marketing technique?

10. In what ways can a bureau work effectively with the media?

11. Why is working with travel writers important to a bureau?

12. Describe and discuss the differences between a press kit and a media kit?

13. What are the three steps suggested for an effective public speaking program by a bureau?

14. Describe and discuss the differences between quantitative and qualitative measurements for public relations programs?

Bibliographic Resources

1. Materials drawn and adapted from "Symptoms of Terminal Community Relations" Presented by Keith Arnold, July 22, 1986 at the Annual Convention of the International Association of Convention & Visitor Bureaus.

2. "Public Relations," *Partners in Profit: An Introduction to Group Travel Marketing,* 2nd ed. (Lexington, Kentucky: National Tour Association, 1987), pp. 38–41.

3. "Publicity and Public Relations," *Principles of Association Management* (Washington, D.C.: American Society of Association Executives, 1975), pp. 199–207.

4. "Public Relations: Creating a Company Image," *Small Business Report,* February 1987, pp. 49–54.

5. Lauffer, Armand, *Strategic Marketing for Not-For-Profit Organizations* (New York: The Free Press/Macmillan, 1984), p. 304.

6. Craig, MaryBeth Vasile, "Listen, Really Listen To Your Members," *Association Management,* September 1982, pp. 79–80; Dalton, William, "Keep Your Finder On Your Association's Pulse: Conduct An Attitude Audit," *Association Management,* March 1983, pp. 103–105; Davis, Nancy M., "The Future of Association Communication," *Association Management,* July 1987, pp. 43–46; Moorman, Lilot and Richard N. Smith, "Are Your Communications On Target? Conduct An Audit and See," *Association Management,* July 1981, pp. 55–58.

7. Lauffer, Armand, Ibid, pp. 305–316.

8. Hanlon, Thomas D., "Travel Publicity: How To Produce It, Place It, Measure It, and Evaluate It" Presentation before the Annual Convention of the International Association of Convention & Visitor Bureaus, July 1986, p. 15.

9. "Public Speaking: A Vital Executive Skill," *Small Business Report,* March 1987, pp. 28–33.

10. Hanlon, Ibid, pp. 10–14.

11. Ronkainen, Ilkka A. and Arch G. Woodside, "Advertising Conversion Studies," in Ritchie, J. R. Brent and Charles R. Goeldner (eds), *Travel, Tourism, and Hospitality Research* (New York: John Wiley and Sons, 1987), pp. 481–488.

12. Adapted from Hanlon, Ibid., pp. 27–29.

EPILOGUE: STRATEGIC PARTNERSHIPS 9

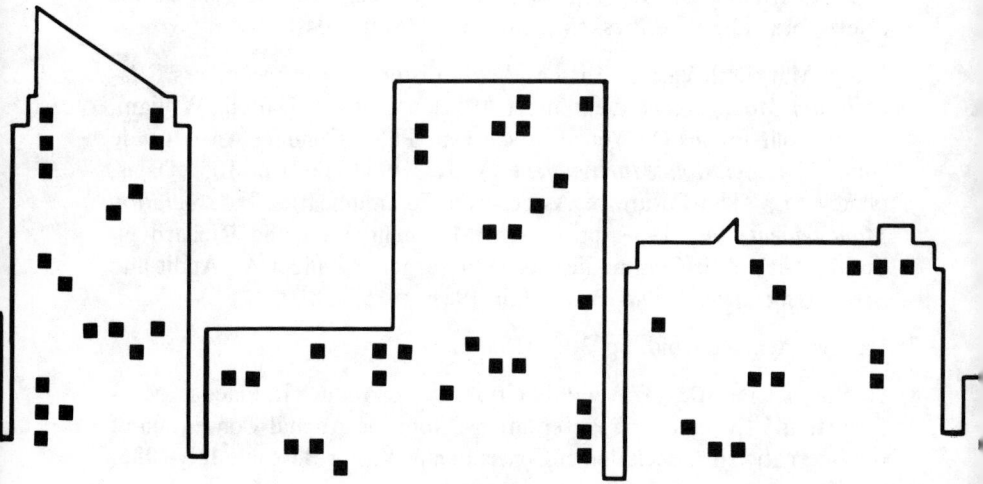

LEARNING OBJECTIVES

Upon reading this chapter, you will learn the
following:

- About the significance and value of an
  industry marketing partnership;

- Why the competitive spirit within the travel
  industry requires cooperation and mutually
  supportive marketing efforts to sell a
  destination;

- How bureaus serve as a stabilizing force
  within a community, and provide dynamic
  leadership.

Convention and visitor bureaus have, for over ninety years, been marketing their destinations with the intent of bringing to their communities group business which would generate new revenues. In fact, these often overlooked, if not underestimated, marketing activities have brought literally hundreds of thousands of visitors and billions of dollars to communities. The impact of these activities can be vividly demonstrated by new attractions, new hotels, new convention facilities, new events and festivals, improved roads and highways, improved air access, employment, expanded tax revenues and a revitalized image for the community. It hasn't happened overnight. Only through steady marketing activities by bureaus have cities come to realize this source of economic and community pride.

The marketplace has grown considerably since those first meetings in 1896. There are now thousands of associations and corporate meeting planners coordinating literally thousands of meetings of various sizes worldwide, each expecting to be treated in a professional manner. Experts indicate that this trend in meeting growth will continue. Though many of these meetings are small, their value is still significant to host facilities and communities as well as to the participants. But the competition has grown, too. Today, there are many cities which have facilities to accommodate meetings, conventions and trade shows. More cities have attractions to lure group tours and visitors. More cities are competing for the visitor's time and disposable income. And the financial investments being made suggest that cities have begun to recognize the importance of this growing travel and tourism industry and its economic impact on them. Today's investments are seen as tomorrow's hopes.

The development of a marketing image and campaign, targeting of specific market segments and execution of marketing plans that result in successful programs do not happen in a vacuum. They require thoughtful planning, knowledgeable and skilled professionals, a viable travel product and resources that will allow dreams to become realities. But more importantly, they require a partnership between the public and private sectors, between normally competitive entities such as hotel, restaurants and attractions, and other diverse constituents within a community.

A partnership means an association, a joint venture. A partner is one who associates with, shares in, and participates. In order to meet the challenges of a growing competitive marketplace, the convention and visitor bureau must engage in a dynamic partnership that includes all the critical elements of a growing travel and tourism industry. Without this partnership, a bureau cannot effectively fulfill its mission and marketing responsibilities.

As the definition suggests, a partner plays an active role and not a passive one. This means that community groups and organizations must be actively engaged in the programs of the bureau, willing to help in their design and development as well as with their execution. The convention and visitor bureau has the difficult task of trying to please everyone, while at the same time fulfilling its task of generating new business and new revenues for the community.

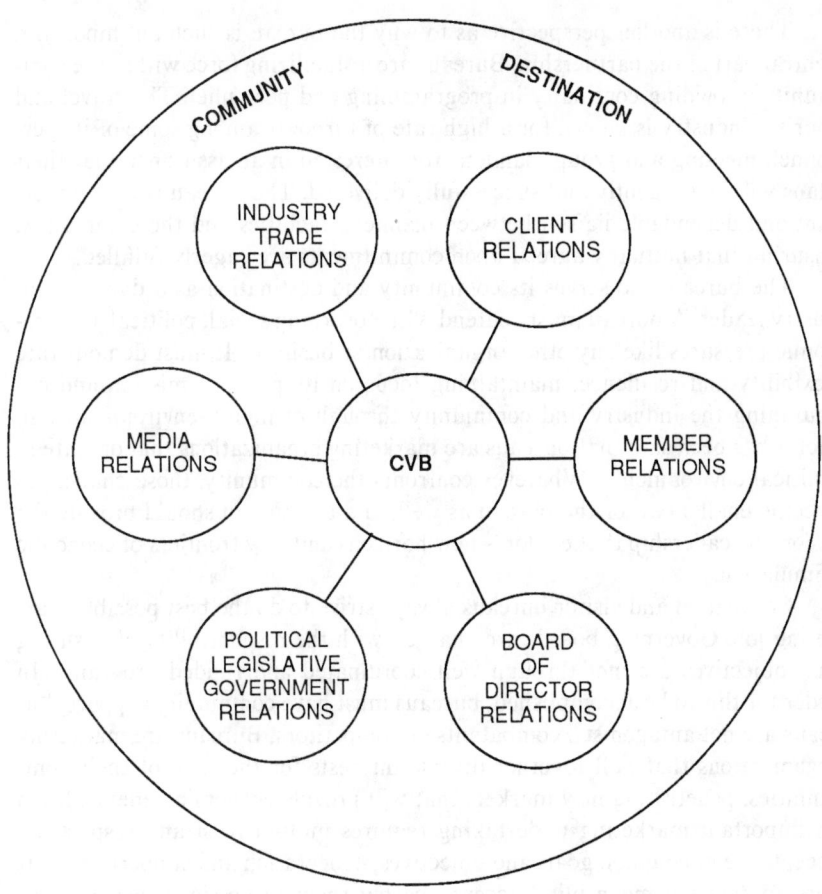

Figure 9.1

The bureau is the umbrella marketing organization and, through this community partnership, can be more effective and efficient with its resources.

For years, convention and visitor bureaus have faced the challenges of relating to many diverse constituents. Each group has its own interests and agenda and they are often not that different from what the bureau is attempting to accomplish. But the competitive spirit often confuses the need for cooperation and mutually supportive marketing activities. At times, relating to all of these audiences seems like an enormous undertaking. But the bureau must work with all groups, sharing their visions for the community and the destination, gaining their confidence and understanding, and pulling together their diverse agendas into a cohesive image and presentation on behalf of the community. This may take time and an abundance of patience, but the end result is affirming and exciting.

There is another perspective as to why the bureau is such an important, central part of the partnership. Bureaus are a stabilizing force within the community, providing continuity in programming and personnel. The travel and tourism industry is known for a high rate of turnover among some of its personnel; meeting and group planners are interested in an assurance that their plans will be diligently and successfully delivered. The bureau is that important and dependable liaison between planners, facilities and the community, ensuring that mutually agreed upon commitments are eagerly fulfilled.

The bureau also serves its community and destination as a dynamic industry leader. A bureau must contend with governing social, political and economic pressures like any other organization or business. It must demonstrate flexibility and resilience, maintaining focus on its primary mission and encouraging the industry and community through changing environments. In fact it has been said that bureaus are marketing organizations that operate in political environments. Whatever confronts the community, those challenges become challenges for the bureau as well, and the bureau should provide the visionary leadership that explores new horizons and new frontiers of economic stimulation.

Convention and visitor bureaus always strive to do the best possible marketing job. Governing boards are charged with the responsibility of ensuring that objectives are met through well coordinated and funded programs. In order for this to be accomplished, bureaus must have community support. Bureaus are not antagonists, combatants or competitors. Bureaus are marketing organizations that pull together diverse interests for the sake of their communities, penetrating new markets that will provide economic benefits. Such an important marketing undertaking requires mutual trust and respect, an acceptance of common goals and objectives, cooperation and support. A partnership does not mean blind acceptance but seeks professional honesty and frankness. In other words, bureaus need the benefit of human interactions to sharpen their own marketing and communication skills. Too often, however, such is not the relationship; for whatever reasons, bureaus often have been plagued by discontent, personality conflicts, program disagreements, power plays and petty jealousies. Misunderstanding is one thing, but issues not quickly resolved consume and misdirect energies that can be more productively used generating business and revenues for the community.

Not unlike sixty years ago, an agenda of the International Association of Convention & Visitor Bureaus suggests that the concerns of yesterday are not unlike the concerns of today; among the agenda items for discussion were the following:

- Relationships between the hotel sales manager and the convention bureau;
- Retail merchant's reaction to conventions;

- Competition with resort hotels;
- What is the proper relationship between the hotel and the convention bureau.

Though the times have changed, it is just as necessary today to attend to the relationships that constitute this strategic partnership of so many diverse constituents.

Exciting programs can be the result of relationships that are natural, supportive and nurturing. That is why this epilogue is entitled "Strategic Partnerships." The bureau may be the central focus for destination marketing, but it requires an active partnership for success. What we sow today will be reaped tomorrow; and with so many communities becoming actively involved in convention, group tour and visitor solicitations, the bureau must be the pivotal focus of a partnership that will generate economic vitality.

Discussion Questions

1. What is meant by "strategic partnership"?

2. What are the three reasons why bureaus are critical to a community?

3. Though issues seem to be the same today as they were over sixty years ago, what might contribute to this lack of resolving them?

4. What is meant by "visionary leadership" when applied to a role for the bureau?

Bibliographic Resources

1. Browne, Elise R., "Vision: The Leadership Difference," *Leadership,* 1986, pp. 30–34.

2. "Hotels, CVBs Lack A United Front: Editorial," *Business Travel News,* August 24, 1987, p. 20.

3. Finley, Dale R., "Working with Elected Officials," Professional Notes for the IACVB Newsletter, No Date.

4. Gillett, Charles, "Working with Cultural Groups," Professional Notes for the IACVB Newsletter, No Date.

5. Shure, Peter, "Miami Communities Must Succeed Together or Perish Individually," *Meeting News,* September 1987, p. 26.

APPENDIX

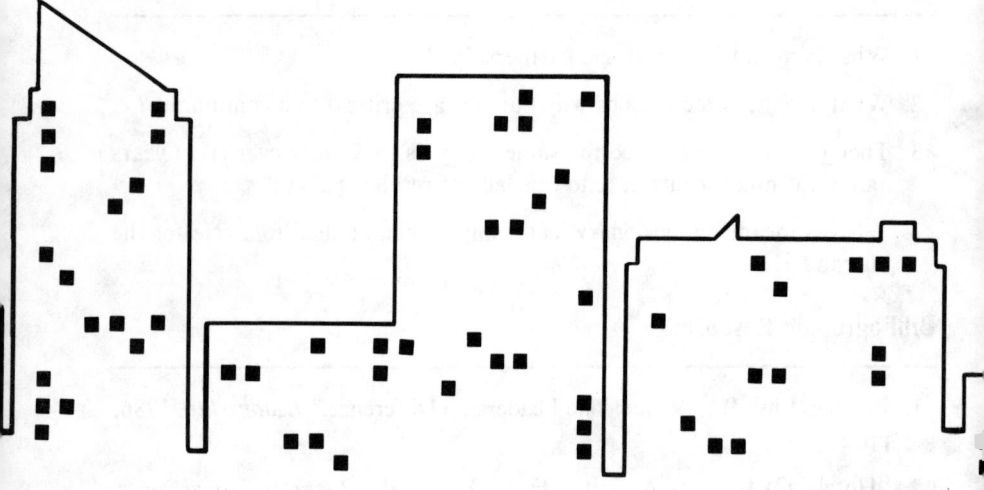

This appendix contains the following information:

A. Member Bureaus of the International Association of Convention & Visitor Bureaus

B. Code of Professional Conduct for IACVB Member Bureaus

C. Bibliography of Trade Articles on Convention and Visitor Bureaus

D. Professional Trade Associations

E. Sample Bylaws for Convention and Visitor Bureaus

F. Sample Bureau Program of Work

G. Sample Site Selection Criteria

H. Rules and Regulations for Registration Assistance Personnel

I. Sample Bureau Organizational Charts

J. Sample Bureau Budget/Chart of Accounts

K. Sample Job Descriptions

L. Sample Festival Survey Form

Appendix A

Abilene Convention and Visitors
  Council
325 Hickory
P.O. Box 2281
Abilene, TX 79604

Adelaide Convention and Visitors
  Bureau
22 Waymouth St., 1st Flr.
G.P.O. Box 351
Adelaide, SA 5001 AUSTRALIA

Akron/Summit Convention and
  Visitors Bureau, Inc.
Cascade Plaza, Sub-Level
Akron, OH 44308

Albany County Convention and
  Visitors Bureau
52 South Pearl St.
Albany, NY 12207

Albuquerque Convention and Visitors
  Bureau, Inc.
625 Silver St., SW, #210
P.O. Box 26866
Albuquerque, NM 87125

Alexandria Convention and Visitors
  Bureau
221 King St.
Alexandria, VA 22314

Netherlands Convention Bureau
Amsteldijk 166
1079 LH Amsterdam,
  NETHERLANDS

Augusta-Richmond County
  Convention and Visitors Bureau
P.O. Box 1331
Augusta, GA 30913

Austin Convention and Visitors
  Bureau
P.O. Box 2990
Austin, TX 78769

Baltimore Convention Bureau, Inc.
One East Pratt St., Suite 14
Baltimore, MD 21202

Polk County Tourist Development
  Council
325 West Main Street
P.O. Box 1909
Bartow, FL 33830

Baton Rouge Area Convention and
  Visitors Bureau
Fontane Hse.-838 N. Blvd.
P.O. Box 4149
Baton Rouge, LA 70821

Greater Battle Creek/Calhoun
  County Visitor and Convention
  Bureau
172 W. Van Buren St.
Battle Creek, MI 49017

Bay County Convention and Visitors
  Bureau, Inc.
315 - 14th Street
Bay City, MI 48708

Anaheim Area Visitor and Convention
  Bureau
800 W. Katella Ave.
P.O. Box 4270
Anaheim, CA 92803

Anchorage Convention and Visitors
  Bureau
201 E. Third Ave.
Anchorage, AK 99501

Ann Arbor Convention and Visitors
  Bureau
211 E. Huron St., Ste. 6
Ann Arbor, MI 48104-1914

Arlington Convention and Visitors
  Bureau
1908 E. Randol Mill, S204
P.O. Box A
Arlington, TX 76004–0927

Asheville Convention and Visitors
  Bureau
151 Haywood St.
P.O. Box 1010
Asheville, NC 28802

Atlanta Convention and Visitors Bureau
233 Peachtree St., N.E., Ste. 2000 - Harris Tower
Atlanta, GA 30303

Atlantic City Convention and Visitors Bureau
2314 Pacific Avenue
Atlantic City, NJ 08401

Beaumont Convention and Visitors Bureau
701 Main Street
P.O. Box 3827
Beaumont, TX 77704

Greater Birmingham Convention and Visitors Bureau
2027 First Ave., North
Suite 300
Birmingham, AL 35203

Birmingham Convention and Visitor Bureau
9 The Wharf
16 Bridge Street
Birmingham, B1 2JS ENGLAND

Bloomington-Normal Area Convention and Visitors Bureau
210 South East St.
Bloomington, IL 61701

Bloomington/Monroe County Convention and Visitors Bureau
2855 N. Walnut
Bloomington, IN 47401

Bloomington Convention and Visitors Bureau
9801 Dupont Ave., South, # 120
Bloomington, MN 55431-3180

Boise Convention and Visitors Bureau
802 W. Bannock, Suite 308
P.O. Box 2106
Boise, ID 83701

Greater Boston Convention and Visitors Bureau, Inc.
800 Boylston St.
Prudential Plz., POB 490
Boston, MA 02199

Boulder Bureau of Conference Services and Cultural Affairs
2440 Pearl Street
P.O. Box 73
Boulder, CO 80306

Bowling Green Tourist and Convention Commission
1755-D Scottsville Rd.
P.O. Box 1040
Bowling Green, KY 42102

Brisbane Visitors and Convention Bureau
Ground Floor, City Hall
King George Square
G.P.O. Box 1434
Brisbane, QLD 4001 AUSTRALIA

Golden Isles Tourist and Convention Bureau
4 Glynn Avenue
Brunswick, GA 31520

Greater Buffalo Convention and Visitors Bureau
107 Delaware Ave.
Buffalo, NY 14202

Calgary Tourist and Convention Bureau
237 - 8th Ave., S.E.,
Calgary, AL T2G OK8 CANADA

Canton/Stark County Convention and Visitors Bureau
229 Wells Ave., N.W.
P.O. Box 1044
Canton, OH 44701-1044

Carbondale Convention and Tourism Bureau
714 E. Walnut St.
Carbondale, IL 62901-3103

Cedar Rapids Area Convention and Visitors Bureau
424 First Avenue, N.E.
P.O. Box 4860
Cedar Rapids, IA 52407

Champaign Urbana Convention and Visitors Bureau
40 E. University
P.O. Box 1626
Champaign, IL 61820

Charleston Trident Convention and Visitors Bureau
17 Lockwood Blvd.
P.O. Box 975
Charleston, SC 29402

Charleston Convention and Visitors Bureau
200 Civic Center Drive, Suite 002
Charleston, WV 25301

Charlotte Convention and Visitors Bureau, Inc.
229 North Church Street
Charlotte, NC 28202

Chattanooga Area Convention and Visitors Bureau
1001 Market St.
Chattanooga, TN 37402

Chicago Convention and Visitors Bureau
McCormick Place On-The-Lake
Chicago, IL 60616

Greater Cincinnati Convention and Visitors Bureau
300 West Sixth Street
Cincinnati, OH 45202

Convention and Visitors Bureau of Greater Cleveland
1301 E. Sixth St.
Cleveland, OH 44114

Coeur d'Alene Con/Vis Bureau
Coeur d'Alene Chamber of Commerce
202 Sherman Avenue
P.O. Box 850
Coeur d'Alene, ID 83814

Southwestern Illinois Tourism and Convention Bureau
206 N. Bluff Rd.
Collinsville, IL 62234

Colorado Springs Convention and Visitors Bureau
104 S. Cascade Avenue, Suite 104
Colorado Springs, CO 80903

Greater Columbia Convention and Visitors Bureau
301 Gervais Street
Coliumbia, SC 29201

Columbus Convention and Visitors Bureau
801 Front Ave.
P.O. Box 2768
Columbus, GA 31902

Greater Columbus Convention and Visitors Bureau
One Columbus Building
10 W. Broad St., #1300
Columbus, OH 43215

Concord Convention and Visitors Bureau
Salvio Pacheo Square
2151 Salvio St., Ste. N
Concord, CA 94520

Corpus Christi Area Convention and Visitors Bureau
1201 N. Shoreline
P.O. Box 2664
Corpus Christi, TX 78403

Council Bluffs Convention and Visitors Bureau
119 South Main Street, Suite 150
Council Bluffs, IA 51501

Northern Kentucky Convention and Visitors Bureau
605 Philadelphia Street
Covington, KY 41011

Culver City Convention and Visitors Bureau
10000 Washington Blvd., Suite N229
Culver City, CA 90232

Dallas Convention and Visitors Bureau
1201 Elm St. # 2000
Dallas, TX 75270

Danville Area Convention and Visitors Bureau
2 East Main, Suite 201
P.O. Box 992
Danville, IL 61834-0992

Dayton/Montgomery County Convention and Visitors Bureau
Chamber Plaza
Fifth & Main
Dayton, OH 45402-2400

DESTINATION DAYTONA!
110 Orange Avenue
P.O. Box 2775
Daytona Beach, FL 32015

Decatur Convention and Visitors Bureau
925 Bank Street, N.W.
P.O. Box 2003
Decatur, AL 35601

DeKalb Convention and Visitors
Bureau
750 Commerce Dr., Suite 201
Decatur, GA 30030

Decatur Area Convention and
Visitors Bureau
118 Merchant St.
Decatur, IL 62523

Denton Convention and Visitors
Bureau
414 Parkway
P.O. Drawer P
Denton, TX 76202

Denver Metro Convention and
Visitors Bureau
225 W. Colfax Ave.
Denver, CO 80202

Des Moines Convention and Visitors
Bureau, Inc.
300 Saddlery Building
309 Court Avenue
Des Moines, IA 50309-2285

Metropolitan Detroit Convention and
Visitors Bureau
100 Renaissance Center, Suite 1950
Detroit, MI 48243

Durban Publicity Association
P.O. Box 1044
Durban 4000, Natau SOUTH
AFRICA

Eau Claire Area Convention and
Tourism Bureau
2127 Brackett Avenue
Eau Claire, WI 54701

Edmonton Convention and Tourism
Authority
9797 Jasper Ave., #104
Edmonton, ALB T5J IN9 CANADA

El Paso Tourist and Convention
Bureau
One Civic Center Plaza
El Paso, TX 79901

Elgin Area Convention and Visitors
Bureau
24 E. Chicago St.
P.O. Box 648
Elgin, IL 60120

North Central Connecticut Tobacco
Valley Convention and Visitors
Dist.
111 Hazard Avenue
Enfield, CT 06082

Eugene-Springfield Convention and
Visitors Bureau, Inc.
305 W. Seventh St.
P.O. Box 10286
Eugene, OR 97440

Eureka/Humboldt County Convention
and Visitors Bureau
1034 Second St.
Eureka, CA 95501

Evansville Convention and Visitors
Bureau
715 Locust St.
Evansville, IN 47708

Fairbanks Convention and Visitors
Bureau
550 First Ave.
Fairbanks, AK 99701

Fayetteville Area Convention and
Visitors Bureau
515 Ramsey Street
Fayetteville, NC 28301

Flint Area Convention and Visitors
Bureau
400 N. Saginaw St., Suite 101A
Flint, MI 48502

Tuscany Convention Bureau
Via Borgognissanti 8
50123 Florence, ITALY

Fort Collins Convention and Visitors
Bureau
#9 Old Town Square, #101
P.O. Box 2018
Fort Collins, CO 80524

Greater Fort Lauderdale Area
Convention and Visitors Bureau
Broward Financial Center
500 E. Broward Blvd.
Suite 104
Fort Lauderdale, FL 33394

Lee County Visitor and Convention
Bureau
2126 First St.
P.O. Box 2445
Fort Myers, FL 33902-9990

Fort Wayne Convention and Visitors
Bureau
826 Ewing St.
Fort Wayne, IN 46802

Fort Worth Convention and Visitors
Bureau
#400, Water Gardens Pl.
100 East 15th Street
Fort Worth, TX 76102

Gatlinburg Tourist and Convention
Bureau
520 Parkway
P.O. Box 527
Gatlinburg, TN 37738

Gold Coast Visitors and Convention
Bureau
First Floor, 115 Scarborough St.
Southport, Queensland, 4215
AUSTRALIA

Granada Convention Bureau
C/ Mariana Pineda, 1
Granada, 18009 SPAIN

Greater Grand Rapids Convention
Bureau
245 Monroe, N.W.
Grand Rapids, MI 49503

Grapevine Convention and Visitors
Bureau
909 S. Main St.
Grapevine, TX 76051

Greeley Convention and Visitors
Bureau
1407 - 8th Avenue
P.O. Box CC
Greeley, CO 80632

Green Bay Area Visitor and
Convention Bureau
1901 S. Oneida St.
P.O. Box 10596
Green Bay, WI 54307-0596

Greensboro Area Convention and
Visitors Bureau
220 South Eugene St.
P.O. Box 1588
Greensboro, NC 27402

Greater Greenville Convention and
Visitors Bureau
803 E. North St.
P.O. Box 10527
Greenville, SC 29603

Mississippi Gulf Coast Convention
and Visitors Bureau
100 Hardy Court Office Plaza, #121
P.O. Box 6128
Gulfport, MS 39506

Greater Hartford Convention and
Visitors Bureau, Inc.
One Civic Center Plaza
Hartford, CT 06103

Heidelberg Convention and Visitors
Bureau
P.O. Box 105860
Heidelberg, 6900 WEST
GERMANY

High Point Convention and Visitors
Bureau
100 West Green Drive
P.O. Box 2273
High Point, NC 27261

Hilton Head Island Visitors and
Convention Bureau
1 Chamber of Commerce Dr.
P.O. Box 5647
Hilton Head Island, SC 29938

Tasmanian Visitor Corporation
7 Franklin Wharf
Hobart, TS 7000 AUSTRALIA

Chicago/South Convention and
Visitors Bureau
900 Ridge Rd., Suite 100
Homewood, IL 60430

Hong Kong Tourist Association
35th Flr., Connaught Ctr.
Connaught Road Central
HONG KONG

Hawaii Visitors Bureau
2270 Kalakaua Ave., Suite 801
Honolulu, HI 96815

Hot Springs Convention and Visitors
Bureau
134 Convention Blvd.
P.O. Box K
Hot Springs, AR 71902

Greater Houston Convention and
Visitors Bureau
3300 Main St.
Houston, TX 77002-9396

Cabell-Huntington Convention and Visitors Bureau
210 11th, #13 Herit. Vil.
P.O. Box 347
Huntington, WV 25708-0347

Huntsville Convention and Visitors Bureau
700 Monroe St.
Huntsville, AL 35801

Indianapolis Convention and Visitors Association
One Hoosier Dome, Ste 100
200 S. Capital Ave.
Indianapolis, IN 46225

Iowa City/Coralville Convention and Visitors Bureau
325 E. Washington
Post Office Box 2358
Iowa City, IA 52244

Irving Convention and Visitors Bureau
3333 N. MacArthur Blvd., Suite 200
Irving, TX 75062

Isle of Man Tourist Board
13 Victoria Street
Douglas, ISLE OF MAN, U.K.

Ithaca/Tompkins County Convention and Visitors Bureau
122 West Court Street
Ithaca, NY 14850

Jackson Convention and Visitors Bureau
1510 N. State, Ste. 200
P.O. Box 1450
Jackson, MS 39205

Jackson Convention and Tourist Bureau
401 South Jackson
Jackson, MI 49201

Convention and Visitors Bureau of Jacksonville and its Beaches
6 E. Bay St., Suite 200
Jacksonville, FL 32202

Clark-Floyd Counties Convention and Tourism Bureau
540 Marriott Dr.
P.O. Box 608
Jeffersonville, IN 47131

Johnson City Conventions and Visitors Bureau
603 E. Market St.
P.O. Box 1674
Johnson City, TN 37605

Juneau Convention and Visitors Bureau
76 Egan Drive, Ste. 140
Juneau, AK 99801

Kalamazoo County Convention and Visitors Bureau
128 North Kalamazoo Mall
Kalamazoo, MI 49007

Convention and Visitors Bureau of Greater Kansas City
Suite 2550, 1100 Main St.
Kansas City, MO 64105

Kingsport Convention and Visitors Bureau
408 Clay Street
P.O. Box 1403
Kingsport, TN 37662

Kissimee-St. Cloud Convention and Visitors Bureau
1925 Space Coast Pkwy.
P.O. Box 2007
Kissimmee, FL 32742

Knoxville Convention and Visitors Bureau
500 Henley St.
P.O. Box 15012
Knoxville, TN 37901

Kodiak Island Convention and Visitors Bureau
100 Marine Way
Kodiak, AK 99615

La Crosse Area Convention and Visitor Bureau
P.O. Box 1895
Riverside Park
La Crosse, WI 54602-1895

Greater Lafayette Convention and Visitors Bureau, Inc.
3530 State Road 26 East
P.O. Box 5547
Lafayette, IN 47903

Lafayette Convention and Visitors Commission
310 16th St.
P.O. Box 52066
Lafayette, LA 70505

Southwest Louisiana Convention and Visitors Bureau
1211 N. Lakeshore Dr.
P.O. Box 1912
Lake Charles, LA 70602

Lake Geneva Convention and Visitors Bureau
201 Wrigley Dr.
Lake Geneva, WI 53147

Pennsylvania Dutch Convention and Visitors Bureau
501 Greenfield Rd.
Lancaster, PA 17601

Convention/Visitors Bureau of Greater Lansing
Suite 302, Civic Center
Lansing, MI 48933

Las Cruces Convention and Visitors Bureau
311 N. Downtown Mall
Las Cruces, NM 88001

Las Vegas Convention and Visitors Authority
3150 Paradise Rd.
Las Vegas, NV 89109-9096

Greater Lexington Convention and Visitors Bureau
430 W. Vine St., Ste. 363
Lexington, KY 40507

Lima/Allen County Convention and Visitors Bureau
53 Town Square
Lima, OH 45801

Lincoln Convention and Visitors Bureau
1221 "N" St., Suite 606
Lincoln, NE 68508

Little Rock Convention and Visitors Bureau
Robinson-Markham and Brdwy.
P.O. Box 3232
Little Rock, AR 72203

London Tourist Board and Convention Bureau
26 Grosvenor Gardens
London, SWIW ODU ENGLAND

Long Beach Area Convention and Visitors Council
180 E. Ocean Blvd, Suite 150
Long Beach, CA 90802

Longview Convention and Visitors Bureau
100 Grand Boulevard
P.O. Box 1952
Longview, TX 75606

Lorain County Visitors Bureau, Inc.
611 Broadway
Lorain, OH 44052

Greater Los Angeles Visitors and Convention Bureau
ManuLife Plaza, 11th Flr.
515 South Figueroa St.
Los Angeles, CA 90071

Louisville Convention and Visitors Bureau
400 S. First
Louisville, KY 40202

Greater Madison Convention and Visitor Bureau, Inc.
121 W. Doty St.
Madison, WI 53703

Madrid Convention Bureau
Recinto Feria de la Casa de Campo-
Avd. Portugal
28011 Madrid, SPAIN

Philippine Convention and Visitors Corporation
4th Flr, Legaspi Twrs 300
Roxas Boulevard
Metro Manila, 2808 PHILIPPINES

Delaware County Convention and Tourist Bureau
602 East Baltimore Pike
Media, PA 19085

Melbourne Tourism Authority and Melbourne Convention Bureau
20th Level, Nauru House
80 Collins St.
Melbourne, VC 3000 AUSTRALIA

Memphis Convention and Visitors
  Bureau
50 North Front St., Suite 450
Memphis, TN 38103

Mesa Convention and Visitors Bureau
120 N. Center Street
Mesa, AZ 85201

Mexico City Convention and Visitors
  Council
Donato Guerra #25
Col. Centro
Mexico City, D.F. 06048 MEXICO

Greater Miami Convention and
  Visitors Bureau
4770 Biscayne Blvd.
Miami, FL 33137

Greater Milwaukee Convention and
  Visitors Bureau, Inc.
756 N. Milwaukee St.
Milwaukee, WI 53202

Greater Minneapolis Convention and
  Visitors Association
15 S. Fifth St.
Minneapolis, MN 55402

Mobile Convention and Visitors
  Corporation
63 S. Royal St., Suite 909
Mobile, AL 36602

Monaco Tourist Board and
  Convention Bureau
2A, Bulevard des Moulins
Monte Carlo, 98000 MONACO

Convention and Visitor Division,
  Montgomery Chamber of
  Commerce
41 Commerce St.
P.O. Box 79
Montgomery, AL 36101

Greater Montreal Convention and
  Tourism Bureau
1010 Ste-Catherine Street West -
  Room 410
Montreal, QB H3B 1G2 CANADA

Mt. Vernon Convention and Visitors
  Bureau
215 Potomac
P.O. Box 2580
Mt. Vernon, IL 62864

Myrtle Beach Area Convention
  Bureau
Hampton Park
710 N. 21st Ave., Suite J
Myrtle Beach, SC 29577

Convention and Visitors Division,
  Nashville Area Chamber of
  Commerce
161 Fourth Ave., North
Nashville, TN 37219

Nassau/Cable Beach/Paradise Island
  Promotion Board
255 Alhambra Circle Suite 435
Coral Gables, FL 33134

Natchez-Adams County Convention
  and Visitor Comission
311 Liberty Rd.
Natchez, MS 39120

Greater New Orleans Tourist and
  Convention Commission, Inc.
1520 Sugar Bowl Drive
New Orleans, LA 70112

New York Convention and Visitors
  Bureau
Two Columbus Circle
New York, NY 10019

Niagara Falls Convention and
  Visitors Bureau
Carborundum Ctr.-Ste. 101
345 Third Street
Niagara Falls, NY 14303

Association Nice-Congres
Acropolis
1 Esplanade Kennedy
06300 Nice, FRANCE

Trumbull County Convention and
  Visitors Bureau, Inc.
650 Youngstown Warren Rd.
Niles, OH 44446

Norfolk Convention and Visitors
  Bureau
236 East Plume Street
Norfolk, VA 23510

Oakland Convention and Visitors
  Bureau
1000 Broadway, Ste. 200
Oakland, CA 94607-4020

**Ocean City Visitors and Convention
Bureau, Inc.**
4001 Coastal Highway
P.O. Box 116
Ocean City, MD 21842

**Oklahoma City Convention and
Tourism Bureau**
4 Santa Fe Plaza
Oklahoma City, OK 73102

**Greater Omaha Convention and
Visitors Bureau**
1819 Farnam St., Suite 1200
Omaha, NE 68183

**Greater Ontario Visitors and
Convention Bureau**
421 North Euclid Avenue
Ontario, CA 91762

**Oneida County Convention and
Visitors Bureau**
Oneida County Airport
P.O. Box AA
Oriskany, NY 13424

**Orlando/Orange County Convention
and Visitors Bureau**
7680 Republic Dr., Suite 200
Orlando, FL 32819

Osaka Convention Bureau
c/o Osaka Cham. of Comm. and
Industry
58-7, Uchihommachi-
Hashizume-cho, Higashi-ku
Osaka, 520 JAPAN

**Canada's Capital Visitors and
Convention Bureau**
222 Queen St., 7th Floor
Ottawa, ON K1P 5V9 CANADA

**Overland Park Convention and
Visitors Bureau**
Corporate Woods
10975 Benson, Suite 360
Overland Park, KS 66210

**Desert Resorts Convention and
Visitors Bureau**
Fred Waring Building
44–100 Monterey, Ste. 203
Palm Desert, CA 92260

**Greater Palm Springs Convention and
Visitors Bureau, Inc.**
255 N. El Cielo Rd., Suite 315
Palm Springs, CA 92262

Paris Convention Bureau
127 Champs-Elysees
75008 Paris, FRANCE

Park City Chamber/ Bureau
528 Main Street
P.O. Box 1630
Park City, UT 84060

**Pasadena Convention and Visitors
Bureau**
171 South Los Robles
Pasadena, CA 91101

**Peoria Convention and Visitors
Bureau**
331 Fulton, Suite 625
Peoria, IL 61602

Perth Convention Bureau
16 St. George's Terrace
G.P.O. Box J732
Perth, WA 6000 AUSTRALIA

**Philadelphia Convention and Visitors
Bureau**
1515 Market St. Suite 2020
Philadelphia, PA 19102

**Phoenix and Valley of the Sun
Convention and Visitors Bureau**
505 N. Second St., Suite 300
Phoenix, AZ 85004

**Greater Pittsburgh Convention and
Visitors Bureau**
Four Gateway Center, Suite 514
Pittsburgh, PA 15222

**Convention and Visitors Bureau of
Greater Portland**
142 Free St.
Portland, ME 04101

**Greater Portland Convention and
Visitors Association**
26 S.W. Salmon
Portland, OR 97204-3299

**Greater Providence Convention and
Visitors Bureau**
Commerce Center
30 Exchange Terrace
Providence, RI 02903

**Quebec City Region Tourism and
Convention Bureau**
53 D'Auteuil
Quebec, QB G1R 4C2 CANADA

Quincy Convention and Visitors Bureau
Villa Kathrine
Quincy, IL 62301

Greater Racine Area Convention and Visitors Bureau
345 Main Street
Racine, WI 53403

Raleigh Convention and Visitors Bureau
255 Hillsborough St.
P.O. Box 1879
Raleigh, NC 27602

Rapid City Area Convention and Visitors Bureau
444 Mt. Rushmore Rd., N.
P.O. Box 747
Rapid City, SD 57709

Reno-Sparks Convention and Visitors Authority
4590 S. Virginia
P.O. Box 837
Reno, NV 89504

Metropolitan Richmond Convention and Visitors Bureau
300 E. Main St., Suite 100
Richmond, VA 23219

Rio Convention Bureau
Rua Visconde de Piraja,
547-Gr. 610 a 617
Rio de Janeiro, 22410 BRAZIL

Riverside Visitors and Convention Bureau
3443 Orange St.
Riverside, CA 92501

Roanoke Valley Convention and Visitors Bureau
14 W. Kirk Ave.
P.O. Box 1710
Roanoke, VA 24008

Rochester Convention and Visitors Bureau
220 S. Broadway, Ste. 100
Rochester, MN 55904

Rochester/Monroe County Convention and Visitors Bureau, Inc.
120 E. Main St.
Rochester, NY 14604

York County Visitor and Convention Bureau
201 East Main Street
P.O. Box 11377
Rock Hill, SC 29731

Rockford Area Convention and Visitors Bureau
220 E. State St.
Rockford, IL 61104

Rosemont/O'Hare Convention Bureau
9291 West Bryn Mawr Ave.
Rosemont, IL 60018

Sacramento Convention and Visitors Bureau
1421 "K" Street
Sacramento, CA 95814

Saginaw County Convention and Visitors Bureau
901 S. Washington Ave.
Saginaw, MI 48601

St. Louis Convention and Visitors Commission
10 S. Broadway, Suite 300
St. Louis, MO 63102

Saint Paul Convention Bureau
#600, N Central Life Twr
445 Minnesota Street
Saint Paul, MN 55101-2108

Salt Lake Convention and Visitors Bureau
180 South West Temple
Salt Lake City, UT 84101

Salzburg Convention and Visitors Bureau
Kngrsbtrb. der Std. Slzbg
Auerspergstrasse 7
Salzburg, A-5020 AUSTRIA

San Angelo Convention and Visitors Bureau
500 Rio Concho Dr.
San Angelo, TX 76903

San Antonio Convention and Visitors Bureau
Alamo Plaza South Bldg.
P.O. Box 2277
San Antonio, TX 78298

San Diego Convention and Visitors Bureau
1200 Third Avenue, Suite 824
San Diego, CA 92101-4190

San Francisco Convention and
Visitors Bureau
201 Third St., #900
San Francisco, CA 94103

San Jose Convention and Visitors
Bur.
333 W. San Carlos St., Suite 1000
RiverPark Bldg., 10th Fl.
P.O. Box 6299
San Jose, CA 95150-6299

San Juan Puerto Rico Convention
Bureau
1110 Ashford Avenue, 2nd Floor
Santurce, PR 00907

San Mateo County Convention and
Visitors Bureau
601 Gateway Boulevard, Suite 970
South San Francisco, CA 94080

San Salvador Convention and Visitors
Bureau
Htl Presid, 221/222, ave. Revolu.,
Col. San Benito
San Salvador, ES C.A.

Santa Barbara Conference and
Visitors Bureau
P.O. Box 299
Santa Barbara, CA 93102

Santa Clara Chamber of Commerce
and Convention-Visitors Bureau
4699 Old Iron Side Dr., Suite 410
P.O. Box 387
Santa Clara, CA 95052

Santa Cruz Conference and Visitors
Council
Division of Santa Cruz
Chamber of Commerce
105 Cooper Street, #243
P.O. Box 921
Santa Cruz, CA 95061

Santa Fe Convention and Visitors
Bureau
201 W. Marcy St.
P.O. Box 909
Santa Fe, NM 87504

Sonoma County Convention and
Visitors Bureau
10 Fourth St., Suite 101
Santa Rosa, CA 95401

Sao Paulo Convention Bureau
Avenida Paulista 2202 150, Conj.
151 01310
Sao Paulo, SP BRAZIL

Sarasota Convention and Visitors
Bureau
655 North Tamiami Trail
Sarasota, FL 34236

Saratoga Convention and Tourism
Bureau
522 Broadway, Room 106
Saratoga Springs, NY 12866

Savannah Area Convention and
Visitors Bureau
222 W. Oglethorpe Avenue
Savannah, GA 31499

Greater Woodfield Convention and
Visitors Bureau
1375 E. Woodfield Rd., Suite 210
Schaumburg, IL 60173

Scottsdale Chamber of Commerce
7333 Scottsdale Mall
P.O. Box 130
Scottsdale, AZ 85251

Seattle/King County Convention and
Visitors Bureau
1815 Seventh Ave.
Seattle, WA 98101

Korea National Tourism Corp.
10, Ta-Dong, Chung-ku
C.P.O. Box 903
Seoul 100, KOREA

Tourist Promotion Board of Seville
Avda. de la Constitucion, 24–3.0
Seville, SPAIN 41001

Sheboygan Area Convention and
Visitors Bureau
631 New York Ave.
P.O. Box 687
Sheboygan, WI 53082

Shreveport-Bossier Convention and
Tourist Bureau
629 Spring St.
P.O. Box 1761
Shreveport, LA 71166

Sioux City Convention and Visitors
Bureau
600 Fourth St., Suite 312, Terra
Centre
Sioux City, IA 51101

St. Tammany Parish Tourist and Convention Commission
2020 First St.
P.O. Box 432
Slidell, LA 70459

Convention and Tourism Div., South Bend/Mishawaka Area Cham. of Comm.
401 E. Colfax, Suite 310
P.O. Box 1677
South Bend, IN 46634-1677

South Padre Island Visitor and Convention Bureau
600 Padre Boulevard
P.O. Box 3500
South Padre Island, TX 78597

Spartanburg Tourism and Convention Bureau
145 North Church Street
P.O. Box 1636
Spartanburg, SC 29304

Spokane Regional Convention and Visitors Bureau
W. 926 Sprague Ave., Suite 180
Spokane, WA 99204

Springfield Convention and Visitors Bureau
P.O. Box 1269
Springfield, IL 62705

Greater Springfield Convention and Visitors Bureau
56 Dwight St.
Springfield, MA 01103

Springfield Convention and Visitors Bureau
320 N. Jefferson
P.O. Box 1687
Springfield, MO 65805

Stevens Point Area Convention and Visitors Bureau
600 Main Street
Stevens Point, WI 54481

Stockholm Site and Development Company
Hantverkargatan 5
S-112
Stockholm 21, SWEDEN

Association Pour la Promotion de Strasbourg
Palais de Congres
Strasbourg, 67000 FRANCE

Hill and Harbor Convention and Visitors Bureau
605 Broad Street
Stratford, CT 06497

Sydney Convention and Visitors Bureau, Ltd.
Ste 2, Lvl 1-Centrepoint
100 Market Street
Sydney, NSW 2000 AUSTRALIA

Syracuse Convention and Visitors Bureau
100 E. Onondaga St.
Syracuse, NY 13202

Tacoma-Pierce County Visitor and Convention Bureau
950 Pacific Ave., #300
P.O. Box 1933
Tacoma, WA 98401

Tourism Bureau of the Republic of China
P.O. Box 1490
Taipei, Taiwan, REP. OF CHINA 10514

Tampa/Hillsborough Convention and Visitors Assn., Inc.
100 S. Ashley, Ste. 850
P.O. Box 519
Tampa, FL 33601

Convention/Tourism Department, City of Temple
Municipal Building - Mayborn Center Box
Temple, TX 76502

Terre Haute Convention and Visitors Bureau of Vigo County
3509 Dixie Bee Road
HoneyCreek Sq, P.O.B. 6000
Terre Haute, IN 47802-6000

Greater Toledo Office of Tourism and Conventions, Inc.
218 Huron St.
Toledo, OH 43604

Topeka Convention and Visitors Bureau
3 Townsite Plaza
120 E. Sixth
Topeka, KS 66603

Metropolitan Toronto Convention and Visitors Association
Queen's Quay Terminal at Harbour Front
207 Queen's Quay West, Suite 509
P.O. Box 126
Toronto, ON M5J 1A7 CANADA

Grand Traverse Convention and Visitors Bureau
900 E. Front St., Suite 100
Traverse City, MI 49684

Metropolitan Tucson Convention and Visitors Bureau
130 S. Scott Ave.
Tucson, AZ 85701

Tulsa Convention and Visitors Bureau
616 S. Boston Ave.
Tulsa, OK 74119

Long Island Tourism and Convention Commission, Inc.
Nassau Coliseum - Hempstead Turnpike
Uniondale, L.I., NY 11553

Valdez Convention and Visitors Bureau
321 Egan
P.O. Box 1603
Valdez, AK 99686

Valley Forge Convention and Visitors Bureau
One Montgomery Plaza, 611
P.O. Box 311
Norristown, PA 19404

Greater Vancouver Convention and Visitors Bureau
#1625 1055 W. Georgia St.
P.O.B. 11142, Royal Ctr.
Vancouver, BC V6E 4C8 CANADA

Greater Victoria Visitors and Convention Bureau
6th Floor, 612 View Street
Victoria, BC V8W 1J5 CANADA

Vienna Tourist Board
Kinderspitalgasse 5
1095 Vienna, AUSTRIA

Virginia Beach Convention Bureau
1000 19th Street
P.O. Box 136
Virginia Beach, VA 23458

Waco Convention and Visitors Bureau
100 Washington Blvd.
P.O. Box 2570
Waco, TX 76702-2570

Washington, DC Convention and Visitors Association
1575 Eye Street, N.W.
#250
Washington, DC 20005

Waterloo Convention and Visitors Bureau
215 East 4th Street
P.O. Box 1587
Waterloo, IA 50704

Palm Beach County Convention and Visitors Bureau
1555 Palm Beach Lakes, Suite 204
West Palm Beach, FL 33401

Wheeling Convention and Visitors Bureau
607 Central Union Bldg.
Wheeling, WV 26003

Wichita Convention and Visitors Bureau
100 S. Main, Suite 100
Wichita, KS 67202

Williamsburg Area Convention and Visitors Bureau
201 Penniman Rd.
P.O. Box GB
Williamsburg, VA 23187

Greater Wilmington Convention and Visitors Bureau
1300 Market St.
Wilmington, DE 19801

Winston-Salem Convention and Visitors Bureau
500 West Fifth St.
P.O. Box 1408
Winston-Salem, NC 27102-1408

Worcester County Convention and Visitors Bureau
33 Waldo Street
Worcester, MA 01608

York County Convention and Visitors Bureau
1 Market Way East
P.O. Box 1229
York, PA 17405

Appendix B

CODE OF PROFESSIONAL CONDUCT

Preamble

The purpose of the International Association of Convention & Visitor Bureaus (IACVB) shall be:

1. To raise the level of professionalism in the convention and visitor industry through an ongoing educational effort.
2. To serve as a vehicle for the systematic exchange of information pertinent to the convention and visitor industry.
3. To exert its collective influence in matters which may impact the national or international convention and visitor industry.
4. To position the convention and visitor industry as an important economic generator in member communities.

During the pursuit of this stated purpose, the convention and visitor bureau executive and the bureau staff shall be guided by the Golden Rule. . ."do unto others as you would have them do unto you". . . and by striving to adhere to the following principles of professional conduct:

A. To be loyal to and to recognize and discharge your responsibilities to your bureau with dedication to achieving the objectives of your bureau.
B. To uphold all laws and regulations relating to your bureau.
C. To serve all members of your bureau impartially, and to provide no special privilege to any individual member, nor to accept special personal compensation from an individual member, except with the knowledge and consent of your employers.
D. To comply with all levels of governmental regulations concerning lobbying and political activities and to use only legal, ethical and moral means when attempting to influence legislation or regulations affecting your bureau or the convention and visitor industry.
E. To issue no false or deliberately misleading statements of advertisements concerning your bureau or community, any other bureau or community, or the convention and visitor industry, to the media, the public or to any other persons, either affiliated with or unrelated to the convention and visitor industry.
F. To uphold the Bylaws, Rules and Regulations of IACVB, including strict adherence to the principle of confidentiality of all information so designated, whether that information be in the form of CCR printouts, special surveys, or any other data or report which itself or through interpretation, ranks cities or in any other way violates the confidentiality or Bylaws, Rules and Regulations of IACVB. Only the designated IACVB member or full time paid staff personnel of that member who have signed this understanding of confidentiality of IACVB data, shall have access to IACVB confidential information. IACVB Rules and Regulations (Sections 110, 111, 112, 113, 114 and 115) specify that full compliance with requirements regarding confidential information is implicit for continuing membership.

    G. To exercise professional and ethical courtesy, cooperation and communication when dealing with your peers in IACVB, and with other professionals in the convention and visitor industry.

Acceptance as a member of IACVB implies that you fully understand and agree to the terms of the Code of Professional Conduct. Adherence to this Code assures those associated with the convention and visitor industry that IACVB members and their staffs constantly strive to achieve and maintain the highest standards of professionalism and integrity. Deliberate and intentional violation could subject you to censure and possible suspension.

Appendix C

Convention and Visitors Bureau Bibliography

This is a bibliography of trade articles written on convention and visitor bureaus.

Beckleman, Jeff and John Marks, "Working Effectively with Convention Bureaus," *Convention World,* May/June 1984, pp. 22–25.

Benchley, Bob, "CVBs: Your Secret Weapon," *Corporate Meetings and Incentives,* September 1985, pp. 63–69.

"City Convention Bureaux," *C&E International,* May 1986, pp. 27–30.

"Convention and Visitors Bureau," *Medical Conference Planner,* September 1979, pp. 31–33.

"Convention and Visitors Bureau Update," *Association Management,* November 1985, pp. 131–132.

Cumings, Robert, "Good Service is Mandatory," *Meetings and Conventions,* date unknown.

Englander, Todd, "CVBs On The March," *Meetings and Conventions,* May 1985, pp. 65–82.

———, "Big-League Mayors Who Pitch For Their Cities," *Meetings and Conventions,* May 1986, pp. 48–56.

Fernicola, Karen, "CVBs Predict More Competition," *Association Management,* November 1986, pp. 57–61.

Flatley, Karen, "Convention Bureaus: Partners in Planning," *Medical Conference Planner,* September 1979, pp. 28–30.

Gartrell, Richard B., "Convention Bureaus One-Stop Convention Shopping," *Association Management,* November 1984, pp. 101 and 103.

"Gold Service Convention Bureaus Can Be Planner's Best Friend," *Meetings and Conventions,* May 1984, pp. 28, 32, 34–38, 42–49.

Griffin, Marie, "C&VB Spells H-E-L-P," *Successful Meetings,* March 1985, pp. 35–40, 45–47.

Hodesblatt, Susan, "Turn to Convention Bureaus," *Corporate Meetings and Incentives,* November/December 1982, pp. 59–60.

"How Convention Bureaus Differentiate Their Services," *Meetings and Conventions,* February 1986, pp. 81, 93, 98, 102–109.

Hughes, Ann, "The Computer Age Dawns for Convention and Visitors Bureaus," *Successful Meetings,* March 1985, pp. 49–56.

LaForge, Ann E., "C&VB's Test New Strategies," *Successful Meetings,* March 1986, pp. 61–80.

Lassiter, Eric, "A Planner's Advocate," *Corporate Meetings and Incentives,* October 1984, pp. 27–44.

MacDonald, Betty, "CVBs and the Corporate Planner: Marriage of Convenience," *Meetings and Conventions,* May 1986, pp. 77–88.

Mecariello, Cheryl, "Convention and Visitors Bureaus—Maximizing Benefits," *Association and Society Manager,* April/May 1982, pp. 25–30.

Meltzer, Erica, "Boards Lure Meetings Overseas," *Successful Meetings,* March 1986, pp. 75–80.

Miller, Griffin, "What CVBs Can Do For You," *Corporate and Incentive Travel,* June 1987, pp. 35–39.

Moline, Julie, "The Convention Bureau: Ally and Partner," *Meetings and Conventions,* May 1983, pp. 80, 82, 86, 88, 93, 95, 98.

Nichols, Don, "CVBs: Allies in Your Corner," *Corporate Meetings and Incentives,* October, 1987, pp. 77–81.

Phillips, Cheryl, "CVBs: A City's Information Center," *Association and Society Manager,* February/March 1982, pp. 73–78.

Pike, Janet, "Mapping Your Meeting: Convention and Visitor Bureaus Serve As Liaison Between a City and You," *Meeting Place,* April 1983, pp. 14–16.

Rolston, Leonard, "CVB Beat," *Meetings and Conventions,* pp. 36, 45, date unknown.

Rosci, Frank, "Put A Convention Bureau Pro On Your Team," *Successful Meetings,* February 1982, pp. 45–46, 48, 50–53, 56–58, 62, 64, 66, 73–74.

Rubin, Joan S., "The Scramble To Stay On Top," *Association Management,* May 1986, pp. 50–54.

Sabo, Sandra R., "Convention Bureaus Favor Cooperation Over Competition," *Association Management,* October 1983, pp. 81–85.

Satterfield, Joel, "New Bureaus Go For The Silver," *Successful Meetings,* March 1985, pp. 63–68.

Segal, Judith, "Convention Bureaus: The Meeting Planner's Best Friend," *Meetings and Conventions,* May 1982, pp. 42, 59–80, 85–89.

———, "Convention Bureaus: They Stand Beside You and Guide You," *Meetings and Conventions,* May 1979, pp. 98, 102, 107, 114, 116–117.

Sherry, E. C. "Buzz", "Convention and Visitors Bureaus: One-Stop Shopping," *Best Insurance Convention Guide,* date and pages unknown.

"Small and Medium Sized CVB's Offer Substantial Services to Planners," *Convention World,* September/October 1986, pp. 40–41.

Smith, Eileen Robinson, "Convention Bureaus: Budgets a Key Issue," *Meetings and Conventions,* May 1980, pp. 56, 58, 60, 62, 64, 68, 70, 72, 74, 76, 113, 136.

Snyder, William F., "Just What Is A Convention Bureau?" *Meetings and Conventions,* date unknown, pp. 20, 91.

Swanbrow, Diane, "CVBs—A City's Host for Associations," *Association and Society Manager,* February/March 1983, pp. 33–35.

Walters, Jonathan, "Selling Downtown USA," *Association Management,* November 1982, pp. 43–47.

Wichman, Abbe, "Convention Bureaus Are On The Ball," *Corporate Meetings and Incentives,* November 1986, pp. 23, 27–28, 30, 32–33.

———, "Convention Bureaus Go Corporate," *Corporate Meetings and Incentives,* November 1983, pp. 67–76.

Wynn, Mary, "CVB Success: Service with a Smile," *Association and Society Manager,* February/March 1983, pp. 103–104.

Appendix D

Professional Trade Associations

Convention/Meetings Market

American Hotel and Motel Association (AH&MA)
The AH&MA represents the interests of the lodging industry and is composed of more than 8,000 hotel and motel properties. The association serves the industry through a variety of membership services including marketing assistance, educational programs and governmental action. The AH&MA Educational Institute (located in East Lansing, Michigan) is also a major producer of educational publications for the lodging industry.
888 Seventh Avenue, New York, NY 10019 (212)265–4506

American Society of Association Executives (ASAE)
Organized in 1920, the ASAE is the largest and oldest of major meeting associations. The main goal is educational development, including programs covering law, managing a non-profit business, publication and membership development, certification, meeting, conference and exposition planning, and government relations.
1575 Eye Street N.W., Washington, D.C. 20005 (202) 626–2723

American Society for Training and Development (ASTD)
The ASTD provides employer-initiated employee education and training programs, publishes a monthly journal, a newsletter and textbooks, and provides "Train the Trainer" institutes.
600 Maryland Avenue S.W., Suite 305E, Washington, D.C. 20024 (202) 484–2390

Association Internationale De Palais Des Congres (AIPC)
Founded in 1958, this association brings together 78 convention centers from 30 countries, establishing close contact between managers of convention centers. The association also studies technical problems relating to international meetings and the standardization of services, and encourages the exchange of information. Technical services also are provided to organizations wishing to establish a convention center.
c/o Mazjski Prostor, Jezuitski TRG 4, P.O. Box 19, 41000 Zagreb, Yugoslavia.

Convention Liaison Council (CLC)
The CLC is a group of organizations which represent the convention, meeting, trade show and exposition industry by exchanging information, recommending and developing programs, monitoring legislation, and publishing the "Legal Review" and the "Convention Liaison Manual."
1573 Eye Street, Suite 1200, Washington, D.C. 20005 (202) 626–2764

Council on Engineering and Scientific Society Executives (CESSE)
CESSE's objective is to promote the art and science of the management of engineering and scientific societies.
2000 Florida Avenue N.W., Washington, D.C. 20009

European Federation of Conference Towns (EFCT)
The EFCT acts as a focal point for meeting planners in arranging events in Europe, making information on European destination and facilities available, and assisting in finding the city or town that meets their particular requirements. The federation collaborates with international authorities, associations, and other institutions and acts as spokesman on behalf of the European conference industry.
40 Rue Washington, 1050 Brussels, Belgium

Health Care Exhibitors Association (HCEA)
The purpose of the association is to encourage ethical practices at health care meetings and to develop a closer cooperation between managers and exhibitors at conventions.
49 Locust Avenue, Suite 107, New Canaan, CT 06840 (202) 966–6909

Insurance Conference Planners Association (ICPA)
The ICPA is responsible for meeting planning for the insurance industry by providing a network for the exchange of ideas and information, by improving communication with hotels and suppliers, and by aiding members' career growth.
8721 Indian Hills Drive, Omaha, NE 68114 (402) 390–7300

International Association of Auditorium Managers (IAAM)
The IAAM is a professional organization of auditorium, exhibit hall and stadium managers who host large trade and industrial shows.
500 N. Michigan Avenue, Chicago, IL 60611 (312) 661–1700

International Association of Conference Centers (IACC)
This is an association of executive, corporate, college/university and resort conference centers concerned with the problems of providing a total meeting environment.
362 Parsippany Road, Parsippany, NJ 07054 (201) 887–3505

International Association of Professional Congress Organizers (IAPCO)
IAPCO was founded in 1968 by and for professionals engaged in the organization and management of international congresses, conventions and special events. The association's goal is to increase the professionalism of its members through education and interaction with other professionals. IAPCO has 38 members in 19 countries.
40 Rue Washington, 1050 Brussels, Belgium.

International Congress and Convention Association (ICCA)
The ICCA, an international organization of 400 members from 70 countries, specializes in organization, promotion and handling of international conventions and exhibitions.
P.O. Box 5343, 1007 AH Amsterdam, Netherlands (020) 76–5941

Joint Industry Council (JIC)
The Joint Industry Council is composed of ten international convention, meeting, trade show, exhibit and travel industry organizations whose purpose is to provide an open forum for exchanging information, addressing industry issues, developing voluntary policies/guidelines for the industry and disseminating to the various publics it serves information on the contributions made by the industry to the world economy and the public welfare.
JIC c/o International Association of Convention & Visitor Bureaus, P.O. Box 758, Champaign, Illinois 61820 USA

Meeting Planners International (MPI)
Over 6,800 members in 22 countries have contributed to increased professionalism in the meeting industry by initiating educational and networking opportunities.
1950 Stemmons Freeway, Dallas, TX 75207 (214) 746–5250

National Association of Exposition Managers (NAEM)
The NAEM is a professional society of individuals who plan, produce and manage trade shows and public expositions.
P.O. Box 377, Aurora, OH 44202 (216) 562–8255

Professional Convention Management Association (PCMA)
The PCMA was formed in 1957 to increase effectiveness of meetings and conventions in the health care profession. The association plans annual educational seminars, produces newsletters and provides innovative services for membership.
2027 1st Avenue N., Suite 1007, Birmingham, AL 35203 (205) 251–1717

Religious Conference Management Association (RCMA)
This multi-denominational association plans and manages meetings and conventions for religious organizations. The RCMA also provides educational programs concerning the effective use of community and volunteer personnel.
One Hoosier Dome, Suite 120, Indianapolis, IN 46225 (317) 632–1888

Society of Company Meeting Planners (SCMP)
The SCMP was founded primarily as a networking organization but also focuses on education and career development by sponsoring annual national meetings and providing a newsletter, a job bank and a resource center.
2600 Garden Road, Suite 208, Monterey, CA 93940 (408) 649–6544

Society of Government Meetings Planners (SGMP)
The SGMP was organized in 1981 to improve quality and cost effectiveness of governmental meetings by focusing on communication between planners and suppliers and by helping suppliers deal with restrictions of government agencies.
1133-15th Street N.W., Washington, D.C. 20005 (202) 293–5913

Society of Incentive Travel Executives (SITE)
SITE is a professional society that is devoted to the pursuit of excellence in incentive travel through educational programming and professional conferences. It is involved with travel to domestic and international destinations.
271 Madison Avenue, New York, NY 10016 (212) 889–9340

Trade Show Bureau (TSB)
The TSB acts as a unified voice for the trade show industry to increase awareness of marketing management and to serve as an information bureau.
49 Locust Avenue, New Canaan, CT 06840 (203) 996–7133

Union of International Associations (UIA)
The UIA was founded in 1907. The association's membership is comprised of individuals involved in international organizations and includes diplomats, international civil servants, association executives, directors of foundations and professors of international relations. The association also has an associate membership. Programs include the Yearbook of International Associations, the International Congress Calendar and the annual statistics on international association meetings.
40 Rue Washington, 1050 Brussels, Belgium.

Tourism/Leisure Market

American Association of Travel Editors (AATE)
AATE is the world's most influential group of travel journalists. It's more than 400 active editor-members representing media with a total circulation of more than 100 million copies. Associate members receive the monthly newsletter and the official Working Press Pass.
342 Madison Avenue, New York, New York 10017 (212) 661–0656

American Automobile Association (AAA)
Established in 1902 as a not-for-profit corporation, AAA is a federation of 161 affiliated motor clubs with more than 1000 offices throughout the United States and Canada. It offers personal service to members through its network of nearly 29,000 full-time employees. Emergency road service is coordinated through a network of more than 14,000 contract garages and service stations. More than 800 accredited full-service AAA travel agencies are located in North America. AAA tour books list and rate 25,000 accommodations and restaurants. The AAA researches and produces its own maps and provides other services for tour operators and travelers.
8111 Gatehouse Road, Falls Church, VA 22047–0001 (703) AAA–6000

American Bus Association (ABA)
The association is a private nonprofit organization that promotes and protects the interests of bus companies, tour operators and suppliers to the industry. The ABA provides up-to-date information through various publications, services and training programs to help members stay abreast of industry developments.
1025 Connecticut Avenue N.W., Suite 308, Washington, D.C. 20036 (202) 293–5890

American Society of Travel Agents (ASTA)
The American Society of Travel Agents is the largest travel trade association in the world, representing 23,000 members in 129 countries. Founded in 1931, ASTA continuously provides new and comprehensive educational programs to sustain the professionalism of its members and provides products and services to permit travel agents to conduct their businesses with integrity and competency. ASTA represents its members throughout the world in an interface with components of the industry, government and the general public.
4400 MacArthur Blvd.N.W., Washington, D.C. 20007 (202) 965–7520

Association of Retail Travel Agents (ARTA)
The Association of Retail Travel Agents was founded in 1962 to provide the retail travel industry with a platform from which it could articulate its views, particularly in the area of regulations and legislation affecting the industry. In addition to its efforts in Washington, ARTA also orchestrates educational experiences to help agents become more cost effective, productive and professional in their dealings with the traveling public.
25 South Riverside, Croton-on-Hudson, NY 10520 (914) 271–9000

Cruise Lines International Associaton (CLIA)
Cruise Lines International Association is a marketing-promotional trade organization composed of 26 major cruise lines serving the North American marketplace, working in affiliation with over 16,000 travel agents. Formed in 1975 to act as a vehicle to promote the general concept of cruising, CLIA exists to educate, train, promote and explain the value, desirability and profitability of the cruise product.
17 Batery Place, Suite 631, New York, NY 10004 (212) 425–7400

Foremost West (FW)
The Foremost West, founded in 1974, currently consists of five Western states. It is supported by the public and private sectors with the objective of economic development through tourism. The organization markets the West through representation at international trade shows, product development "Familiarization Tours" and an extensive publicity/public relations program. Regional educational seminars are conducted to inform and upgrade the industry in the area.
770 East South Temple, Suite B, Salt Lake City, UT 84102 (801) 532–3113

Hotel Sales and Marketing Association International (HSMAI)
The HSMAI provides a variety of programs that benefit members. Each year the association offers more than 60 courses, seminars, workshops and clinics designed to enhance the professional performance of hotel sales and marketing executives. The HSMAI conducts studies and publishes books and reports based on their research. An Executive Referral Service is also provided.
1400 K Street, N.W. Washington, D.C. 20005 (202) 789–0089

International Association of Amusement Parks and Attractions (IAAPA)
The IAAPA represents amusement parks and attractions and aims to promote the progress and development of the industry as well as the establishment of standards.
4230 King Street, Alexandria, Virginia 22302 (703) 671–5800

Midwest Travel Writers (MTW)
Midwest Travel Writers is a professional association whose members' work is found in Midwest magazines and newspapers. The organization also includes public service organizations for Midwest states and cities.
Newman Associates, P.O. Box 758, Champaign, IL 61820 (217) 359–8881

National Motorcoach Marketing Network, Inc. (NMMN)
The National Motorcoach Marketing Network, Inc. was founded in 1983. It is the largest marketing consortium in the motorcoach charter and tour industry. As a for-profit corporation, the Network sets the toughest affiliation requirements in the motorcoach industry. A carrier is selected on the basis of its reputation, continuous service and performance in its region.
P.O. Box 399 Fairfax Station, VA 22039 (703) 250–7897

National Restaurant Association (NRA)
The National Restaurant Association is the leading trade association for the $198 billion food service industry. The association's 11,000 members represent more than 100,000 food service outlets. Since its founding in 1919, the NRA has worked to promote the ideals and interests of the food service industry by providing members with a wide range of education, research, communications, convention and government services.
311 First St. N.W., Washington, D.C. 20001 (202) 638–6100

National Tour Association (NTA)
The National Tour Association is the primary domestic tour industry association in North America. NTA's 3000+ membership is comprised of tour companies, suppliers such as hotels, restaurants, attractions and travel promotion agencies. NTA is committed to assisting its members to deal effectively with public policy issues and to addressing the broad needs of society in the travel and tourism field.
546 East Main Street, P.O. Box 3071, Lexington, KY 40596 (606) 253–1036

Old West Trail Foundation (OWTF)
The Old West Trail Foundation is a non-profit marketing organization that promotes the lore and history, the outstanding attractions, and the travel opportunities available in Montana, Nebraska, North Dakota, South Dakota and Wyoming. State travel departments and private-sector members pool dollars and ideas—utilizing a wide variety of marketing techniques to attract more visitors to the Old West region and to encourage them to stay longer.
900 Jackson Blvd., P.O. Box 2554, Rapid City, SD 57709 (605) 343–7677

Ontario Motorcoach Association (OMA)
The Ontario Motorcoach Association is a professional trade association of tour operators and bus company owners in Ontario. Supplier members include hotels, restaurants, destinations, attractions and other industry suppliers in the United States and Canada.
234 Eglinton Ave. E., Suite 602, Toronto, Ont. M4P 1K5 Canada (416) 488–8855

Pacific Asia Travel Association (PATA)
The Pacific Asia Travel Association was born in Hawaii in 1951. The purpose is to bring together governments, airlines and cruiselines, hotels, tour operators, travel agencies and other tourism-related organizations with the common goal of promoting and developing travel to and among the countries of the Pacific and Asia. PATA serves as the central resource for research, development and marketing expertise by offering support for members in marketing their destinations.
228 Grant Avenue, #4, San Francisco, CA 94108 (415) 986–4646

Recreation Vehicle Industry Association (RVIA)
Recreation Vehicle Industry Association, the national trade association representing more than 600 RV manufacturers, serves as the industry's voice to the government and general public, and as a primary source of shipment statistics, market research, technical data, and consumer and media information. The association maintains an inspection program and hosts two annual trade shows of the industry's new-model RVs, engineering developments and aftermarket innovations.
P.O. Box 2999, 1896 Preston White Dr., Reston, VA 22090 (703) 620–6003

Society of American Travel Writers (SATW)
The Society of American Travel Writers, founded in 1956, is a nonprofit, public service organization dedicated to serving the interest of the traveling public, to promoting international understanding and good will, and to further promoting unbiased, objective reporting of information on travel topics. The Society's five regional chapters represent approximately 700 members.
1120 Connecticut Ave., Suite 940, Washington, D.C. 20036 (202) 785–5567

Travel Industry Association of America (TIAA)
The primary purpose of the Travel Industry Association of America is to facilitate travel in the United States, to indicate the importance of travel to the national economy and cultural development, to encourage international exchange of travelers and to influence government policies that affect the travel industry.
1133-21st Street, N.W., Washington, D.C. 20036 (202) 293–1433

Travel South USA (TS)
Travel South USA, founded in 1968, is the nation's largest multi-state travel organization. It is a nonprofit promotional agency which was organized to increase travel by domestic and international travelers to and within the eleven member states. The organization provides education, research and government affairs programs.
3400 Peachtree Rd., N.E., Atlanta, GA 30326 (404) 231–1790

United States Tour Operators Association (USTOA)
The United States Tour Operators Association was founded in 1972 to establish a voice for the U.S. tour operator community and to uphold the principles of its motto, "Integrity in Tourism." USTOA members maintain the highest standards of professional conduct and aim to inform, educate and protect the traveling public as well as retail travel agents.
211 E. 51st Street, Suite 12B, New York, NY 10023 (212) 944–5727

United States Travel and Tourism Administration (USTTA)
The United States Travel and Tourism Administration promotes travel to the United States in overseas markets. It also calculates and disseminates statistical information on the number of visitors from foreign countries and the total revenues they generate. The administration also tabulates the number of U.S. citizens traveling abroad. Thirty-one offices in the United States are joined by three offices in Canada and one each in Mexico, Australia, the Netherlands and Italy.
United States Department of Commerce, Washington, D.C. 20230

World Tourism Organization (WTO)
The WTO aims at promoting tourism with a view of contributing to economic expansion of countries, international understanding, peace, prosperity and universal respect for human rights and fundamental freedoms. The WTO works closely with units of the United Nations. 109 countries plus associate members are represented in the WTO. Calle Capitan Haya 42, Madrid 28020 SPAIN.

Education/Research Market

The Society of Travel and Tourism Educators (STTE)
Founded in 1980, the society has a membership of more than 200 individuals representing all levels of travel and tourism education and related businesses. The society promotes increased professional knowledge through interaction, the development of networking among peers, the sharing of ideas, strategies and research. These objectives are accomplished through conferences, workshops and a newsletter.
T. Powderly, CTC, Brandywine College, P.O. Box 7139 Concord Pike, Wilmington, Delaware 19803 (302) 478-3000.

Travel and Tourism Research Association (TTRA)
Travel and Tourism Research Association is the only international organization of travel research and marketing professionals devoted to improving the quality, scope and acceptability of travel research and marketing information. The 750 active members are from accommodations, attractions, transportation companies, media, advertising and consulting firms, government agencies, convention and visitor bureaus and other organizations interested in travel research and marketing.
TTRA, P.O. Box 8066, Foothill Station, Salt Lake City, Utah 84108

U.S. Travel Data Center (USTDC)
The U.S. Travel Data Center is the national non-profit center for travel and tourism research, devoting its resources to measuring the economic impact of travel and producing consumer research for broad distribution in the industry. A free Guide to Data Center programs and publications is available by writing USTDC at Two Lafayette Center, 1133 21st Street N.W., Washington, D.C. 20036 (202) 293-1040

Appendix E

Index of Bylaws
(Eastern U.S. City)
CONVENTION AND VISITORS BUREAU

Section 6. Manner of Acting.
Section 7. Presumption of Assent.
Section 8. Informal Action by Directors.
Section 9. Committees of the Board

Article VI. Officers:

Section 1. Officers of the Corporation.
Section 2. Election and Term.
Section 3. Compensation of Officers.
Section 4. Removal.
Section 5. Bonds.
Section 6. President.
Section 7. Vice-Presidents.
Section 8. Secretary.
Section 9. Assistant Secretaries.
Section 10. Treasurer.
Section 11. Assistant Treasurers.

Article VII. Contracts, Loans, Checks and Deposits:

Section 1. Contracts.
Section 2. Loans.
Section 3. Checks and Drafts.
Section 4. Deposits.

Article VIII. General Provisions:

Section 1. Distribution upon Dissolution.
Section 2. Seal.
Section 3. Indemnification.
Section 4. Fiscal Year.

Bylaws
(Eastern U.S. City)

Article I. Offices

Section 1. *Principal Office.* The principal office of the corporation shall be located in (name of city).

Section 2. *Registered Office.* The registered office of the corporation required by law to be maintained in the State of (name of state) may be, but need not be, identical with the principal office.

Section 3. *Other Offices.* The corporation may have offices at such other places, either within or without the State of (name of state) as the Board of Directors may designate or as the affairs of the corporation may require from time to time.

Article II. Members

Section 1. *Membership.* The corporation shall have members who shall be those persons, corporations, associations or firms elected to membership by the Board of Directors as hereinafter provided. The members shall not have any voting rights.

Section 2. *Active Members.* Any person, corporation, association or firm interested in the purpose of the corporation shall be eligible for active membership.

Section 3. *Election of Active Members.* Any person, corporation, association, or firm eligible for active membership under these bylaws may be elected on written application by a majority vote of the Board of Directors. The written application shall be in such form as may be prescribed by the Board of Directors and shall state the name, address and occupation of the applicant and, if a corporation, association or other organization, the name of the individual who shall represent such organization.

Section 4. *Honorary Members.* The Board of Directors, by unanimous action, may elect as an honorary member any person distinguished for his or her achievements or contributions to the community. Honorary members shall be exempt from all dues and assessments.

Section 5. *Dues and Assessments.* Active members shall pay dues and assessments in such amounts and at such times as the Board of Directors may prescribe from time to time. Any member who shall fail to pay any dues or assessments for a period of thirty days after the due date thereof shall be notified in writing of such nonpayment and if the amount due is not then paid within thirty days after the mailing of such written notice the Board of Directors may terminate the membership of such member without further notice.

Section 6. *Termination or Suspension of Membership.* Any member may resign as a member at any time by giving written notice of resignation to the corporation. Any member may be suspended or terminated from membership by the Board of Directors for cause, including without limitation the nonpayment of dues or assessments after notice as provided in Section 5 above or any other conduct by the member that is in the good faith judgment of the Board of Directors a violation of the charter or bylaws of the corporation or is inimical to the purpose of the corporation.

Article III. Meetings of Members

Section 1. *Place of Meetings.* All meetings of members shall be held at the principal office of the corporation, or at such other place, either within or without the State of (name of state) as shall be designated in the notice of the meeting.

Section 2. *Annual Meetings.* There shall be an annual meeting of the members of the corporation in the month of May of each year, unless otherwise ordered by the Board of Directors, for delivering reports and the transaction of any other business.

Section 3. *Special Meetings.* Special meetings of the members may be called at any time by the Chairman of the Board, the President, Secretary or Board of Directors of the corporation.

Section 4. *Notice of Meetings.* Written or printed notice stating the time and place of the meeting shall be delivered to each member not less than ten nor more than fifty days before the date of any meeting of members, either personally or by mail, by or at the direction of the President, the Secretary, or the Board of Directors. If mailed, such notice shall be deemed to be delivered when deposited in the United States mail, addressed to the member's address as it appears on the records of the corporation, with postage thereon prepaid.

Article IV. Board of Directors

Section 1. *General Powers.* The business and affairs of the corporation shall be managed by its Board of Directors.

Section 2. *Number, Term and Qualifications.* The number of directors constituting the Board of Directors shall be sixteen regular directors and four ex officio directors. The regular directors shall have the sole right to vote and otherwise act on all matters acted upon by the Board of Directors. The ex officio directors shall not have the right to vote or otherwise act upon any matter and shall not be counted or deemed to be directors in determining a quorum or the number of votes required on any matter; they shall only have the right and privilege to attend and participate in the discussions at all meetings of the Board of Directors.

The regular directors shall be (1) the President of the corporation elected by the Board of Directors, (2) a member of the City Council appointed by such City Council, (3) a member of the Coliseum-Auditorium-Civic Center Authority appointed by such Authority, (4) a member of the Executive Committee of the Chamber of Commerce appointed by such corporation and (5) twelve elected directors who shall be divided into three classes, as nearly equal in number as may be, to serve in and first instance for terms of one, two and three years, respectively, and until their successors shall be elected and shall qualify, and thereafter the directors in each class of elected directors shall be elected to serve for terms of three years and until their successors shall be elected and shall qualify. In the event of any increase or decrease in the number of elected directors, the additional or eliminated directorships shall be so classified or chosen that all classes of elected directors shall remain or become equal in number, as nearly as may be. In the event of death, resignation, retirement, removal or disqualification of an elected director during his term of office, his successor shall be elected to serve only until the expiration of the term of his predecessor.

The ex officio directors shall be the persons who hold the following offices: (1) President of the Chamber of Commerce; (2) President of Hotel/Motel Association, Inc., or some other member of its Executive Committee appointed by such Association to serve as an ex officio director in lieu of its President; (3) City Manager or some other employee of the City appointed by the City Manager to serve as an ex officio director in lieu of the City Manager; and (4) Managing Director of the Coliseum-Civic Center-Auditorium Authority, or some other person appointed by such Authority to serve as an ex officio director in lieu of its Managing Director.

Section 3. *Election of Directors.* The elected directors shall be elected by the vote of
a majority of the directors then in office. If any director so demands, the
election of directors shall be by ballot. No elected director shall be elected
to serve more than two consecutive terms of three years.

In electing directors the Board of Directors shall, to the extent practicable,
choose persons as follows: four representatives from the lodging industry
divided as fairly as practicable according to size and geographic location;
four representatives from the travel industry, including without limitation
restaurants, attractions, meeting and show planners, transportation (air &
ground), festivals and similar groups; and four business community leaders,
including without limitation finance, retail, purveyors, news media, manufacturing and wholesale.

Section 4. *Removal.* Any regular director may be removed at any time with or without
cause by the vote of a majority of the directors then in office.

Section 5. *Vacancies.* Any vacancy occurring in the elected directors may be filled
by the affirmative vote of a majority of the remaining directors even though
less than a quorum, or by the sole remaining director. A director elected
to fill a vacancy shall be elected for the unexpired term of his predecessor
in office.

Section 6. *Chairman of Board.* There may be a Chairman of the Board of Directors
elected by the directors from their number at any meeting of the Board.
The Chairman shall preside at all meetings of members and all meetings
of the Board of Directors and perform such other duties as may be assigned by the Board.

Section 7. *Honorary Co-Chairmen.* The Mayor of the City and the Chairman of the
County Commission shall be Co-Chairmen of the Board of the corporation
and as such shall have a standing invitation to attend and participate in,
but not vote at, all meetings of the Board of Directors and all meetings of
members of the corporation.

Section 8. *Compensation.* The Board of Directors may compensate directors for their
services as such and may provide for the payment of any or all expenses
incurred by directors in attending regular and special meetings of the Board
and otherwise performing their duties as directors.

Article V. Meetings of Directors

Section 1. *Regular Meetings.* A regular meeting of the Board of Directors shall be
held immediately after, and at the same place as, the annual meeting of
members. In addition, the Board of Directors may provide, by resolution,
the time and place, either within or without the State of (name of state)
for the holding of additional regular meetings.

Section 2. *Special Meetings.* Special meetings of the Board of Directors may be called
by or at the request of the President or any two directors. Such a meeting
may be held either within or without the State of (name of state) as fixed
by the person or persons calling the meeting.

Section 3. *Notice of Meetings.* Regular meetings of the Board of Directors may be
held without notice. The person or persons calling a special meeting of the
Board of Directors shall, at least two days before the meeting, give notice
thereof by any usual means of communication. Such notice need not specify
the purpose for which the meeting is called.

Section 4. *Waiver of Notice.* Any director may waive notice of any meeting. The attendance by a director at a meeting shall constitute a waiver of notice of such meeting, except where a director attends a meeting for the express purpose of objecting to the transaction of any business because the meeting is not lawfully called or convened.

Section 5. *Quorum.* A majority of the number of directors fixed by these bylaws shall constitute a quorum for the transaction of business at any meeting of the Board of Directors.

Section 6. *Manner of Acting.* Except as otherwise provided in these bylaws, the act of the majority of the directors present at a meeting at which a quorum is present shall be the act of the Board of Directors.

Section 7. *Presumption of Assent.* A director of the corporation who is present at a meeting of the Board of Directors at which action on any corporate matter is taken shall be presumed to have assented to the action taken unless his contrary vote is recorded or his dissent is otherwise entered in the minutes of the meeting or unless he shall file his written dissent to such action with the person acting as the secretary of the meeting before the adjournment thereof or shall forward such dissent by registered mail to the Secretary of the corporation immediately after the adjournment of the meeting. Such right to dissent shall not apply to a director who voted in favor of such action.

Section 8. *Informal Action by Directors.* Action taken by a majority of the directors without a meeting is nevertheless Board action if written consent to the action is signed by all the directors and filed with the minutes of the proceedings of the Board, whether done before or after the action so taken.

Section 9. *Committees of the Board.* The Board of Directors, by resolution adopted by a majority of the number of directors fixed by these bylaws, may designate two or more directors to constitute an Executive Committee and other committees, each of which, to the extent authorized by law and provided in such resolution, shall have and may exercise all of the authority of the Board of Directors in the management of the corporation.

Other committees not having and exercising the authority of the Board of Directors in the management of the corporation may be designated by a resolution adopted by a majority of the directors present at a meeting at which a quorum is present.

The designation of any committee and the delegation thereto of authority shall not operate to relieve the Board of Directors, or any member thereof, of any responsibility or liability imposed upon it or him by law.

Article VI. Officers

Section 1. *Officers of the Corporation.* The officers of the corporation shall consist of a President, a Secretary, a Treasurer and such Vice Presidents, Assistant Secretaries, Assistant Treasurers, and other officers as the Board of Directors may from time to time elect. Any two or more offices may be held by the same person, but no officer may act in more than one capacity where action of two or more officers is required.

Section 2. *Election and Term.* The officers of the corporation shall be elected by the Board of Directors and each officer shall hold office until his death, resignation, retirement, removal, disqualification or his successor shall have been elected and qualified.

Section 3. *Compensation of Officers.* The compensation of all officers of the corporation shall be fixed by the Board of Directors and no officer shall serve the corporation in any other capacity and receive compensation therefor unless such additional compensation be authorized by the Board of Directors.

Section 4. *Removal.* Any officer or agent elected or appointed by the Board of Directors may be removed by the Board whenever in its judgment the best interests of the corporation will be served thereby; but such removal shall be without prejudice to the contract rights, if any, of the person so removed.

Section 5. *Bonds.* The Board of Directors may by resolution require any officer, agent, or employee of the corporation to give bond to the corporation, with sufficient sureties, conditioned on the faithful performance of the duties of his respective office or position, and to comply with such other conditions as may from time to time be required by the Board of Directors.

Section 6. *President.* The President shall be the principal executive officer of the corporation and, subject to the control of the Board of Directors, shall in general supervise and control all of the business and affairs of the corporation. He shall sign, with the Secretary, and Assistant Secretary, or any other proper officer of the corporation thereunto authorized by the Board of Directors, any deeds, mortgages, bonds, contracts, or other instruments which the Board of Directors has authorized to be executed, except in cases where the signing and execution thereof shall be expressly delegated by the Board of Directors or by these bylaws to some other officer or agent of the corporation, or shall be required by law to be otherwise signed or executed; and in general he shall perform all duties incident to the office of President and such other duties as may be prescribed by the Board of Directors from time to time.

Section 7. *Vice Presidents.* In the absence of the President or in the event of his death, inability or refusal to act, the Vice Presidents in the order of their length of service as such, unless otherwise determined by the Board of Directors, shall perform the duties of the President, and when so acting shall have all the powers of and be subject to all the restrictions upon the President. Any Vice President shall perform such other duties as from time to time may be assigned to him by the President or Board of Directors.

Section 8. *Secretary.* The Secretary shall: (a) keep the minutes of the meetings of the members, of the Board of Directors and of all committees in one or more books provided for that purpose; (b) see that all notices are duly given in accordance with the provisions of these bylaws or as required by law; (c) be custodian of the corporate records and of the seal of the corporation and see that the seal of the corporation is affixed to all documents the execution of which on behalf of the corporation under its seal is duly authorized; (d) keep a register of the post office address of each member which shall be furnished to the Secretary by such member; and (e) in general perform all duties incident to the office of Secretary and such other duties as from time to time may be assigned to him by the President or by the Board of Directors.

Section 9. *Assistant Secretaries.* In the absence of the Secretary or in the event of his death, inability or refusal to act, the Assistant Secretaries in the order of their length of service as Assistant Secretary, unless otherwise determined by the Board of Directors, shall perform the duties of the Secretary, and when so acting shall have all the powers of and be subject to all the restrictions upon the Secretary. They shall perform such other duties as may be assigned to them by the Secretary, by the President, or by the Board of Directors.

Section 10. *Treasurer.* The Treasurer shall: (a) have charge and custody of and be responsible for all funds and securities of the corporation; receive and give receipts for moneys due and payable to the corporation from any source whatsoever, and deposit all such moneys in the name of the corporation in such depositories as shall be selected in accordance with these bylaws; and (b) in general perform all of the duties incident to the office of Treasurer and such other duties as from time to time may be assigned to him by the President or by the Board of Directors, or by these bylaws.

Section 11. *Assistant Treasurers.* In the absence of the Treasurer or in the event of his death, inability or refusal to act, the Assistant Treasurers in the order of their length of service as such, unless otherwise determined by the Board of Directors, shall perform the duties of the Treasurer, and when so acting shall have all the powers of and be subject to all restrictions upon the Treasurer. They shall perform such other duties as may be assigned to them by the Treasurer, by the President, or by the Board of Directors.

Article VII. Contracts, Loans, Checks and Deposits

Section 1. *Contracts.* The Board of Directors may authorize any officer or officers, agent or agents, to enter into any contract or execute and deliver any instrument in the name of and on behalf of the corporation, and such authority may be general or confined to specific instances.

Section 2. *Loans.* No loans shall be contracted on behalf of the corporation and no evidences of indebtedness shall be issued in its name unless authorized by a resolution of the Board of Directors. Such authority may be general or confined to specific instances.

Section 3. *Checks and Drafts.* All checks, drafts or other orders for the payment of money, issued in the name of the corporation, shall be signed by such officer or officers, agent or agents of the corporation and in such manner as shall from time to time be determined by resolution of the Board of Directors.

Section 4. *Deposits.* All funds of the corporation not otherwise employed shall be deposited from time to time to the credit of the corporation in such depositories as the Board of Directors may select.

Article VIII. General Provisions

Section 1. *Distribution upon Dissolution.* Upon dissolution of the corporation its assets shall, after all of its liabilities and obligations have been discharged or adequate provision made therefore, be distributed to the city or to any association or associations organized for purposes similar to the purposes of the corporation as may be designated by a majority of the directors of the corporation then holding office.

Section 2. *Seal.* The corporate seal of the corporation shall consist of two concentric circles between which is the name of the corporation and in the center of which is inscribed SEAL; and such seal is hereby adopted as the corporate seal of the corporation.

Section 3. *Indemnification.* Any person who at any time serves or has served as a director, officer, employee or agent of the corporation, or in such capacity at the request of the corporation for any other corporation, partnership, joint venture, trust or other enterprise, shall have a right to be indemnified by the corporation to the fullest extent permitted by law against (a) reasonable expenses, including attorneys' fees, actually and necessarily incurred by him in connection with any threatened, pending or completed action, suit or proceedings, whether civil, criminal, administrative or investigative, and whether or not brought by or on behalf of the corporation, seeking to hold him liable by reason of the fact that he is or was acting in such capacity, and (b) reasonable payments made by him in satisfaction of any judgment, money decree, fine, penalty or settlement for which he may have become liable in any such action, suit or proceeding.

The Board of Directors of the corporation shall take all such action as may be necessary and appropriate to authorize the corporation to pay the indemnification required by this bylaw, including without limitation, to the extent needed, making a good faith evaluation of the manner in which the claimant for indemnity acted and of the reasonable amount of indemnity due him.

Any person who at any time after the adoption of this bylaw serves or has served in any of the aforesaid capacities for or on behalf of the corporation shall be deemed to be doing or to have done so in reliance upon, and as consideration for, the right of indemnification provided herein. Such right shall inure to the benefit of the legal representatives of any such person and shall not be exclusive of any other rights to which such person may be entitled apart from the provision of this bylaw.

In addition to all of the foregoing, the Board of Directors shall have the right and power to purchase and maintain insurance on behalf of any person who is or was a director, officer, employee or agent of the corporation, or is or was serving at the request of the corporation as a director, officer, employee or agent of another corporation, partnership, joint venture, trust or other enterprise against any liability asserted against him and incurred by him in any such capacity, or arising out of his status as such, whether or not the corporation would have the power to indemnify him against such liability.

Section 4. *Fiscal Year.* The fiscal year of the corporation shall be fixed by the Board of Directors.

Bylaws
(Western U.S. City)
CONVENTION AND VISITORS BUREAU

Article I. Name and Location

Section 1. *Name.* The name of the corporation, herein called "corporation", shall be the (name of city) *Convention & Visitors Bureau.*

Section 2. *Location.* The principal office for the transaction of business of the corporation shall be in (name of state).

Article II. Membership

Section 1. *Membership.* Any person, natural or corporate, partnership or association interested in promoting the convention and visitor business in the area may make application for membership, and upon payment of the membership fee, and upon compliance with such conditions as may be prescribed by the Board of Directors for membership, may become an active member of the corporation. Each membership shall entitle the holder to one vote on membership matters. The Board of Directors shall have the power to reject any membership application if such rejection is deemed by the Board to be in the best interest of the corporation.

Section 2. *Membership Fee.* The membership fee and frequency of payment shall be determined from time to time by the Board of Directors of said corporation. The amount of such fee may be changed or otherwise fixed by resolution of the Board of Directors.

Section 3. *Expiration of Membership.* Upon the expiration of any term of membership, the rights of the member cease without further notice of the member.

Section 4. *Termination of Membership.* Membership in the corporation may be terminated:
   a. By resignation
   b. By expulsion
   Any member may, for refusal to comply with the Bylaws or the rules and regulations of the corporation, or for any breach thereof, or for conduct unbecoming a member, may be expelled from membership by the affirmative vote of two-thirds of the Board of Director members present at the meeting of the Board.

Section 5. *Members' Rights Upon Termination of Membership.* In the event of a termination of membership, regardless of how terminated, the corporation shall not be liable for the return of dues.

Article III. Meetings of Membership

Section 1. *Annual Meeting.* An annual meeting of the members of the corporation shall be held each fiscal year at a time and place to be designated by the Board of Directors.

Section 2. *Special Meetings.* Special meetings may be called at any time by the Board of Directors or by written petition signed by not less than five percent (5%) of the members entitled to vote thereat. Notice of special meetings shall be given in the same manner as for annual meetings of the members.

Section 3. *Notice of Meetings.*
   a. *Time and Content.* Written notice of every meeting of members shall be sent or otherwise given in accordance with the provisions of this article not less than twenty (20) nor more than fifty (50) days before the date of the meeting. The notice shall specify the place, date and hour of the meeting and the general nature of the business to be transacted. The agenda for the annual meeting shall include a category designated "new business for discussion" during which any member may present any matter for discussion except the election of Directors and other matters, if any, voted upon by mail ballot as hereinafter provided. Each item discussed under "new business for discussion" shall be approved or disapproved by the members present in person or by

proxy. If a majority of the members present approve an item, the Board of Directors shall consider and vote upon that item before the next annual meeting and shall report the Board's decision to the members not later than the time when notice of the next annual meeting is mailed to the membership. The agenda for a special meeting shall specify the nature of the business to be transacted.

    b. *Manner of Giving Notice.* Notice of a members' meeting shall be given by mail or other means of written communication, addressed to the member at the address of such member appearing on the books of the Bureau or given by the member to the Bureau for purposes of notice. Notice shall be deemed to have been given at the time when delivered personally or deposited in the mail or sent by telegram or other means of written communication.

    c. *Affidavit of Mailing Notice.* An affidavit of the mailing or other means of giving any notice of any members' meeting may be executed by the Secretary, Assistant Secretary, or any other authorized representative of the Bureau giving the notice, and if so executed, shall be filed and maintained in the minute book of the Bureau.

    d. *Adjourned Meetings.* If a members' meeting is adjourned for more than forty-five (45) days or if after the adjournment a new record date is fixed for the adjourned meeting, a notice of the adjourned meeting shall be given to each member of record entitled to vote at the meeting.

Section 4. *Quorum.*

    a. *Number Required.* The presence in person or by proxy of twenty-five (25) members entitled to vote shall constitute a quorum for the transaction of business.

    b. *Loss of Quorum.* The members present at a duly called or duly held meeting at which a quorum is present may continue to transact business until adjournment, notwithstanding the withdrawal of enough members to leave less than a quorum, if any action taken (other than adjournment) is approved by at least a majority of the members required to constitute a quorum.

Section 5. *Adjournment.* Any members' meeting, whether or not a quorum is present, may be adjourned from time to time by a vote of the majority of the members represented at the meeting, either in person or by proxy, but in the absence of a quorum, no other business may be transacted except as provided in this article.

Section 6. *Voting.*

    a. *Eligibility to Vote.* Persons entitled to vote at any meeting of members or by ballot shall be members in good standing as of the date determined in accordance with Section 10 of this Article III.

    b. *Manner of Casting Votes.* Voting may be by voice or balloting, provided that any election of Directors must be by ballot.

    c. *Proxy Voting.* Members entitled to vote, as set forth in this Section 6, shall have the right to vote either in person or by a written proxy executed by such person or his or her duly authorized agent and filed with the Secretary of the Bureau, except as otherwise expressly provided in these Bylaws, provided, however, that a proxy shall not be valid after the expiration of eleven (11) months from the date thereof unless otherwise provided in the proxy. The maximum term of any proxy shall be three (3) years from the date of its execution. Every proxy shall continue in full force and effect until revoked by the person executing it prior to the vote pursuant thereto.

Section 7. *Majority Vote.* At all membership meetings all questions shall be determined by a majority vote of the members present in person or by proxy who are entitled to vote except as herein expressly provided to the contrary.

Section 8. *Waivers, Consents, and Approval.*

    a. *Written Waiver or Consent.* The transactions of any meeting of members, however called and noticed, and wherever held, shall be as valid as though had at a meeting duly held after regular call and notice, if a quorum is present either in person or by proxy, and if, either before or after the meeting, each of the persons entitled to vote but not present in person or by proxy, signs a written waiver of notice, a consent to the holding of the meeting, or an approval of the minutes of the meeting. All such waivers, consents, and approvals shall be filed with the corporate records.

    b. *Waiver by Attendance.* Attendance by a person at a meeting shall also constitute a waiver of notice of that meeting, except when the person objects at the beginning of a meeting to the transaction of any business due to the inadequacy or illegality of the notice. Also, attendance at a meeting is not a waiver of any right to object to the consideration of matters not included in the notice of the meeting, if that objection is expressly made at the meeting.

Section 9. *Action by Written Ballot.*

    a. *Ballot Requirement.* Any action which may be taken at any regular or special meeting of members may be taken without a meeting. If an action is taken without a meeting, the Bureau shall distribute a written ballot to every member entitled to vote on the matter. The ballot shall set forth the proposed action, provide an opportunity to specify approval or disapproval of any proposal, and provide a reasonable time within which to return the ballot to the Bureau. Approval by written ballot shall be valid only when the number of votes cast by ballots within the time period specified equals or exceeds the quorum required to be present at a meeting authorizing the action, and the number of approvals equals or exceeds the number of votes that would be required to approve at a meeting at which the total number of votes cast was the same as the number of votes cast by ballot.

    b. *Directors to be Elected by Ballot.* Directors shall be elected by written ballot.

    c. *Solicitation of Ballots.* Ballots shall be solicited in a manner consistent with the requirements of giving notice of members' meetings set forth in Section 3 of this Article III and of voting by written ballot set forth in Paragraph (d) of this Section 8. All such solicitations shall indicate the number of responses needed to meet the quorum requirements and, with respect to ballots other than for the election of Directors, shall state the percentage of approvals necessary to cast the measure submitted. The solicitation shall specify the time by which the ballot must be received in order to be counted.

    d. *Voting by Written Ballot.* The form of written ballot distributed shall afford an opportunity to specify on the form a choice between approval and disapproval of each matter or group of related matters intended, at the time the written ballot is distributed, to be acted on by such written ballot. The form shall also provide, subject to reasonable specified conditions, that where the person solicited specifies a choice with respect to any such matter the vote must be cast in accordance therewith. In any election of Directors, any form of written ballot in which the directors to be voted on are named therein as candidates and which is marked by a member "withhold" or otherwise marked in a manner indicating that the authority to vote for the election of directors is withheld shall not be voted either for or against the election of a Director.

e. *Revocation of Ballots.* A written ballot may not be revoked.

Section 10. *Record Date for Member Notice and Voting.* For the purpose of determining which members are entitled to receive notice of any annual meeting, to vote, to cast written ballots, or to exercise any right in respect to any other lawful action, the Board of Directors shall fix, in advance, a "record date", which shall be forty-five (45) days before the date of any such action. With respect to a notice of a special meeting, the record date shall be twenty (20) days before the date of any such meeting. Only members of record on the date so fixed are entitled to notice, to vote, to cast ballots, or to exercise any other lawful right, as the case may be.

Article IV. Board of Directors

Section 1. *Members and Qualifications.* The members of the Board of Directors shall, by virtue of their responsibility, be selected from the membership of the corporation. They will include:

1. General Business is defined as: *Members*

   All businesses not regularly identified with the tourism/convention business which directly or indirectly derive benefits from tourists/conventioneers.   *8*

                                                                    8

2. Hospitality, Visitor Service Industry and Transportation

   A. Hospitality and Visitor Service Industry is defined as:

   All businesses directly serving the visitor and/or conventioneer in the following capacities: lodging, food service, attractions, convention servicing, and any like hospitality-oriented service.

   i. Lodging—Innkeepers President   *1*
          —Other lodging representatives   *5*
   ii. Restaurant Assoc.   *1*
   ii. Visitor service   *2*

   B. Transportation Industry is defined as:
   All airlines, bus lines, tour companies, trains and, in general, any business which transports visitors or conventioneers in normal business conditions.   *2*

                                                                    11

3. Government
   A. City Manager or Assistant City Manager   1
      (non-voting member)
   B. County Manager or Assistant   1
      County Manager (non-voting member)
   C. Member of City Council   1
   D. Member of County Board of Supervisors (non-   *1*
      voting pending funding at a level approved by the   4
      Board of Directors)

Total 20 voting and 3 non-voting = 23

Section 2. *Terms of Director*

No director from categories (1) or (2) may serve more than two consecutive three-year terms. In the event the Board member's initial term was less than three years, he may serve an additional two three-year terms.

Directors from categories (1) and (2) shall serve the following terms on the initial Board of Directors: 3 members for three years; 3 members for two years and three members for one year.

Section 3. *Powers and duties of the Board of Directors.* The Board of Directors shall serve without remuneration. Subject to the provision of any law, the Articles of Incorporation or these Bylaws, the Board of Directors shall have the power and authority granted by law to the Corporation except as may be specifically excepted by law, by the Articles of Incorporation or by these Bylaws. This power shall include but not be limited to the following:

a. To prescribe the qualifications and the requirements of membership, and cause to be issued appropriate certificates of membership.

b. To select, appoint and remove at will, the Executive Director of the corporation and to prescribe the duties and delegate such powers to the officers and employees of the corporation as may be necessary and required in the transaction of the business of the corporation not inconsistent with these Bylaws.

c. To fix the compensation of the Executive Director and to require security for the faithful performance of his duties.

d. To borrow money and to make and issue notes, bonds and other negotiable and transferable instruments, mortgages, deeds of trust and trust agreements, and to do every act and thing necessary to effectuate the same.

e. To procure, adopt, amend, and rescind from time to time such rules and regulations as in their discretion may be necessary and desirable for the conduct of the business and affairs of the corporation and to prescribe penalties for the breach thereof.

f. To make amendments or recisions of the Bylaws of the corporation by a two-thirds vote of the whole Board of Directors at any regular or special meeting of the Board of Directors.

g. To fix a schedule of charges to be paid to the corporation for the facilities and services furnished and rendered by the corporation.

h. The Board of Directors shall at least once in each year, employ a competent certified public accountant or auditor to make a detailed examination and audit of the books and accounts of the corporation and to render a report in writing in respect thereto, which said report shall be submitted to the Board of Directors.

Section 4. *Nominations.*

a. *Nominating Committee.* Each year, approximately two months prior to the annual meeting, the current Chairman of the Board shall appoint a Nominating Committee composed of the retiring members of the current Board of Directors, to prepare a ballot to nominate new candidates for the Board of Directors of the corporation. The Nominating Committee shall secure the consent of all candidates prior to the annual meeting. Only members in good standing are eligible to hold office.

b. *Notice to Members.* As soon as practicable after the record date, a written notice containing the names of the candidates nominated by the Board of Directors for election as Directors to succeed those Directors whose terms of office are expiring shall be mailed to each member who is entitled to vote for the election of Directors. Such notice shall also specify the date for the close of nominations.

c. *Nomination by Members.* Nominations may also be made by any group of five (5) percent of members of the voting membership, provided such nominations are written, signed by the nominating members and presented to the Secretary/Treasurer not later than the thirty-fifth (35th) day prior to the annual meeting.

Section 5. *Election.*

a. *Ballots.* The Directors shall be elected by written ballot. A ballot together with notice of meeting, ballot envelope, return envelope, agenda, candidates' resumes and other items the Board wishes the membership to vote upon shall be sent to each member entitled to vote not later than twenty (20) days before the meeting. No ballot or proxy shall be valid unless received by the corporate office by 5:00 P.M. of the fifth (5th) day before the meeting. A proxy must be dated and signed by a member entitled to vote.

b. *Vote Required.* The elected Directors shall be those nominees receiving the highest number of mail votes. In the event of a tie, the voting members present in person or by proxy at the Annual Meeting shall elect as between the tied nominees.

Section 6. *Meetings.*

a. *Regular Meetings.* Regular meetings of the Board of Directors shall be held monthly at places as shall from time to time be designated by the Chairman of the Board. Written notice of the time and place of each regular meeting shall be mailed to each Director at least five (5) days prior to the meeting. Board of Directors may choose not to meet up to two (2) meetings per year.

b. *Special Meetings.* A special meeting of the Board of Directors may be called at any time by the Chairman of the Board, the Chairman Elect or a majority of Directors in office. Written notice of the time and place of each special meeting shall be mailed to each Director at least five (5) days prior to the meeting.

Section 7. *Quorum.* A quorum for conducting business at any meeting shall be fifty-one percent (51%) of the Directors then holding office.

Section 8. *Waiver of Notice.* The transactions of any meeting of the Board of Directors, however called and noticed or wherever held, shall be as valid as though taken at a meeting duly held after regular call and notice, if (a) a quorum is present, and (b) either before or after the meeting, each of the Directors not present signs a written Waiver of Notice, a Consent to Holding the Meeting, or an Approval of the Minutes. The Waiver of Notice or Consent need not specify the purpose of the meeting. All Waivers, Consents, and Approvals shall be filed with the corporate records or made part of the Minutes of the meeting. Notice of a meeting shall also be deemed given to any Director who attends the meeting without protesting before or at its commencement about the lack of adequate notice.

Section 9. *Absences.* The office of any member of the Board of Directors shall be automatically vacated ninety (90) days after such Director has failed to attend three (3) consecutive meetings or after he or she has failed to attend five (5) out of twelve (12) consecutive meetings unless the Board of Directors, before the expiration of such ninety-day period, has acted favorably on such Director's petition to relieve him or her of the loss of office provided for herein. After the failure to attend three (3) consecutive meetings or five (5) of twelve (12) consecutive meetings a Director shall not be entitled to vote unless and until his or her petition for relief has been favorably acted upon by the Board.

Section 10. *Filling Vacancies.* In case of a vacancy in the Board of Directors from any cause, the remaining members of the Board may elect from nominees submitted by the nominating committee, a member to fill the vacancy, such member to serve the unexpired portion of such term and until his successor is elected and duly qualified.

Article V. Officers

Section 1. *Titles.* The Board officials of this corporation shall be the Chairman of the Board, Vice-chairman, Immediate Past Chairman and Secretary/Treasurer. These individuals (except Immediate Past Chairman) shall be elected from the Board of Directors at the meeting of the Board immediately following the annual meeting of the members.

Section 2. *Term of Office.* The Officers of the Board of Directors shall serve a one-year term.

Section 3. *Removal and Resignation.* Any Board official may be removed by a majority of the Board of Directors at any meeting of the Board. Any officer may resign at any time by giving written notice to the Chairman of the Board.

Section 4. *Vacancy.* A vacancy in any office shall be filled by the Board of Directors at any meeting of the Board. The officer holds office for the unexpired term of his predecessor.

Section 5. *Duties of Board Officials.*
    a. *Chairman of the Board.* The Chairman of the Board shall be the principal official of the corporation and shall, subject to the control of the Board of Directors, have general supervision, direction, and control of the business of the corporation. He shall preside at all meetings of the Board of Directors, and shall cast the deciding vote in the event of a tie. He shall appoint all standing committees and special committees as needed. In addition, he shall have such other powers and duties as may be prescribed by the Board of Directors or these Bylaws. In the absence or disability of the Chairman, the Board of Directors shall designate the Vice-Chairman to act in his stead, or in the absence of both the Chairman and Vice-Chairman, the Board shall designate one of their members to act in their stead.

b. *Vice-Chairman.* In the absence or disability of the Chairman, the Vice-Chairman shall perform all of the duties and have all powers of the Chairman. In addition, he shall have such other powers and perform such other duties as may be prescribed for him by the Chairman, the Board of Directors, or these Bylaws.

c. *Immediate Past Chairman.* This individual is an ex-officio Board member who may attend meetings of the Board of Directors and participate in an advisory capacity.

d. *Secretary/Treasurer.* The Secretary/Treasurer shall provide stewardship over all financial aspects for the Bureau. His responsibilities include check signing for all amounts over $1,000, participation in the annual budget process and monitoring staff's adherence to the established budget.

Article VI. Management Structure

Section 1. *Management.* The managers of this corporation shall be the Executive Director, Director of Tourism Development, Director of Convention Sales, and Director of Membership and Communications. The Executive Director shall be selected by the Board of Directors and the other managers shall be selected by the Executive Director.

Section 2. *Executive Director.*

a. *Qualifications.* The Executive Director must be able to qualify the Bureau as a member of the International Association of Convention and Visitors Bureaus. Other qualifications for the Executive Director shall be determined by the Board of Directors. Qualifications and job description shall be incorporated into and made a part of his employment contract.

b. *Duties and Responsibilities.*

1. The Executive Director shall perform such responsibilities as may be assigned to him by the Chairman of the Board and/or Board of Directors.

2. The Executive Director will oversee all financial aspects of the Bureau and provide administrative management of its operations under the direction of the Board of Directors.

3. He shall prepare monthly financial statements for the review of the Board of Directors, coordinate the preparation of statistical reports for the Annual Report and develop an annual budget.

4. The Executive Director shall present a schedule of salaries for all paid employees of the Bureau to the Board of Directors for their approval. The Executive Director shall prepare an operating budget covering all activities of the corporation, subject to approval of the Board of Directors.

5. He shall assemble information and data, and prepare special reports on such matters as the Chairman of the Board and/or the Board of Directors may designate.

6. The Executive Director, the Chairman of the Board, the Vice-Chairman, the Secretary/Treasurer and designated members of the Board of Directors are authorized to sign checks of the organization, with two signatures of the above being required for validity; however to facilitate the internal operations of the corporation the Executive

Director may be authorized to sign checks drawn upon the operation's account with only one signature for the purpose of covering payroll and for expenditures of less than $1,000.

7. He shall serve as advisor to the Chairman of the Board and the Board of Directors. He shall prepare and maintain a statement of all corporation policies as determined by the Board of Directors and shall recommend a plan whereby such policies may be reexamined, reaffirmed or rescinded by the Board.

8. The Executive Director shall be responsible for production of the program of work, in accordance with policies and regulations of the Board of Directors, and present it to them for their approval.

9. He shall be responsible for employment, direction, supervision and termination of all salaried personnel with the exception of himself. All employees at the administrative level, and others as designated, shall report directly to him. He shall call and conduct regular staff meetings.

10. He shall be responsible for preparing a General Procedures Manual, outline the duties, responsibilities and working relationships of the Board of Directors, committees, committee chairmen and the salaried staff. He shall assign the secretarial duties required by project (action) committees to other appropriate members of the staff.

11. He shall perform such other duties as may be assigned to him by the Chairman of the Board.

12. He shall oversee the membership solicitation department and develop the private sector funding for the organization.

13. He shall oversee the Convention Services and Reservations Departments. Convention Services include registration assistance and materials for conventions held in this area as well as housing for the larger conventions as requested by the meeting planner. The Reservations Department includes the booking of tourism business to the metropolitan area and acts in a supportive capacity to service the various marketing programs undertaken by the Tourism Department.

Section 3. *Other Management.*

    a. *Qualifications.* The qualifications of the Director of Tourism, Convention Sales and Membership shall be determined by the Executive Director with the approval of the Board.

    b. *Duties and Responsibilities.* The Directors of Tourism, Convention Sales and Membership report directly to the Executive Director. The responsibilities of these managers shall be as determined from time to time by the Executive Director.

Article VII. Committees

Section 1. *Committees.* The Chairman of the Board with the approval of the Board of Directors shall appoint such administrative, standing and project committees as he deems necessary to fulfill the purposes of this corporation. These committees shall include but not be limited to an Executive Committee.

    a. Executive Committee shall consist of Chairman of the Board, Chairman Elect and Secretary/Treasurer. In the first year of incorporation if the last two positions named are the same person, the Board shall elect a third from the Board at large. In succeeding years the third member of the Executive Committee shall be the Immediate Past Chairman of the Board, or if he is unable to serve the Board shall elect a third member. The purpose of this committee is:

1. To act on behalf of the full Board only in case of an emergency. Actions taken pursuant to this paragraph shall be ratified by the majority of the Board of Directors at the next regularly scheduled meeting.
2. Formulate a full job description for the Executive Director.
3. To review the Executive Director's job performance once a calendar year. This review should address areas included in his job description. The review should also address salary issues if called for in the Executive Director's contract.
4. All Executive Committee decisions must be brought before the Board for their approval.

Section 2. *Duties.* These committees shall report to and operate under the authority and power delegated by the Board of Directors and these Bylaws.

Section 3. *Chairmen.* Committee chairmen shall be appointed by the Chairman of the Board or by the individual committees at the Chairman's option.

Section 4. *Meetings.* Meetings of Committees may be called at any time by the Chairman of the Board or chairman of a committee, and with whatever frequency is required in order that the committee dispatch its responsibility in accordance with Section 2, Article VII, of these Bylaws.

Section 5. *Minutes.* The committee chairman shall have the option to have minutes taken at all committee meetings. These minutes shall be promptly mailed to each member of the committee and a copy shall be filed in the corporation office.

Article VIII. Finances

Section 1. *Fiscal Year.* The fiscal year of the corporation shall commence on the first day of July of each year and end on the thirtieth day of June of the next succeeding year.

Section 2. *Budget.* As soon as practicable after the first day of February each year, the Board of Directors shall adopt a tentative budget for the next fiscal year.

Section 3. *Operating Statements.* The Executive Director shall submit to the Board of Directors each month, an operating statement, showing the financial condition of the corporation as of the end of the preceding month.

Article IX. Voting

All questions put to the Board, or their subcommittees, shall be considered validated upon a simple majority vote of the voting members of the full Board.

Article X. Indemnification

The corporation shall have the power to indemnify its directors, officers, employees and agents in accordance with the provisions of (appropriate legal reference).

Article XI. Inspection of Books

The books of the corporation may be inspected for specific and proper purposes by persons determined by the Board of Directors to be entitled thereto at such reasonable times and places as the Board of Directors may determine, upon application by the persons desiring inspection thereof.

Article XII. Amendments

These Bylaws may be amended, added to or altered by a majority vote of the voting members at any Annual Meeting (subject to the provisions of Article III) or at any special meeting called for that purpose. The Board of Directors shall also have power to adopt, add to or alter the Bylaws for the governance of this corporation by a two-thirds vote of the whole Board of Directors.

By-laws amended June 1, 1982 by Board of Directors to add Article XIII.

Article XIII. Earnings

No part of the next earnings of the corporation shall insure to the benefit of, or be distributable to its members, directors, officers or other private persons, except that the corporation shall be authorized and empowered to pay reasonable compensation for services rendered and to make payments and distributions in furtherance of the purposes set forth in these By-Laws. Notwithstanding any other provision of these articles, the corporation shall not carry on any other activities not permitted to be carried on by a corporation exempt from federal income tax under Section 501(c)(6) of the Internal Revenue Code of 1954 (or the corresponding provision of any future United States Internal Revenue law).

Appendix F

PROGRAM OF WORK
Goals and Objectives

Convention Department

Convincing association executives and corporate meeting planners to convene in the Portland area, or at our member hotels and resorts throughout Oregon, is the ongoing task of GPCVA's Convention Department. This role will become increasingly important should Portland area voters approve a general obligation bond issue in November, 1986 to fund construction of a 400,000 sq. ft. world class convention center in downtown Portland.

Convention Sales

During fiscal 1986/87 the Convention Sales thrust will continue with direct marketing efforts to increase future convention, meeting and trade show activity. We will also be actively working to create a "hot prospect" list of organizations seriously interested in considering Portland, should a suitable convention facility be built. These would be convention groups which cannot currently consider Portland because of its lack of larger convention facilities, but who otherwise are seriously interested in a site in the western United States for 1990 or later.

Besides targeting the "mid-sized" convention market, our Convention Sales effort will continue to emphasize smaller, self-contained group business, as well as multiple-hotel or "city-wide" conventions which our existing facilities can accommodate.

After a nearly 73% increase in lead productivity this past fiscal year, we are continuing to project an upsurge in directing potential business to member hotels, motels and resorts through our GPCVA Convention Sales lead program. In fiscal 1986/87, we anticipate in excess of a 20% increase over levels of 1985/86.

This should result in 370 GPCVA-initiated group sales leads, with a potential of 505,000 room nights*—or in excess of $116,000,000 in potential delegate, association, and exhibitor expenditures. Of these 370 new leads and those from earlier years, the department is expected to confirm 202 new bookings attributable to GPCVA efforts. A total of 258,000 new room nights representing a 17% increase over last fiscal year's results, will equate to $60,000,000 in direct future economic impact.

*One room for one night = one room night.
Reprinted with permission of the Greater Portland Convention and Visitors Association (Oregon).

Convention Services

The department's Convention Services personnel will provide assistance to groups representing in excess of a quarter million delegates attending meetings in the greater Portland area. The objective is to encourage repeat business and pre- and post-convention activity by providing a successful meeting and convention experience, and encouraging attendees to enjoy all that Oregon has to offer.

Convention Housing

This GPCVA activity functions as a centralized reservation service for organizations which require accommodations in more than one hotel. In fiscal 1986/87 GPCVA expects to place nearly 50,000 room nights into area hotels and motels.

Tourism Department

Increasing the number of pleasure travel visitors to the Portland area is the primary objective of the Tourism Department, which directs its efforts at both domestic and international tourism.

Travel Trade Promotion

Participation in industry trade shows will continue to generate increased tour programs to Oregon by strengthening the area's presence among domestic and international tour wholesalers who can build traffic from targeted markets.

GPCVA will also increase its participation in travel shows which target the retail trade, or travel agents as the next logical major development in our tourism promotion efforts.

The Tourism Department will also orchestrate a repeat performance of the successful "Fall Fun Fam Trip" first organized in 1984. This effort will host selected tour operators to review Portland and its environs to increase their awareness of our offerings to their clients.

The level of Group Tour Operator leads generated for follow-up by member supplier firms to the travel trade is projected to exceed 300. We also anticipate 410 travel agent leads to be generated, providing opportunities for member supplier firms to solicit from this additional audience.

Visitor Services

During 1986/87 GPCVA's Visitor Information Service will answer some 180,000 consumer inquiries. In addition to our dedicated staff of volunteers and Visitor Services Manager, we have added a full-time weekend staff person for our downtown Visitor Information Center. During this fiscal year we will also look into expanding our visitor information capabilities in and beyond the downtown area.

Media Services

GPCVA's output of publicity and assistance will include servicing hundreds of travel writer visits and inquiries, and providing convention planners and tour operators with the tools to assist them in promoting Portland to their audiences. We will also orchestrate a familiarization weekend for travel writers in May, 1987 to further provide opportunities to get Portland's message out to both domestic and international travelers.

Administration and Finance Department

The Administration and Finance Department is responsible for coordinating such key support functions as accounting, budgeting, personnel, word processing, etc., as well as membership development, services, and activities and community relations.

General Operations

In addition to upgrading the tools for the responsible financial management of GPCVA's activities, the department oversees the day-to-day workings of the Association's office and personnel.

Having recently completed an office expansion, which provides an additional 2,500 sq. feet of working space for the organization, the next major step is computerization. The first priority during fiscal 1986/87 will be to automate our membership billings and mailings and take our accounting function in-house. Ultimately we hope to computerize the convention sales data contained in our thousands of sales files as well as a host of other functions, including automating our Housing Bureau operation.

Membership Development

A key ingredient in GPCVA's private sector support is the ongoing expansion of the Association's drive for new member investment. One of the major developments that came out of the 1985/86 fiscal year was the debut of a new advertising supported visitor publication called "The Portland Book." This twice-a-year publication has not only answered a host of visitor needs, it has also provided greater incentive for potential member firms to consider supporting the organization, since it provides a substantive return to any operation which can potentially serve the visiting public. The availability of display advertising also provides an opportunity for member companies to further increase their share of visitor dollars by reaching the over 1,000,000 pleasure and business travelers and 250,000 convention delegates who will potentially seek out their services through this all-encompassing visitor portfolio of the Portland area.

Communications

Another ongoing effort of the Association is to heighten public awareness of the economic development role of tourism, in the Portland area and throughout the state. With the industry being focused on in an unprecedented manner, this role will be particularly important in the coming year.

It is also the responsibility of the Association to be responsive to input from the public, and civic and business leaders, as to how to best meet the needs of the community in fulfilling our responsibilities.

Appendix G

MEMORANDUM

TO: IACVB Members

FROM: Chairman
Convention Site Committee

DATE: October 17, 1985

RE: Request for Invitation for 1989 and 1990 Annual Conventions

On behalf of the IAVCB membership, I invite your bureau to submit a proposal for hosting an upcoming IACVB annual convention. As described by the IACVB President, our committee's charge is to make a recommendation to the board of directors regarding sites for the 1989 and 1990 annual conventions.

The committee asks that proposals be submitted no later than **December 1, 1985,** so the committee can review all bids and recommend a site to the board at the January board of directors meeting.

Proposals must include, but are not limited to, the following information:

1) **Dates for the annual convention**
   Traditionally, the annual convention opens with a reception on Saturday evening, with the first official convention function beginning on Sunday morning. The convention normally concludes Wednesday evening. In the past, the board of directors and some committees meet on Saturday prior to the opening reception.

   The convention is normally held during the middle to latter part of July since many members prefer to use it as a family vacation. When submitting possible dates, please keep in mind that other associations in our industry also hold their annual meetings during the month of July. So as to not conflict with these meetings, it is important to verify other meetings scheduled for the same dates.

2) Hotel
   Please submit the name and location and five copies of the brochure describing the hotel you propose to house the convention. If you wish to propose more than one hotel from which a choice of one can be made, you may do so. If you elect to submit more than one hotel for consideration, please send five brochures on each property.

   Please note, that while not imperative, normally the hotel selected as the convention site sponsors either the opening reception or a meal function during the convention. Such sponsorships may be done in conjunction with the host convention and visitors bureau or independently.

3) **Room Requirements**

For purposes of bidding, you should anticipate a convention attendance of 600; 275 members, 175 bureau staff members, 125 accompanying persons and 25 guests. Room pick-up should be based on 300 singles and 150 doubles. Flat rates are preferred, either flat single and double or flat regardless of room type. Please provide the committee with an idea of the 1985 rates for the hotel(s) you propose.

At a minimum, the proposed hotel(s) should provide a 1/50 complimentary room policy. IACVB requires two suites during the convention; one for the current IACVB President and one for the convention chairman. In addition, the hotel's complimentary room policy should have allowance for four IACVB staff rooms.

4) **Meeting room requirements**

Traditionally, the IACVB annual convention requires the following meeting space:

Saturday: AM & PM
            1 room to set "U" for 21, 100 theatre

Sunday: AM
            1 room to seat 125 schoolroom
            4 breakout rooms to seat 12 each conference style (committee meetings)

            PM
            1 room to seat 500 schoolroom

Monday: AM
            7 breakout rooms to seat 50 each in hollow square
            1 breakout room to seat 125 theatre
            1 breakout room to seat 25 conference

            PM
            1 breakout room to seat 200 schoolroom
            3 breakout rooms to seat 100 schoolroom
            1 breakout room to seat 75 schoolroom

Tuesday: AM
            1 breakout room to seat 200 schoolroom
            3 breakout rooms to seat 100 schoolroom
            1 breakout room to seat 75 schoolroom

            PM
            7 breakout rooms to seat 50 each in hollow square
            1 breakout room to seat 125 theatre
            1 breakout room to seat 25 conference

Wednesday: AM
            1 room to seat 500 schoolroom

            PM
            1 room to seat "U" for 21, 100 theatre

5) **Food and beverage requirements**

The convention may also require the following food and beverage functions:

Saturday: Reception for 600

Sunday: Reception and/or dinner for 600

Monday:	Luncheon for 475
	Evening reception for 600
Tuesday:	Luncheon for 475
	Evening reception and/or dinner for 600
Wednesday:	Evening reception for 600
	Dinner/Banquet for 600

6) **Exhibit Space Requirements**
The following space will be required to accommodate the annual Idea Fair:

Saturday (AM) thru	1 exhibit room to hold 100 6' tables for table-
Wednesday (AM)	top displays only

7) **Attractions/Activities**
Please describe attractions, special activities and/or programs available in your area you feel would be of interest to IACVB delegates and their families. In addition to the above meeting specifications, the convention will also have an accompanying persons program and possibly a children's program.

8) **Golf and tennis facilities/recreational activities**
During the annual convention, IACVB normally sponsors both a golf and tennis tournament for registered delegates. In past years, the tournaments have been held either Sunday morning or Monday afternoon. Anticipated attendance is 80 golf and 40 tennis.

An alternate convention activity should be recommended for delegates not participating in either the golf or tennis tournaments.

9) **Accessibility to Host City**
Since convention delegates will be arriving from around the world, the accessibility to the host city is an important consideration. Please provide a list of air carriers that presently serve your city and the number of daily inbound flights per carrier. In addition, please advise if your city is served by an international airport; if not, the location of the nearest international airport.

In addition to the above specifications, the International Office will require the assistance of the host bureau personnel for pre-convention planning and administration. Specifically, the International Office will seek advice as to appropriate outside suppliers for such services as bus charters, accompanying persons and children's programming, equipment rental, etc. During the convention, registration clerks are normally provided to IACVB on a complimentary basis.

Hosting the IACVB annual convention is both a privilege and a pleasure. Your Convention Site Committee hopes that many members will respond to this invitation. If you would like additional information about activities traditionally held during an IACVB annual convention, please contact the International Office.

Please submit 5 sets of your proposal by **December 1st** to:

> Chairman
> IACVB Convention Site Committee
> c/o IACVB
> P.O. Box 758
> Champaign, Illinois 61820 USA

Thank you.

Appendix H

Atlanta Convention and Visitors Bureau
Registration Assistance

Rules and Regulations

The Atlanta Convention and Visitors Bureau's registration personnel are skilled professionals with a genuine devotion to their position in representing the City. As registrars, you should take pride in your work with the associations and be dedicated to doing the best job you possibly can do, not because you have to, but because you *want* to. You are representing our City and know that you *must* perform professionally and accurately. Any task you perform is a direct reflection on the Atlanta Convention and Visitors Bureau and the City of Atlanta; we must insist on perfection plus.

To help us keep this reputation, the following rules and regulations have been established to insure complete satisfaction to anyone using the Atlanta Convention and Visitors Bureau's registration personnel.

1. Greetings . . . always remember to greet the attendees with a smile regardless of any trouble you may be having. Be courteous and helpful at all times.
2. Never, under any circumstances, complain about your job assignment or make derogatory statements to the association executive. Try to keep a positive attitude and remember that the association is always right.
3. Be prepared to come in early and stay late during an assignment. Since the first day of any meeting is the most important, we would be most appreciative if you could arrive early to get yourself acclimated and go over any of the association's procedures and directions you are to follow.
4. Locating the registration area and association executive . . . in the event that you cannot locate the registration area to which you have been assigned, go directly to the convention services office or sales department; they will lead you to the proper location. Under no circumstances should you leave the hotel or exhibit facility if you are unable to locate the association contact.
5. Personal appearance . . . The official ACVB uniform and name tag is to be worn at all times unless otherwise specified. (Black suit or skirt with a white blouse and the ACVB Burgundy tie.) We expect everyone to give a neat, business-like appearance and prefer that skirts or dresses be worn as opposed to slacks or culottes.
6. Work area . . . Be neat in your work area! Straighten your materials, empty ashtrays and *never* bring food or drink to the work area unless the association has offered. Under *no* circumstances will smoking or chewing gum be permitted while you are on duty. This is permitted only during designated break periods.

7. Lunch breaks . . . Lunch breaks are to be scheduled by your supervisor. If no supervisor is on duty, we ask that you check with the meeting planner or the association executive and take your lunch break (30 minute limit unless otherwise specified by the association), during the slowest period of the day. Do not eat your lunch, dinner or snack in your work area.
8. Anticipatory factor . . . Always anticipate a possible problem ahead of time in order to prevent its occurrence later in the meeting. However, if a problem does occur, report it to your supervisor *immediately*.
9. Scheduling . . . Please be flexible and accommodating where scheduling changes can occur; hours may be increased or decreased depending upon the needs of the association. If you personally must make a change in your assignment, contact the ACVB Convention Services Manager as soon as possible so that changes can be made immediately. Do not accept a job assignment if there is any doubt of your being able to work. Continued job cancellations will be taken into consideration for future job assignments.
10. Time sheets . . . It is very important to turn in your time sheets to your supervisor or the ACVB office as soon as the Convention/Meeting worked has concluded. No one can be paid for that particular meeting until all time sheets are in our office. If you do not know how to figure out your time sheets, put the number of hours worked and we will complete it for you. If you do not have a blank time sheet, write your hours worked on a piece of paper and send it to our office; we will complete a time sheet for you. Do not write in the association's column.

Job Guidelines

Supervisor:

Reviews all instructions and procedures from the association
Checks to see that all registrars are on time
Collects and checks time sheets for accuracy and completeness
Designates lunch breaks and dinner breaks
Acts as liaison between the ACVB registrars and association executives
Makes sure all ACVB Registration Procedures are followed completely
Reassigns jobs if needed, and cuts when so requested by the association

Typists:

ACCURACY . . . Practice, practice, practice! Make sure your typewriter is in proper working condition and all delegate badges are accurate.

Advance Registration:

Your job is to keep the line moving. Please limit your conversation with each delegate to a minimum in order to keep the lines moving.

Cashiers:

ACCURACY
1) Count your cash at the beginning of the day and keep accurate records.

Cashiers:

ACCURACY

1) Count your cash at the beginning of the day and keep accurate records.
2) Under no circumstances should you let anyone in your cash box—you are responsible for *your* cash box.

CRT Operators:

All CRT machines are not alike, which means it is very important that you follow procedures during orientation and ask questions about any procedures you do not understand. If you have problems with your terminal, notify the staff immediately. If you do not understand the procedures, ASK! Keep fraternizing with the attendees to a minimum. The lines must keep moving.

Embossers:

Please refer to CRT Operators' instructions

Information/Message Desk:

Be familiar with the hotel or exhibit facility so you can answer any questions intelligently. Please write all messages legibly and accurately.

Receptionist/Secretary:

Be professional and courteous to the association staff. Keep your work area organized. Learn association executives' names and positions, and keep their telephone numbers close at hand in case of an emergency. Familiarize yourself with the convention program so you can answer any questions. Dates, times, meeting locations, and exhibitor locations are particularly important in this area.

Monitors:

Make sure all delegates attending the meetings/exhibitions are properly badged; if not, refer them back to the registration area where someone can assist them.

Please help us present a positive image for the City of Atlanta

REGISTRATION QUESTIONNAIRE   Date: _____

Name: _____ Social Security Number: _____

Address: _____

Phone Number: _____

How long have you worked with the Bureau? _____

1. Do you do any other part-time work? _____ If so, when? _____

2. Do you have anything you do on a regular basis (like bridge or garden clubs)?

   _____

   If so, when? _____

3. Do you want to work as much as possible? _____ Occasionally? _____

   Rarely? _____

4. Do you mind working late hours? _____ Are you available most of the

   time? _____

   If not, please explain: _____

   _____

5. Do you mind working on National holidays? _____ or Sundays?

   _____

6. Do you have private transportation? _____ If not, do you rely on busses

   or other workers? _____ List all workers with whom you ride: _____

   _____

7. Do you type? _____ If so, would you describe your speed as slow _____,

   average _____, or fast _____? Do you feel comfortable using a manual bul-

   letin _____, an electric bulletin _____, an electric standard _____, an

   IBM Selectric _____?

8. Do you cashier? _____ Do you have a cash box? _____

9. Can you type and cashier at the same time without slowing everything up? _____

10. Can you operate a CRT machine? _____ If so, do you enjoy operating them?

    _____

11. Have you ever operated a telephone switchboard? _____

11. Have you ever operated a telephone switchboard? _____

12. List all office machines with which you are familiar: _____

    _____

13. Do you believe you are capable of operating an information booth? _____

14. Do you mind working a publications booth? _____ , or a ladies hospitality
    room? _____

15. Do you mind working on pre-registration? _____ , or filing? _____

16. Do you mind taking orders from the supervisor on large meetings? _____
    If so, why? _____

17. Do you seem to get along with the other ladies/men? _____ ,
    or do you feel better working by yourself? _____

18. Occasionally we need outside help in our office (mainly for typing or filing); would
    you like to work in our office? _____

19. Do you have a uniform? _____ If not, what size jacket do you wear? _____

20. Please use this space for any comments, complaints, concerns, etc., that you may
    have. What you say *will not* be used against you, and *will not* affect the number
    or quality of jobs you will be given. This information will go no further than this
    office and will only be used to improve your job as a registration person.

    _____

    _____

    _____

    _____

Appendix I

WICHITA CONVENTION AND VISITORS BUREAU

STAFF ORGANIZATIONAL CHART

PRESIDENT

INTERNSHIP PROGRAM
PART-TIME
(1)

NAT'L CONVENTION
SALES MANAGER
(3)

CONVENTION
SERVICES
COORDINATOR

DIRECTOR
OF
TOURISM

EXECUTIVE ASSISTANT
BOOKKEEPER

CONVENTION
SALES MANAGER
(APPRENTICE)
(1)

REGISTRATION
HOSTESSES
PART-TIME
(10)

ADMINISTRATIVE
ASSISTANT
TOURISM DIV.

WORD PROCESSING
SPECIALIST

VISITOR
INFORMATION
RECEPTIONIST

AIRPORT VISITOR
INFORMATION
PERSONNEL-
CONTRACT EMPLOYEES
(4)

ORGANIZATION CHART
MARKETING DEPARTMENT

Reno-Sparks Convention and Visitors Authority

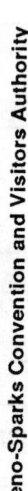

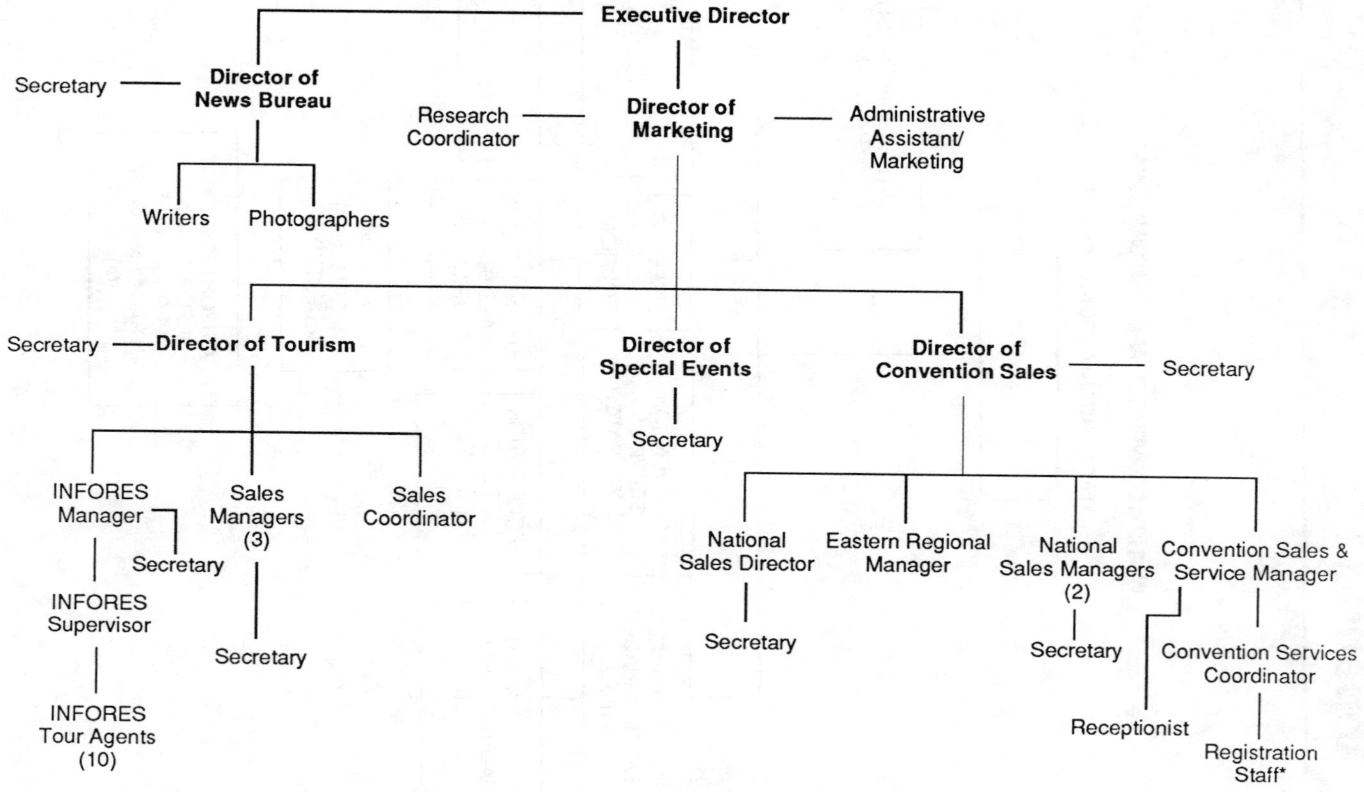

Executive Director

— Administrative Assistant/ Marketing

Research Coordinator —

Director of News Bureau

Secretary —

Writers — Photographers

Director of Marketing

Director of Special Events

— Secretary

Director of Tourism

Sales Coordinator

Sales Managers (3)

— Secretary

INFORES Manager

— Secretary

INFORES Supervisor

INFORES Tour Agents (10)

Secretary —

Director of Convention Sales

— Secretary

National Sales Director

— Secretary

Eastern Regional Manager

National Sales Managers (2)

— Secretary

Convention Sales & Service Manager

Convention Services Coordinator

— Receptionist

Registration Staff*

METROPOLITAN TORONTO CONVENTION AND VISITORS ASSOCIATION

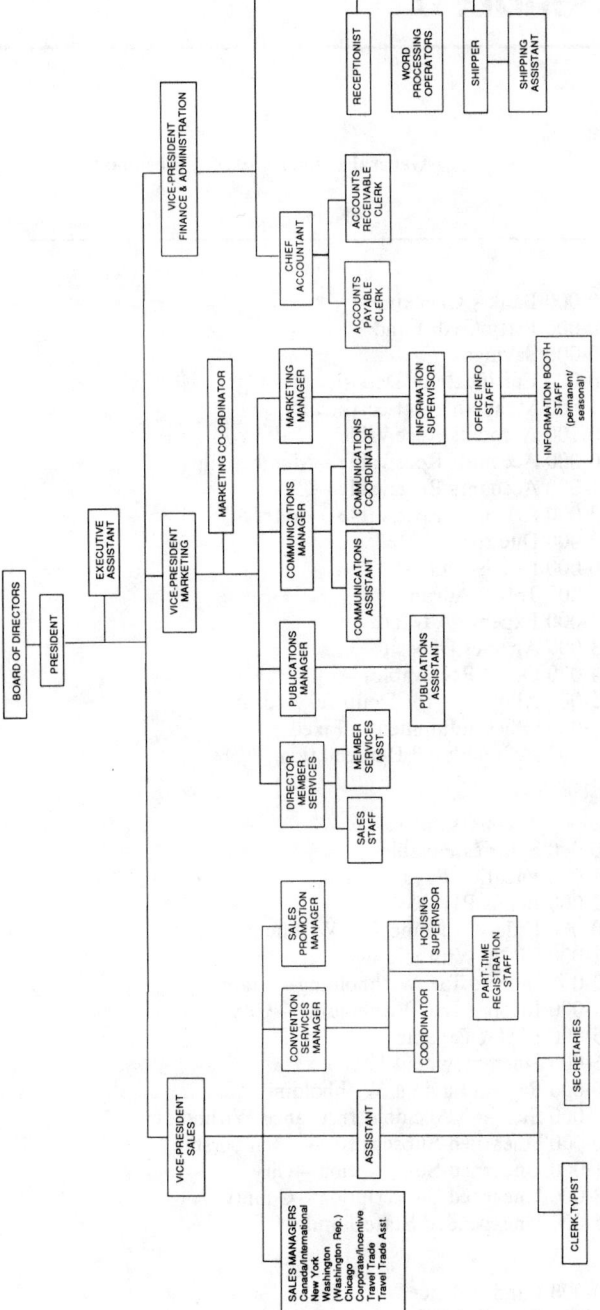

Appendix J

Account Number	Name

Income
0-410-000 Room Tax
0-420-000 Membership
0-421-000 City
0-423-000 County
0-425-000 Billings for Special Services
0-431-000 Interest
0-440-000 Grant from State

Expenses
0-510-000 Salaries—Regular Staff
S-510-000 Salaries—Regular Staff—State Account
0-511-000 Staff Bonus
0-512-000 Salaries—Extra Office Staff
0-513-000 Salaries—Registration Staff
0-520-000 Taxes—FICA
0-521-000 Taxes—FUTA
0-522-000 Taxes—unemployment
0-530-000 Pension Fund
0-540-000 Group Insurance—Life
0-542-000 Group Insurance—Health
0-550-000 Travel—Convention Sales
S-550-000 Travel—Convention Sales—State Account
0-551-000 Travel—Group Tour/International
S-551-000 Travel—Group Tour/International—State Account
0-552-000 Travel—Corporate
S-552-000 Travel—Corporate—State Account
0-560-000 Local—Convention Sales
S-560-000 Local—Convention Sales—State Account
0-561-000 Local—Group Tour/International
0-562-000 Local—Corporate
0-572-000 Advertising
S-572-000 Advertising—State Account
0-573-000 PR and Membership
0-574-000 Publications
S-574-000 Publications—State Account
0-575-000 Incentives
0-576-000 Audio/Visual
S-576-000 Audio/Visual—State Account
0-577-000 Exhibits
S-577-000 Exhibits—State Account
0-578-000 Registration Services
0-579-000 Research
0-580-000 Rent
0-581-000 Light
0-582-000 Telephone
S-582-000 Telephone—State Account

Account Number	Name

0-583-000 Office Supplies
0-584-000 Office Equipment
0-585-000 Postage
S-585-000 Postage—State Account
0-586-000 Insurance
0-587-000 Professional Fees
0-588-000 Membership Dues and Subscriptions
0-589-000 Administrative
0-590-000 Automobile (Lease, gas and parking)
0-591-000 Depreciation
0-592-000 Doubtful Accounts
0-595-000 Governor's Conference on Tourism

Income Transfer
x-xxx-xxx Income Transfer

Sample Budget and Comparison to Earlier Budget

Revenues	1987	1986 Estimated	Increase (Decrease)
Assessment	$3,000,000	$2,000,000	$61,000
Membership:			
General	908,550	862,000	46,550
Special billings	50,000	50,000	0
Interest income	11,000	11,000	0
State Grant	13,500	13,500	0
Total Revenues	$3,983,050	$2,936,500	$1,046,550
Expenses	$1,198,500	$1,073,750	$116,750
Salaries and related:	0	62,000	62,000
Regular staff	40,000	32,000	8,000
Bonus	89,000	88,394	606
Extra office help	115,840	98,000	17,840
Registration	32,000	32,582	(582)
Taxes	130,490	111,163	19,327
Pension expense			
Group insurance			
Promotional expenses:			
Travel—			
Convention sales	280,000	200,000	80,000
Group tour/international	34,305	21,000	13,306
Corporate	16,750	12,000	4,750
Local—			
Convention sales	38,000	38,500	(500)
Group tour/international	13,050	10,000	3,050
Corporate	10,700	2,400	8,300

Revenues	1987	1986 Estimated	Increase (Decrease)
Political party bids	0	32,000	(32,000)
Advertising	19,000	19,200	(200)
PR & membership	60,000	125,000	(65,000)
Publications	450,000	400,000	50,000
Incentives	39,300	32,000	7,300
Audio/visual	168,500	198,000	129,500
Exhibits	10,000	21,000	(11,000)
Registration services	34,500	45,000	(10,500)
Research	16,000	24,000	(8,000)
	7,000	3,000	4,000
	3,500	3,500	0
General administrative:			
Rent	190,500	190,500	0
Light	9,300	9,000	300
Telephone	54,000	54,000	0
Office supplies	53,600	52,000	1,600
Office equipment	45,600	69,000	(23,400)
Postage	45,600	45,000	600
Insurance	35,000	34,300	700
Professional fees	40,000	49,000	(9,000)
Dues and subscriptions	10,500	11,500	(1,000)
Administrative	12,700	16,900	(14,200)
Auto expense	17,800	17,800	0
Depreciation	43,100	35,000	8,100
Doubtful accounts	6,500	6,375	125
Total Expenses	$2,852,635	$2,746,864	($105,771)
Excess/(Deficit)	$1,130,415	189,636	($1,320,051)

Appendix K

SAMPLE JOB DESCRIPTION

JOB TITLE: President & CEO

REPORTS TO: Executive Committee and Board of Directors

SPECIFIC DUTIES:

The President and Chief Executive Officer shall be responsible for the administrative, operating and marketing functions of the Bureau.

The President & CEO shall serve as advisor to the Chairman of the Board, the Board of Directors and such other committees as may from time to time be designated.

The President & CEO shall assemble information, and cause to be prepared, such reports as may be required by the Chairman of the Board and the Board of Directors.

The President & CEO shall attend all meetings of the membership, the Board of Directors, and other duly designated committees in an advisory, non-voting capacity.

The President & CEO shall be responsible for the hiring, firing, discharging, directing and supervising of all employees of the Bureau.

The President & CEO shall be responsible for the preparation of an annual operating budget encompassing all activities and operations of the Bureau, which budget shall be subject to review and approval of the Board of Directors.

The President & CEO shall perform such other and additional duties as may be assigned by the officers, the Board of Directors and such other committees as may be designated, and as provided for in the bylaws.

Develop and supervise plans to promote (DESTINATION) as a convention and visitor destination to area, state, regional, national and international convention holding groups and organizations; as a center for business conferences, workshops and sales meetings; and as a tourism area through individual leisure travel and motorcoach development.

Develop and supervise plans and procedures to disseminate information about facilities available in (DESTINATION) which are conducive to conventions; for greeting executives in charge of associations holding conventions; for assisting groups in preparing programs and preconvention literature.

Develop and supervise master listings of conventions and exhibits and special events scheduled to be held in (DESTINATION); filing of IACVB listings and confidential convention reports to IACVB and maintain records required for efficient functioning of the Bureau.

Develop and supervise implementation of an annual operating and marketing plan for the Bureau.

Develop and supervise plans to promote (DESTINATION) as an area visitor destination. Work in conjunction with other cities to create a new tourist programs and publicize the existing tourist attractions more fully.

Develop and supervise an annual budget for support of activities.

Interview and hire candidates for positions in the Convention and Visitors Bureau.

Supervise and monitor work flow and dissemination of information.

Supervise all staff.

Receive inquiries pertaining to conventions and tourism and assign members of the staff for follow-up or makes personal follow-up.

Write promotional literature as required.

Contact travel industry representatives by telephone, mail or personal visits to present the advantages of meeting or visiting (DESTINATION).

As an assigned staff member of Board committees, take minutes of meetings and assist in conducting meetings as requested by committee chairs.

Participate and maintain membership in local, state, regional, national and international organizations and attend their respective meetings.

Write annual and quarterly reports of performance.

Formulate and direct the marketing, advertising, sales and promotion programs.

Be responsible for monthly financial reports and annual audit reports in accordance with written financial procedures approved by the Board.

SAMPLE JOB DESCRIPTION

JOB TITLE: Director of Convention Sales

REPORTS TO: President

SPECIFIC DUTIES:

In addition to the specific duties of an Account Executive, the Director of Convention Sales will:

• Direct and train Account Executives in all matters pertaining to Convention Sales.

• Read and approve all memos and bulletins pertaining to Convention Sales before they go out of the office.

• Read, approve and sign all firm, tentative and cancellation of date letters to Hall pertaining to Convention Sales and Corporate Sales.

• Be liaison with Hall regarding expansion and business already on the books for future years.

• Reassign files whenever necessary.

• Review files that are to be destroyed.

• Send out letters to new prospects.

• Assign all new accounts.

• Receive calls from Account Executives when they call in sick.

• Gather requests for vacation time from the Convention Sales Staff.

• Submit information for the review process of each Account Executive.

• Other responsibilities to be assigned at later dates.

SAMPLE JOB DESCRIPTION

JOB TITLE: Account Executive—Convention Sales

REPORTS TO: Director of Convention Sales

SPECIFIC DUTIES:

To provide as a destination for conventions and trade and shows and other defined activities by soliciting assigned sales accounts. Also working to direct this business towards member and/or assessed hotels and motels and other member firms supplying support services to these groups.

Account Executive is responsible for achieving individual sales goals assigned annually to include: total conventions booked and estimated total attendance and room nights generated by conventions booked.

Under the general supervision of the Director of Convention Sales preparing and implementing a well coordinated sales effort to attract these accounts to include:

- Identify, recruit and encourage local people affiliated with state, regional, national and international organizations to hold future activities here (bookings).
- Develop, coordinate and implement comprehensive "bid" strategies including but not limited to:
  —Daily review of assigned files for the purpose of determining and triggering appropriate action
  —Verbal presentations
  —Audio-visual presentations
  —Bid book preparation and distribution
  —Invitation packet preparation and distribution
  —Ongoing communications through correspondence, phone calls and meetings
  —Place dates in date books
  —Knowledge of key personalities and issues effecting site selection decisions
  —Develop new customers whenever possible
  —Distribute sales leads to appropriate local businesses via letter, memorandum, bulletin, etc.
  —Conduct site inspection visits by individuals or groups interested in the area
- Maintain a well informed, working knowledge of the facilities, attractions and services, both private and public, available in the area to customers and act as liaison between these entities and the customer
  —Also maintain a familiarity with competing areas or issues that impact on the Bureau's ability to promote effectively
  —Promote good will towards the Bureau among members, assessed hotels and motels, and the community at large
- Represent the Bureau with appropriate industry groups for the purpose of generating interest in as a destination or promoting attendance at events already scheduled for this area.
  —Holding membership with selected organizations
  —Attending and/or exhibiting at appropriate trade shows or events
- Participate in special promotions sponsored by the Bureau such as "sales blitzes" or "airlifts" and other activities as assigned.

- Coordinate with the Convention Services Department and Housing Bureau manager to effectively service groups scheduled to meet in the area to ensure success of activity to include but not be limited to:
  —Pre-convention meetings with customers and appropriate representatives of local organizations involved in servicing the group
  —On-site visits to conventions in progress as required
  —Distribution of brochures and equipment as required
- Complete and submit on a timely basis, appropriate reports as assigned by the Director of Convention Sales.
  —Accept and implement other duties as assigned by the Director of Convention Sales, and/or President
- Work in a cohesive way with other Bureau personnel to ensure unified and effective promotional effort.

SAMPLE JOB DESCRIPTION

JOB TITLE: Director of Tourism

REPORTS TO: President

SPECIFIC DUTIES:

To promote (DESTINATION) as a visitor destination to individual and tour groups.

Assist tourism officials at the state level in elevating tourism awareness for (DESTINATION)

Develop preliminary tourism market plans and budgets and presents to President for approval.

Responsible for timely submission of quarterly reports as required by City/Bureau contract.

Develop and author articles on tourism in (DESTINATION) as requested by media and publishers.

Supervise the staff and the activities of the three visitor information centers at the:

1. Airport
2. Chamber of Commerce
3. Convention and Visitor Bureau

Maintain attendance records on all local visitor attractions and consolidate for quarterly reporting.

Insure that all visitor inquiries from mail, walk-in and telephone are answered in a prompt and courteous manner.

Compile and prepare a quarterly and annual Calendar of Events for (DESTINATION) and supervise distribution to interested parties.

Insure that a daily recording of the Fun Fone is prepared on events and activities taking place in (DESTINATION).

Oversee the production and development of all visitor brochures and materials including the annual printing of the *Official Visitors Guide.*

Be responsible for maintaining accurate inventory counts of all visitor brochures and notify President of any projected shortfalls in printed materials.

Monitor inventories of printed materials distributed through Visitor Information Centers.

Develop tourism advertising program with Bureau President and advertising agent.

Participate and promote (DESTINATION) as a visitor destination at major industry trade shows.

Develop a group tour manual and distribute to motor coach tour operators.

Coordinate local FAM (familiarization) tours for tour operators and travel writers, working with local airlines, hotels and attractions to generate more interest and travel articles featuring (DESTINATION).

Develop and implement a weekend promotional program for out-of-city residents on an annual basis.

Maintain memberships in tourism-related professional organizations.

SAMPLE JOB DESCRIPTION

JOB TITLE: Convention Services Manager

REPORTS TO: President or Dir. of Administration or Director of Convention Sales

SPECIFIC DUTIES:

To develop, strengthen and promote the many services provided by the bureau.

1. Supervise Housing Supervisor.
2. Supervise Visitor Information staff.
3. Maintain, update and print annual Convention Services Directory.
4. Maintain, update and print semi-annual Convention Services Directory.
5. Supervise Registration personnel staff.
6. Develop a strong, active registration personnel staff.
7. Maintain Services reports including monthly attendance/revenue reports and IACVB CCR's.
8. Visit each convention which utilizes the Bureau's services.
9. Develop services promotion package which would be sent to meeting planners of forthcoming conventions.
10. Produce services seminar for membership to be entitled "How to market your services to the Meeting Planner."
11. Work closely with Membership Account Executive to solicit and maintain service members.
12. Produce, update and distribute Non-hotel Meeting Facilities Guide.
13. Maintain video library.
14. Act as liaison between meeting planner and service member. Offer suggestions and planning of entertainment, tours, shopping, spouse and children's programs and other attractions.
15. Handle inquiries for large brochure requests, lure pieces, lapel stick-ons and honorariums.
16. Fulfill any other reasonable request of the association that assists in a productive and successful meeting.

SAMPLE JOB DESCRIPTION

JOB TITLE: Vice President of Communications

REPORTS TO: President

SPECIFIC DUTIES:

Under the general supervision of the President, is responsible for the development, implementation and management of the Bureau's communications with the public, media, industry professionals, members and other civic and community organizations.

Also responsible for the development, production and distribution of marketing tools including the advertising and publicity programs, audio-visual aids, publications and exhibits.

- Supervise the Communications Department staff of specialists to include but not limited to: Work assignments · Hiring and training · Performance review and appraisal · Recommend compensation levels · Establish department objectives and expectations · Ongoing monitoring of work flow and priorities · Advise Communications staff on job related matters
- Act as Senior Editor on all Communications projects including but not limited to, newsletters, news and feature releases, publications, scripts, exhibits and speeches
- Consult with other department heads on their communication needs, suggesting or proposing appropriate uses of communication resources.
- Serve as liaison with the Bureau's advertising agency. This responsibility includes direct involvement in the development of an advertising program, the implementation of that program and the review of the agency's effectiveness.
- Along with the President, serve as liaison with the media. This responsibility requires the coordination of all external communications to inform the local and national news and travel media of local activities and developments and to ensure that inaccuracies, errors or misunderstandings are eliminated.
- Develop and monitor departmental budget to include but not be limited to: Recommend level of spending on various departmental activities · Approval of all departmental expenditures · Periodic revisions to departmental budget as required
- Organize and implement travel writer familiarization tours
- Participate in special bid presentations, promotional projects and events as appropriate, i.e. annual membership reception, "airlifts," major convention bids, etc.

SAMPLE JOB DESCRIPTION

JOB TITLE: Director of Finance and Administration

REPORTS TO: President

SPECIFIC DUTIES:

- Maintain all necessary accounting records for internal operating control, corporate reports and statutory requirements.
- Prepare all financial reports and statements, analysis special statistical reports to assist management in operational and financial planning.
- Handle banking and investment of bureau funds.
- Assemble, review and coordinate all income forecasts and budget expense requests of all departments generating an annual operating budget for approval by the Executive Committee and Board of Directors.

- Manage employee fringe benefit programs.
- Administer general insurance coverage.
- Review expenditures and approve or recommend for approval.
- Assure protection of assets through internal audit, inventory and insurance coverage.
- Administer operation of bureau's data and word processing operations including development of new programs.
- Supervise purchase, rental and maintenance of all furniture and equipment.
- Supervise administration of all office support services. This includes supervisory and administrative responsibilities for all accounting, payroll, purchasing, personnel and inventory control functions serving all departments of the bureau.
- Serve as liaison to bureau's Finance Committee, and to any other designated group or political body that has a financial relationship with the bureau (e.g. city/county boards/commissions).
- Brief Secretary/Treasurer of the Board regularly on the bureau's financial status and matters.
- Participate in senior staff review and planning sessions along with other department heads and the bureau chief executive.
- Serve as the primary staff contact for independent auditors, data processing, insurance and employee benefit consultants.
- Prepare as required monthly/quarterly claims for funds from city/county financial sources; provide city/county organizations with appropriate reports and documentation on the utilization of such funds.

Appendix L

FRI.–SAT.–SUN.   Time _____ am/pm

1. Where is your residence? _____
   city   state   zip

2. Are you staying overnight in the Pendleton area? _____   _____
                                                     yes   no

   If so, what accommodations are you using?

   _____   _____   _____
   friends/relatives   hotel/motel   campground

3. How many people are in your group?   _____   _____
                                           adults   children
                                                        (12 and under)

4. How much do you plan to spend at the festival? $ _____

5. How much do you plan to spend in the area other than on the festival site?
   $ _____

6. How long do you plan to stay at the festival? _____

7. How did you hear about the festival?
   (Check as many as apply)

   _____ newspaper   _____ radio   _____ television   _____ brochure

   _____ poster   _____ word-of-mouth   _____ magazine

   _____ other; describe: _____

8. Do you have any comments or suggestions (to improve the festival)?

THANK YOU

Index